A WINDOW INTO MODERN IRAN

The Ardeshir Zahedi Papers at the Hoover Institution Library & Archives

A WINDOW INTO MODERN IRAN

With its eminent scholars and world-renowned library and archives, the Hoover Institution seeks to improve the human condition by advancing ideas that promote economic opportunity and prosperity, while securing and safeguarding peace for America and all mankind. The views expressed in its publications are entirely those of the authors and do not necessarily reflect the views of the staff, officers, or Board of Overseers of the Hoover Institution.

www.hoover.org

Hoover Institution Press Publication No. 691

Hoover Institution at Leland Stanford Junior University,
Stanford, California 94305-6003

Cover design by Jennifer Navarrette
Photo on cover and on page 18 is by Louis Fabian Bachrach Jr.; appears courtesy of Ardeshir Zahedi.
Text design and composition by Howie Severson

First printing 2019
27 26 25 24 23 22 21 20 19 9 8 7 6 5 4 3 2

Printed and bound by Friesens Corporation in Canada.

The paper used in this publication meets the minimum requirements of the American National Standard for Information Sciences—Permanence of Paper for Printed Library Materials, ANSI/NISO Z39.48-1992. ∞

Cataloging-in-Publication Data is available from the Library of Congress.
Library of Congress Control Number: 2019944507
ISBN: 978-0-8179-2174-3 (cloth : alk. paper)
ISBN: 978-0-8179-2178-1 (PDF)

CONTENTS

FOREWORD

Ardeshir Zahedi

My father had often thought of collecting and archiving the family records. Even long before I finished my studies at Utah State University, he was giving me the necessary directions to continue the work he had begun. Well organized and highly disciplined, he wanted me to be the same, meticulous and attentive to the smallest details.

I learned the importance of every letter, picture, and document, however they are recorded, be it on paper, handwritten or printed, in words or images. When my father moved to Switzerland and bought our residence, Villa les Roses, we decided to devote much of the space in the basement to storing these files and photos. Soon we realized that we needed more room, and some documents were moved to the corridors and other floors.

These files cover almost every aspect of our family life, from childhood to maturity and marriage, from school days to social and political scenes. The coming of the communication revolution corresponded with the beginning of my political career. Documents began to multiply, and our facilities modernized. Every week we had hundreds of letters and reports; social and diplomatic ceremonies, photos, speeches, reunions, conferences, and interviews became almost daily routine during my three ambassadorships in the United States and Great Britain and the five years I served as the minister of foreign affairs of my country. Throughout these decades, I continued to be a confidant and close companion of the late shah and had almost daily contact. He was my friend, father-in-law, and beloved king. Our attentively recorded exchanges constitute an important part of my papers.

After the Revolution of 1979, I, like many of my compatriots, was constrained to a life of exile; I was privileged and fortunate to live in a peaceful corner of Switzerland that was like a second home for us. Now I had plenty of time and began to devote myself to organizing and expanding my archives. It was then that I discovered the diversity and richness of what my beloved father and I had collected through almost a century.

Scholars and researchers who had heard about my files showed great interest. Several came to consult the papers for their research—a book or dissertation. I also had visitors from great universities and centers of Iranian studies such as Harvard, Stanford, and Utah State, my alma mater. At the Defense of Foreign Affairs they had even created the Zahedi Research Center in Washington, DC, hoping to enrich its archives with some of these documents. Mr. Ghoreyshi of the Iranian Studies Department at Harvard University came to see the documents and had an extensive interview with me for the Harvard Oral History series; it was recorded over several days and then transcribed on some six hundred pages. Geneva University's School of International Relations and the Swiss State Library in Bern also showed great interest. They counted on my family attachments to the country.

They all thought that my archives were critical for understanding Iranian society, politics, and international relations in the second half of the twentieth century. I had decided that they should be trusted to specialists of documentation and professional archivists who were equipped with modern technologies of classification and preservation. The aim was to make them easily accessible to the scholars and researchers and others who might be interested in Iran and our recent history.

These papers belong to the Iranian people and are particularly valuable to the younger generation. Students in humanities and the political and social sciences can find a mine of new information for their research. These archives will help them better understand our beloved country, its historical and contemporary missions, its achievements and contributions.

Dr. Milani, of the Hoover Institution and Stanford University, came to Montreux to consult the documents and interview me for his new books, *The Persian Sphinx*, *Eminent Persians*, and *The Shah*. Having discovered his deep interest in the recent history of Iran, my father's documents, and my own records, I invited him to visit Villa les Roses to have easier access to the papers. I was impressed by his intellectual curiosity and indefatigable energy. Sometimes when I woke up at three in the morning, the lights in his room were on and he was still reading and taking notes. I enjoyed the company of this renowned scholar and began to admire his sincerity, intelligence, and lucidity of mind.

After Professor Milani had visited my archives, he explained to me why the Hoover Institution was one of the most suitable archives for my papers and how serious they were in their proposal. I knew Hoover Institution from my time in the United States and through my extensive contacts with the academic world. Several of my distinguished friends were associated with its work. But it was through Professor Milani that I discovered the wide range of research they had been doing on Iran and the Middle East.

The institution always had a keen interest in the region and its global issues, conflicts, and revolutions. This was the main purpose for which President Herbert Hoover created it in 1919. This was just after the First World War, and all parts of the globe were going through revolutionary changes. Even before the official creation of this institute, Stanford University had one of the richest documentation centers, a library and archives that housed nearly two million files on the contemporary crisis in the world. The Iranian section of the collections held at the Stanford University and the Hoover Institution Library & Archives was enriched and considerably expanded under the devoted leadership of Professor Abbas Milani.

When I was approached, the institution had already established its fame as one of the top think tanks in the world. The personal attachment and support of high-profile leaders like Ronald Reagan, Walter Annenberg, George Shultz, and Condoleezza Rice, as well as top scholars from distinguished universities, had made the Hoover Institution a unique and prestigious center.

Meanwhile I received messages and proposals from Professor Marc Tessier-Lavigne, the president of Stanford University; Professor John Raisian, the director of Hoover Institution from 1989 to 2015; and Professor Thomas W. Gilligan, who replaced him. Negotiations for the official transfer of papers, the environmental storage conditions, provisions for classification, preservation, and digital accessibility were soon concluded and translated into a legal document.

On May 2, 2017, I signed the official agreement for the donation; the packing and transfer started with no delay. The progress made in such a short time is more than promising. I cannot but be happy to have taken this initiative.

The work of the professional team assigned to the project was more than delicate. Many documents were photocopies, some on old thermic papers and vulnerable to heat and light. They had to be restored. A majority of files needed to be translated from Persian or other languages and then digitized, classified, and referenced. The kind of access also had to be defined, with public documents separated from those that should have limited access; some sensitive files needed special authorization prior to publication.

I must add that I wanted all these documents to be at the institution's disposal and gave them entire liberty to take whatever they found interesting for their archives, including family records and personal documents—and of course the large and unique collection of photographs, many illustrating crucial contemporary events or signed and dedicated by historical figures and heads of state.

These days I am putting the final touches on the third volume of my memoirs, covering the five years I served as minister of foreign affairs. Volume 4 will be primarily concerned with my second ambassadorship in the United States, the turbulent events of 1978–79 and the aftermath, the sad tale of the last days of the shah, and the story of my own nearly forty years living far from my beloved land. Now my own work will also depend on the Hoover Institution archives, and I think by that time they will all be classified and accessible.

Let me reiterate that I have good memories of working with Hoover and with scholars like Professor Abbas Milani; Dr. Eric Wakin, the Robert. H. Malott Director of the Hoover Institution Library & Archives, and Hoover Institution deputy director; Mr. Bradley Bauer, once in charge of the archive; Professor Abraham David Sofaer; and the very cooperative and diligent archivist Heather Hughes. It was Mr. Bauer who first visited me on behalf of Hoover, looked at my collection, and explained to me the workings of the Archive. It was Dr. Eric Wakin who kindly provided me with a copy of my speech in October 1976 at the Commonwealth Club, San Francisco, which was delivered in the presence of Governor Ronald Reagan, soon to be president of the United States and one of the main supporters of the Hoover Institution. To all these friends I am grateful, and above all to my beloved father, who showed me the way and started collecting this family heritage.

It gives me great satisfaction to see that scholars will soon have access to many hitherto unknown artifacts of recent Iranian history. I do not wish to comment on the content of the files; I leave this to the judgment of readers and researchers. I am certain that in every page of these papers, readers will see traces of the patriotism of my illustrious colleagues, who served the country with devotion and worked with me loyally throughout the seventy-five years of my political career.

A good part of these papers is already accessible to educators and the public through the Library and Archives of Hoover Institution. I am happy and proud of the choice I made and grateful to the Hoover Institution for the importance they have given to the collection and to the great people with whom I worked to realize this project.

I consider it a humble contribution to my beloved Iran and the founders of its future, our highly qualified and most promising younger generation.

—Ardeshir Zahedi
Veytaux. Montreux, May 2018

FOREWORD

Eric Wakin

An archive is the preservation of human memory in physical—and now digital—form. The best of these—and the Hoover Institution Library & Archives, founded twenty years before the US National Archives, is certainly one of the best—strive to collect, preserve, describe, make available, and encourage the use of the documentary riches held for future generations.

The Archive of Ardeshir Zahedi, now housed at the Hoover Institution Library & Archives, is one of the most remarkable political collections in recent memory. It contains over three hundred manuscript boxes of material and two gigabytes of digital files. Particularly rich in material from the 1970s, one of the most turbulent periods in modern Iranian history, the collection spans a century, from 1915 to 2014—as told primarily through the global relationships of Ardeshir Zahedi and his father, Fazlollah Zahedi, in their roles as Iranian political figures.

The collection includes all of the physical matter created in a modern life—letters, speeches, interviews, photographs, and audiovisual material—related to Ardeshir Zahedi's diplomatic career during the Pahlavi dynasty. Zahedi served the shah and his country as ambassador to the United States and ambassador to the United Kingdom in the 1960s, then as minister of foreign affairs, and once again as ambassador to the United States from 1973 to 1979, when the reign of the shah, Mohammad Reza Pahlavi, collapsed, ushering in the religious theocracy that exists today. The collection also contains the papers of Ardeshir's father, Fazlollah Zahedi, a general and prime minister before his son.

This rich collection offers researchers unique access to the inner workings of the shah's government; to Iranian foreign relations across the world—and especially with the United States during the cold war; to the shah's last years: and to Zahedi's life in exile for forty years after the fall of the shah. As the selection of documents in this book amply demonstrates, the collection is a rich resource for understanding the numerous ways a modern state functions.

The collection is arranged in several series. Beginning with the papers of Fazlollah Zahedi, it documents the elder Zahedi's military and political career, including his internment in Palestine during World War II, his tenure as prime minister, and his time as a diplomat at the United Nations.

The next series is the Minister of Foreign Affairs File. Through the documentary record, it delineates the work of Ardeshir Zahedi as foreign minister and his meetings with officials and heads of state.

The Ambassador to the United States Series is perhaps the most voluminous. In Zahedi's second appointment as ambassador, he met repeatedly with Presidents Richard Nixon, Gerald Ford, and Jimmy Carter; his appointment ended with the shah's abdication. Many reports prepared for and annotated by the shah are included in the series.

The Career after Diplomacy Series contains material on Zahedi's life after government service. The collection concludes with the Photographs Series, which contains photographs and albums from Fazlollah

Zahedi's youth through Ardeshir Zahedi's political and post-political careers.

Rarely has such a rich collection, intersecting with global political, social, economic, and military matters, been preserved and made available for research. There is no greater collection on modern Iran outside of Iran today. Complementing the Hoover Institution Library & Archives' other collections on war, revolution, and peace, the Zahedi Collection will be a boon to students, scholars, and researchers for centuries to come.

—ERIC WAKIN,
Robert H. Malott Director of Hoover Institution Library & Archives, Hoover Institution deputy director, and research fellow

INTRODUCTION

The Odyssey of an Archive

The long journey of the monumental Zahedi archive, from the storied Villa les Roses in Montreux to the historic Hoover Archives at Stanford, began unexpectedly one evening some two decades ago. I had gone to Montreux to interview Ambassador Zahedi. My first interview with him occurred even earlier. I was then working on a biography of an Iranian prime minister, Amir Abbas Hoveyda.[1] We met in an ornate niche in a grand ballroom of the Montreux Palais Hotel—itself a landmark in what is rightfully called the Swiss Riviera. The niche, I was told by the host, is called the Zahedi corner.

That first interview was a formal affair, based on previously submitted written questions. Gradually I grew to admire his unusual candor, his attention to detail, his formidable memory, his knack for often sprawling narrative, his brimming compassion, his patriotism, and his dedication and devotion—never blind, but never wavering—to the shah. Though in my youth I had been an opponent of the shah, by then I was studying the Pahlavi era not through the warped ideological prism of my youth but from the point of view of scholarship. By that auspicious evening, much to my delight, Ambassador Zahedi had grown to trust me as someone who no longer had a political ax to grind, someone who was trying to find the truth about a tumultuous part of Iran's modern history. Indeed, I was then meeting Zahedi in preparation for a book on the Shah himself.[2]

That night as we arrived at the hotel, having talked for about four hours, he reached into the backseat of his always impeccably clean car, pulled out a folder, and said, almost in passing, "This file might interest you. I took it out of the bank." We bid farewell and agreed to meet early the next morning. Ardeshir Zahedi is nothing if not hardworking, dedicated to punctual, detailed planning for each day's activities, always mapped out at least a day, if not weeks and months, in advance. This penchant for planning and preparation would later be more than confirmed by his archives. Known more as a debonair diplomat, his archives show him to have been an indefatigable, born archivist, and a diplomat who believed in carefully planning and preparing for each meeting or contingency, and documenting and preserving each step of the process. His old habit of jotting down ideas, preserving every note, keeping every memento, his willingness to spare no effort or expense to haul his archive around the world, finally his success in keeping the records pristine and complete for posterity will, I think, be considered a great historic accomplishment.

That first night in my hotel room, I opened the folder and was amazed. Much of the night I stayed awake, stunned by the explosive novelty of what I was reading, and wondering how many more of these equally revealing documents he had "at the bank." The file he had so casually given me included correspondence between Ardeshir Zahedi, then Iran's foreign minister, the shah, and Yasser Arafat, then head of the Palestinian Liberation Organization (PLO). Also included were copies of two checks dated September 14, 1969, payable to Yasser Arafat, totaling five hundred thousand dollars. In those days, Arafat and his PLO were a crucial source of "training for Iranian guerrillas" and a growing source of anxiety for the shah. And though the Iranian regime and the Palestinian group had been publicly at war, here was incontrovertible evidence that behind the scenes Arafat gladly accepted the shah's donation, both sides also agreeing to "keep this unusual transaction away from the eyes of American and Israeli officials. In his letter confirming receipt of the check and thanking the shah for his generous assistance, Arafat called the shah his Akhi, "brother" or "comrade."[3]

The next morning, at exactly the designated hour, Zahedi arrived at the hotel. He soon observed in my face the signs of astonishment, exhaustion from a sleepless night, avid curiosity, and anxious trepidation. I asked permission to copy the file, particularly the checks. I told him it would be more credible to incredulous readers if in my book I could produce a copy of the actual checks. I thought given the sensitive, even sensational nature of the file, and given the fact that he was already working on his own memoir, he would want to delay its publication till his own book was ready. But he readily and selflessly agreed to my request, went on to answer my many questions, and as we parted, said that when I next came to town, he would share a few more files.

After a couple of years, with intermittent visits and long hours of interviews, occasional access to a few files, and tantalizing hints of more to come, he invited me to stay in his house. I knew enough about him to know that such an invitation was a clear sign that the cautious formality of our initial contacts had given way to a bond of friendship and complete trust. Outside the room where I slept, there was a metal drawer. He told me it was full of documents from his days at the Iranian embassy and that I was welcome to read them. I was excited that another joyfully sleepless night was ahead. At around five in the morning, having noticed the light in my room, Zahedi came to the door and told me he thought I should now sleep. "There is plenty more of these," he said enigmatically, adding, "they won't go anywhere."

During my next visit, before going out to dinner, he asked me to come with him to the cellar. He was always known to have an eye for excellent wines and champagnes. With a big metal key, darkened by time, reminiscent of the keys that open gates to moated castles, he opened the heavy door to a room full of metal file cabinets, all of equal sizes, lining two walls, metal armoires filling one wall, boxes, antiques, and books piled on the floor, large red-covered volumes neatly arranged on top of the cabinets, and a few handsome but worn leather bags. "All of my papers are here," he said, adding, "they cover my second appointment as Iran's ambassador to the US and most of my papers as the foreign minister." With a generous nonchalance he said, "After dinner you can look and see what is here." He showed me where the key would be kept, and then we went to dinner.

Though his hospitality is legendary, and though he had invited me to yet another delightful Montreux restaurant, as is his wont, that night I could not wait to get back to his house and go into his cellar-turned-archive to look at what I anticipated, based on my experience of the Arafat file, would be a mind-bending experience. We went back to his house around ten, and no sooner had we arrived than I went down to the room and began browsing, opening drawers, glancing at titles of reports, sometimes reading in amazement the first few paragraphs. I immediately realized that this was the motherlode of material outside Iran on the shah's last two decades in power—even more remarkable than the first file I had seen.

Over the next few years, as I spent hours excavating the riches of that collection, he began to talk about his desire to donate his papers to some institution for safekeeping and for use by posterity and by scholars. He was, he said, always particularly keen on making sure the youth of Iran know the truth of what his generation and the shah—whom he usually calls "my beloved monarch"—had done; they should know "our accomplishments and our mistakes." He initially toyed with the idea of turning his villa, with all its historic ornaments and appointments, and tokens of visits by monarchs and ministers, artists and entrepreneurs, into a museum celebrating modern Iran. But there was, he concluded, no way the small town of Montreux could be a functionally efficient host to scholars from around the world, or an expert curator of his vast collection of material.

As he began to search for a university that could be the proper host for his singular archive, he, as he often told me, sought a place that would, in practice and reputation, and by the nature of its other collected papers, be a natural fit for his diplomatic and political archive. I couldn't agree more with his decision and told him that he should consider Hoover Archives. Here was, after all, where people as different as George Shultz, and Warren Chistopher to William Rehnquist and Milton Friedman had deposited their papers. And then one day he told me that he had decided to donate the papers to Hoover and Stanford. It was, for me, one of the happiest days of my professional life at Stanford.

Though he initially told me of his decision verbally, over breakfast, I knew his promise was more reliable than any written document. It took at least three years for the labyrinthine legal process to be completed and another three years for the almost one hundred big boxes of documents and rare photographs to be professionally packed at Montreux and arrive on our campus. The emotional toll of parting company with an archive that had been accumulating in his family for almost 150 years, each page or image of which was a reminder of a moment in his and his father's eventful and remarkable lives, was not hard to understand. His decision not only immediately made Hoover Archives an indispensable source for scholarship on Pahlavi-era politics and diplomacy but will, I am sure, be a critical part of his enduring legacy for modern Iranian history.

—Abbas Milani,
the Hamid and Christina Moghadam Director of Iranian Studies at Stanford University, and research fellow at the Hoover Institution

NOTES

1. Abbas Milani, *The Persian Sphinx* (Washington, DC: Mage Books, 2000).

2. Abbas Milani, *The Shah* (New York: St. Martin's Press, 2011).

3. Ibid., 328.

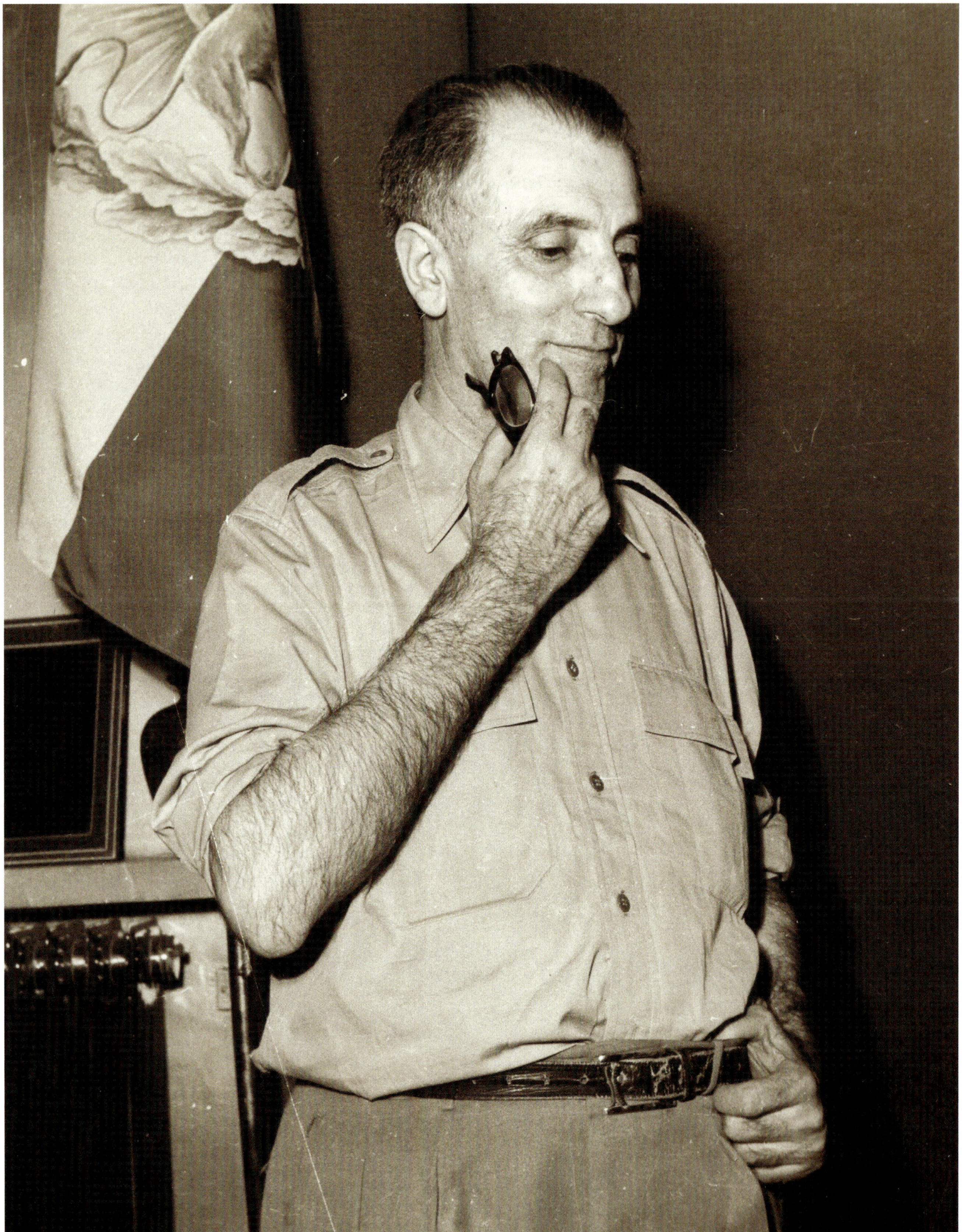

GENERAL FAZLOLLAH ZAHEDI: A PROFILE

Few men in Iran's modern military could match General Fazlollah Zahedi for fame. Early in his career, he had fought some of the most notorious knaves in Iranian politics—characters like Khaz'al, a self-declared king in Iran's oil-rich southern provinces. The general was a kingmaker but also feared by kings; a handsome, charismatic soldier with the reputation of a bon vivant. He was known to have a taste for luxury, fancy cars, and beautiful women. He dressed impeccably and loved films. Humphrey Bogart was one of his favorite actors.[1]

He was one of the most decorated generals of the Iranian army in the twentieth century. The infamous Islamic terrorist group Feda'yan Islam had plans to assassinate him.[2] At the height of his political life, when he was the prime minister, his chief of staff and trusted aide-de-camp was, unbeknownst to him, a communist and a member of the Tudeh Party's secret organization of officers.[3]

He had fought many wars to victory, but his ambition and a widespread reputation for having a following in the Iranian army made him suspect in the eyes of both Pahlavi kings. Though in August 1953 he saved the throne for the shah, he was after about two years exiled to Europe, where he lived the last years of his life eating the bitter bread of banishment.

Zahedi was born in 1893 in the village of Shervin, near the city of Hamadan.[4] His father was known as Basir-Divan (Visionary of the Court) and was among the city's eminent citizens. In the early part of the century, for much of the winter, cold and snow isolated Hamadan from the outside world. The city's benevolent grandees, including Basir-Divan, organized a de facto system of social welfare for the poor: they bought ample supplies of coal, and when winter and want came, they distributed it gratis to the neediest families.[5] Upon his father's death, a number of small villages—Damag, Khorbandeh, and others—were left to the children. As the eldest boy, Fazlollah took care of the properties. Late in life, he directed his son, Ardeshir, to ensure that the rest of the family received a fair share of the paternal inheritance.[6]

Figure 1 General Fazlollah Zahedi on his first day as prime minister, August 19, 1953.

The young Fazlollah went to school at Mozafari and Alliance, both in Isfahan. His love of guns and of a soldier's life, evident even in his youth, led him to the military. Hamadan, like most other urban centers of Iran in the early part of the century, was often prey to bandits and armed hooligans. Fazlollah was barely a teenager when he organized a posse to capture a bandit. He was shot and almost died. Only the fortuitous arrival of a group of American missionaries who happened to have a physician in their midst saved his life. But seven of his ribs had to be removed, and for the rest of his life, he suffered from a weak kidney.[7]

He was only thirteen when he first met Reza Khan, a charismatic commander of the Cossack Brigade traveling through Hamadan on his way to the Kurdistan region. Reza Khan, who would soon become Reza Shah and the founder of the Pahlavi dynasty, stayed in the Zahedi family home, and it was the beginning of a long relationship between the rapidly rising colonel and the aspiring young soldier.[8] At the urging of

Figure 2

A familiy portrait: General Zahedi and his children Ardeshir and Homa Zahedi.

Figure 3

On the road to Kerman, 1936. Mrs. Akhtar Shariar; Brigadier General Fazlollah Zahedi; Homa Zahedi and Ardeshir in childhood; Last person is the late Shahriar; the person talking to the general and the officer standing next to Shahriar were not recognized. The person standing behind the general was Sergeant Sabzali, who accompanied the general in all his battles.

Reza Khan, the young Fazlollah joined the Cossack Brigade. In pictures of the period, he cuts a dashing figure in full Cossack regalia. A picture of him from those days is included in this volume. At that time, he still used his father's title of Basir-Divan in lieu of a surname. Before long, the family, like everyone else in the country, was forced to give up its title and pick a family name. They chose Zahedi, "people of piety," alluding to the fact that there were men known for their piety and faith among their ancestors.

As a young officer, Fazlollah showed himself to be fearless and tactical. One of his first battles was against the forces loyal to Mirza Kuchek Khan Jangali—a nationalist Iranian who, in surprising unity with Iranian and Russian Communists, had created a Soviet Socialist Republic of Iran.[9] By 1922, Reza Khan had become the commander of Iran's armed forces, and Zahedi was promoted to lieutenant general, the youngest to hold that rank in the Iranian army. He was involved in several other important wars against separatist forces in Iran—from the fight against Turkomans to the famous battle to defeat and arrest the army of Sheikh Khaz'al, who had turned the oil-rich province of Khuzestan into a veritable protectorate of the British. It was General Zahedi who, on the order of Reza Shah, arranged the arrest of the sheikh and his son. Zahedi invited Khaz'al to a party, and when the sheikh and his guards were inebriated, he had them arrested.[10] Included in this volume are General Zahedi's recollections of this important episode of modern Iranian history.

After the battle for Khuzestan, Zahedi took his first trip to Europe. He traveled leisurely for three months, picking up a smattering of French. He also had a command of Turkish. Upon his return, he was appointed commander of the Sixth Army, based in the province of Gilan. In that capacity, an enduring aspect of Zahedi's life and character became evident. He arranged for a concert by Saba, one of Iran's most innovative modern musicians. All his life, Zahedi befriended artists, intellectuals, and journalists. His coterie of friends included such figures as Abbas Egbal Ashtiyani, a self-made scholar; Zabih Behrouz, a fiercely nationalist historian; and Ali Asghar Amirani, the controversial editor of the influential magazine *Khandaniha*.[11] The general was also an early advocate of education for girls, and when such schools were started in Iran, the conservative clergy invariably fought against them. On several occasions, General Zahedi used his power and position to keep the schools open.

One of Reza Shah's earliest policies as king was turning the nomads of Iran, often forcibly, into sedentary citizens of the new polity. The nomads fought back, and for several years the government was involved in military skirmishes with various armed tribes. During this period, General Zahedi was named commander of the Iranian Gendarmerie, and quelling these uprisings was part of his responsibilities. But Reza Shah grew suspicious of the way the general handled the assignment and ordered him arrested.[12]

General Zahedi was not long out of favor. After a short time, he was released and appointed to the even more important post of commander of Iran's National Police. He lasted a year in the new post. But then two prisoners, one a British spy named Lawrence, the other a common criminal named Seyyed Farhad, escaped from Gasre Prison in Tehran. An angry Reza Shah demanded their capture within twenty-four hours. When the allotted time elapsed and the prisoners were still at large, the king not only angrily dismissed General Zahedi from his post, but also—in one of his famed theatrical gestures—tore the stars from the general's uniform and ordered him arrested. This time, he was in prison about a month. More important, for the first time in his life he had to look for a job outside the army.

After a yearlong hiatus, General Zahedi was recalled to the army; Reza Shah gave him back his stars and appointed him a special adjutant to the king. But this time, too, his tenure was short. Reza Shah had by then grown wary of charismatic officers and ambitious politicians. He grew suspicious of Zahedi, who was both. Aware of the king's distrust, General Zahedi had no choice but to resign his post. He remained in the army but spent the next few years in perfunctory capacities. In one assignment, he was sent to purchase five hundred Hungarian horses for the cavalry.

In 1929 the general married Khadijeh, the daughter of Motamen-ol-Molk, one of the most respected Iranian statesmen of his generation.[13] It was a rocky marriage from the beginning. Husband and wife were both fiercely independent, and after they had two children together—a boy named Ardeshir and a girl called Homa—they separated.

On the day Reza Shah abdicated, General Zahedi decided to leave Iran with him. He had a history of fighting the Soviet Communists and the British, and as the two armies were converging on the city, it seemed wise for him to leave. He was joined by his son, Ardeshir, and a general. The three left the capital on the same day that Reza Shah's entourage left the city. They were to join the newly abdicated king in the city of Gom. As the general watched soldiers of the army roam the streets aimlessly, often out of uniform, frightened and emaciated, the son "saw [his] father's tears for the first time. . . . 'Look at these people. They are so decent. Anywhere else in the world, these soldiers would be ransacking the city.'"[14]

Forty kilometers outside the city the general met with Reza Shah, who convinced him that he should return to the capital. "I leave my son in your care," Reza Shah is reported to have told General Zahedi. Zahedi returned to Tehran and began almost two decades of a deeply complicated, eventful relationship with the new shah, Mohammad Reza Pahlavi.

His first position in the postwar cabinet was as the commander of the Gendarmerie. His tenure lasted only a few months. The end of Reza Shah's iron-fisted rule brought about a surge of political activity, and the armed rebellion of the nomadic tribes was one of the most serious. General Zahedi was accustomed to fighting these nomads and was known to have close ties to some of the leaders, or khans, of the tribes. For these reasons, he was appointed the commander of the Ninth Army, stationed in Isfahan. The British and the Soviet authorities had another theory about why Zahedi was going to Isfahan.

The Allies had received intelligence that Nazi spies had secretly entered Iran and were on their way to join the nomadic tribes and together act as a "fifth column" for Germany. Indeed, the British believed that the plot included the "arrival [of] paratroops [and] German forces in North Persia."[15] Zahedi was suspected of complicity with the German spies.

Some even in the British government did not believe these charges against Zahedi. The British consulate in Isfahan, for example, wrote that "there is now little likelihood of any coup d'etat" by Zahedi. The only concrete evidence the British had against him was "the matter of the [German wireless] W/T transmitter which he is said to have."[16] Eventually, the British, in coordination with the Soviets, rounded up a couple hundred Iranians from all walks of life. They put some under arrest in Iran, and others they exiled. General Zahedi was one of them. Plans for his arrest were not discussed with the shah or the Iranian government. On December 5, 1941, he was arrested in a cloak-and-dagger operation in Isfahan. Only after his arrest did the British bother to inform the Iranian government.

Aside from the allegations of pro-German sympathies, there are indications that General Zahedi and the British had a number of other confrontations during his tenure in Isfahan. From the distribution of bread to the treatment of Iranian officers by the British, there were constant run-ins between the general and British officials in the city.

The arrest of General Zahedi did not, according to the British, lead to any disturbances in Isfahan. There were faint words of protest from the shah and the Iranian government, and the US embassy and the State Department expressed "deep concern about arrest of General Zahedi."[17] In response, the British prepared talking points to be used by diplomats in response to such criticism. The notes suggest that "Zahedi is a born intriguer and is notorious for his anti-Allied attitude. . . . He is known to have harbored German agents. . . . His past record gives no ground for any confidence in his integrity."[18] The British provided the same answers to the Americans as they did to the shah and the Iranian government. The story of his arrest by a special unit of the British army became the subject of a memoir by Fitzroy Mclean, the commander of the British unit that attacked the general's house and put him under arrest.[19]

General Zahedi spent the next three years in exile. Not long after his arrest, the British, much to his consternation, convinced the Iranian army to announce his retirement.[20] After several months, the general used a family in the Druse community to smuggle a brief note to his son reassuring him of his safety.[21] His recollections of his days in a British prison in Palestine have been included in this collection.

When the general finally returned home, it did not take long for the shah to rescind the retirement order and return him to active duty. When the nomadic tribes of the south rose up against the government again, General Zahedi was entrusted with the task of quelling the uprising. He used a combination of force and finesse to bring peace to the region and was subsequently appointed governor of the Fars region. During this period, he was approached on several occasions by Nasser Ghashgai, of the Ghashgai tribe, and asked to cooperate in a coup against the shah. On each occasion, the general, according to Nasser Khan, refused, saying, "We need this young man. With him we can do much good for Iran."[22] As one of the documents selected for this collection shows, the general maintained close relations with the Gashghais long after the end of the Second World War.

As tensions in the Iranian political scene increased, General Zahedi emerged more and more as a pivotal figure. He became a member of the newly created senate, and his next appointment after the governorship was the command of the Iranian National Police. In February 1951, he was named minister of the interior in what was a caretaker cabinet. During this time, Dr. Mohammad Mossadegh and his allies won seats in Parliament. According to Ardeshir, the fact that his father oversaw a fair election endeared him to Mossadegh but was the subject of snide remarks by the shah, who commented, "It was your father who brought [Mossadegh and his allies] to power."[23]

When Mossadegh finally succeeded in having Parliament ratify his proposed bill to nationalize the Iranian oil industry, he became the prime minister on a wave of nationalist euphoria. He asked General Zahedi to remain at the crucial post of interior minister. The general agreed, and thus began a period of tense cooperation between these two towering and charismatic figures. The cooperation was short lived. Before long, the general resigned in protest over Mossadegh's demand to fire the commander of the National Police.

After his resignation, Zahedi began meeting regularly with a group of retired officers and generals. The government saw them as a cabal of conspirators out to organize a coup. In September 1952, a member of the group, General Mohammad Hejazi, was arrested by the government on charges of conspiring with a foreign government. Evidence from the American and British archives shows that as early as July 31, 1952, the Americans and the British had jointly decided that only a coup against Mossadegh could bring about desired

Figure 4
A photo of Motamen-ol Molk Pirnia, Ardeshir Zahedi's maternal grandfather, and a politician of great stature in his time.

changes, and that the only "army officers who seemed to be best fitted for leadership in effecting coup d'etat were General Zahedi and General Hedjazi."[24] The same report adds that, of the two, "Zahedi sympathized with moderates of National Front." Both governments decided that "neither British nor American government should" participate or encourage such a coup.

The general, however, continued his efforts against what he perceived as Mossadegh's increasing radicalism. In notes prepared for what was to be his memoir—included in this collection—he gives a brief outline of the events that led to his success in toppling the Mossadegh government.

In talks in the senate, where he enjoyed immunity as a senator, he emerged as a focal point of opposition to Mossadegh. In response, Mossadegh arranged for the dissolution of the senate. On February 26, 1953, Zahedi, no longer a senator, was arrested. At the same time, efforts to muster enough votes in Parliament to dismiss Mossadegh and his cabinet came to naught. The US embassy reported that General Zahedi "wishes to become prime minister, and" then referring to the efforts of his allies and supporters to attempt to vote Mossadeq out of office, and show their inclination for the general as the prime minister, added, that Zahedi's "adherents are active in Majlis. It is unlikely that he will succeed."[25]

One major obstacle in the general's way was the fact that the shah, according to the American embassy in Tehran, "did not fully trust Zahedi."[26] Events later confirmed their view. Even Hussein Ala, then court minister, opined to the embassy that "Zahedi was not completely trustworthy."[27] But by April 1953, as the situation deteriorated and the shah was left with few viable options, his attitude toward General Zahedi changed, and for the first time, the court began to regard "Zahedi's candidacy with favor."[28]

At the same time, the British and American governments were also beginning to pressure the shah to act. They wanted him to sign orders dismissing Mossadegh and appointing Zahedi in his place. The shah demurred, insisting that only when it was constitutionally possible would he sign such orders. On May 30, 1953, for example, Loy Henderson, the American ambassador in Iran, met with the shah and "told him I would like frank statement his attitude re General Zahedi. He said although General not intellectual giant, nevertheless he would be acceptable under three conditions." He "would come into office through legal, parliamentary means" and the United States as well as Britain must "be prepared to give new government emergency financial as well as massive economic aid."[29]

But then Mossadegh, through a referendum of dubious legality, dismissed the Parliament, giving the shah the authority to issue a recess *farman* (order). With Parliament in session, the shah could only dismiss a prime minister if he received a vote of no confidence from Parliament. When there was no parliament, there was a long tradition of kings issuing recess orders appointing or dismissing prime ministers. With no parliament in session, the shah signed two such orders, one dismissing Mossadegh, the other appointing General Zahedi as prime minister. After some initial delays and mishaps, the orders were delivered on the night of August 16, 1953. Mossadegh refused to heed the order, arresting the officer who had delivered it late on the evening of August 15 and announcing the next day that his government had defeated a military coup but making no reference to the royal decree. No sooner had the shah learned of Mossadegh's refusal to heed his order than he left the country for Iraq. He assumed his days on the peacock throne had come to an end.[30]

What happened in the next three days is one of the most contested accounts in modern Iranian history. It is clear that after the first two days, both the CIA station in Tehran and the general assumed that the effort to replace Mossadegh had been defeated. General Zahedi was planning to leave the city and go to a western province of Iran to begin an armed struggle against Mossadegh. The CIA ordered its officers to leave Iran forthwith. But on August 19, the situation changed. Crowds appeared on the streets chanting slogans in favor of the shah. To Mossadegh and his followers, the dismissal, the attack on his house on the nineteenth, and the takeover of government offices and radio station by forces loyal to the shah were part of a coup masterminded by the CIA and the British. To the royalists, August 19 was a day of national uprising against the increasingly inept government of Mossadegh. The real coup, they claim, was Mossadegh's refusal to accept the legal dismissal order signed by the sovereign. Ever since those eventful days, the general's son, Ardeshir, has spared no effort to offer his and his father's version of the events. General Zahedi's notes for his memoirs, represented in this collection, offer for the first time his view of the trajectory of the events.

By two-thirty on the afternoon of the nineteenth, General Zahedi came out of hiding and delivered a speech on the radio declaring himself to be the only legitimate prime minister. By four o'clock he was "master of the situation" in the country. Almost immediately, despite the advice of his senior advisers, who suggested that he should keep the shah waiting for at least a few days—thus undermining the shah's ability to reassert authority on his return[31]—he sent a telegram inviting the shah back to Iran. When the shah received the telegram, he was in Rome, planning for his retirement as a gentleman farmer in the United States. He began to plan his return home.

To the surprise of the political cognoscenti, there were few military men in General Zahedi's cabinet. The majority were politicians. At the same time, General Zahedi had to face the fact that the shah was unhappy with the cabinet. Almost immediately after his return, the shah began trying to push Zahedi out of office. There were also tensions between the two over control of the army. The shah had let the general know that he should in no way interfere in matters related to the military.

By far the most pressing and sensitive issue facing the new cabinet concerned oil. After some negotiations, Iran signed an agreement with a consortium of Western oil companies. The agreement was severely criticized by members of the Iranian opposition as a betrayal of Iran's national interests. Even the Iranian architects of the new agreement conceded that it was far from a favorable deal for Iran. We were negotiating from a position of weakness, they said, and had to agree to unfavorable terms.

These small and big differences between the shah and Zahedi—and the fact that the king was, like his father, inherently wary of charismatic and ambitious officers—led the shah to attempt to sack the man who had saved his throne. American and British embassies forcefully dissuaded the shah from such a move. For his part, Zahedi had big plans. He hoped to use a carrot-and-stick approach. A week after the coup, for example, he told the American ambassador, according to the ambassador's notes, that "he hoped [to] put hundred thousand to work on roads. . . . Also necessary begin construction immediately thousands houses."[32] At the same time, he appointed Colonel Teymur Bakhtiar as the military governor of Tehran, and his units began a crackdown on members of the opposition, particularly the Communists.

Another point of contention between the shah and Zahedi was the fate of Mossadegh. Less than two days after the general assumed office, Mossadegh turned himself in. The headquarters of the new government had been set up at the Officers Club, and General Zahedi made every effort to show deference to the fallen prime minister. Zahedi was adamantly opposed to the idea of putting Mossadegh on trial. He favored exiling him to his estate outside Tehran. The shah, however, insisted on having a trial, which led to Mossadegh's apotheosis as the

Figure 5

General Zahedi in his temporary new office as a Prime Minister on the afternoon of August 19, 1953.

Figure 6

The Shah, just returned from his temporary exile, with General Zahedi, standing next to him. Some members of the cabinet also present.

Figure 7 Mossadegh's house on August 19, 1953, after angry mobs had ransacked it.

Figure 8 The body of General Zahedi, in Switzerland, awaiting to be returned to Iran. The year is 1963.

nationalist leader unjustly pushed out of power by a coup.

Starting in late 1954, the shah began creating a cabal of trusted aides and entrustig them with preparing the ground for Zahedi's dismissal. The group dubbed itself the "polit-bureau." In mid-March 1955, the shah stated unambiguously that he wanted the general to resign. Zahedi was equally unequivocal that he would not abide by the shah's wishes. On March 23, he sent for General Bakhtiar and told him "he supposed General Bakhtiyar knew that his relations with the Shah were not good and that it was all the fault of that wretched fellow Ebtehaj [head of Iran's Plan Organization]: he did not see why he should lose his job after all that he had done for his country and he could not understand why the Shah wanted to get rid of him. . . . He was damned if he would go gracefully. If he were thrown out he would not go to Europe but to South America, where he would be able to speak his mind about the present rulers of Persia. He added that it would be perfectly open for him to invoke the assistance of foreigners in order to maintain himself in power."[33]

By early April, after several unsuccessful attempts to secure the general's resignation, the shah finally dispatched his trusted friend Assadollah Alam to convince Zahedi to step aside. After some detailed negotiations, the two worked out the text of a letter of resignation, as well as the shah's response.[34] General Zahedi finally resigned on April 7, 1955, citing ill health. The US embassy reported that Zahedi left believing that "his own return to power in not too distant future will be necessary" and thus "conducted himself in loyal and dignified manner at departure." The same report contends that Zahedi's devotion "to certain cronies among ministers who were neither particularly effective nor interested in the Shah's program," along with his "opposition to Plan Director Ebtehaj," contributed to his demise.[35]

Only hours after submitting his resignation, Zahedi was asked to leave Iran and put on a plane. Lest the rift become a sore point used by the opposition, the general, in spite of his initial refusal to accept any job in the government, was appointed ambassador at large. The job was ceremonial. The general tried to go back to Iran as little as possible but did make a special trip to attend his son's wedding to the shah's daughter, Princess Shahnaz.

Zahedi lived his last years in Europe, isolated and disheartened. He grew increasingly concerned about the future of the throne in Iran. His hoped-for return to power never materialized. The shah had begun to consolidate power; a strong and charismatic prime minister who, like Mossadegh or General Zahedi, insisted that the shah should reign, not rule, was no longer tolerable. General Zahedi made his home in the city of Montreux, in a villa called Les Roses.

In documents about the Zahedi family published by the Islamic Republic, letters from the general to his son show his character and concerns. He emerges as a father deeply concerned about his son—about his education, his mastery of the English and Persian languages, even his penmanship. When his son asks him what subject he should pursue in college, the general writes, "Choose a field according to your own taste; in other words, choose a field that is necessary but to your liking."[36] But in another letter he writes, "I want you to be like a soldier; a soldier is absolutely obedient in the face of his commander. . . . If you want to be my loving son, you have to be absolutely obedient."[37] He invites his son to forgo using profanities in his letters and his daily discourse. He tries to educate Ardeshir in the history of Iran, asking Zabih Behrouz, the famed historian, to send them some material on the subject.[38]

On the day of his departure from Iran, he wrote to his son lamenting leaving Tehran "with a world of sorrow. . . . You should not get too mad about this. I swear to God that the trip has been a blessing, and it was good, and it was God's wish. God is always with us. The hand of fortune worked in my favor." He goes on to tell his son to accept any post he is offered, adding, "Don't stay alone, but also be careful. People have no honor. Be very very careful. You and I have no friend or ally other than God. You are now the light of the Zahedi family."[39] In another letter, he writes, "I have lived my life. . . . It was necessary and preferred that I step aside. . . . Those who had escaped during the Mossadeq days, or had sided with him, are now surrounding the Shah. I am worried that they might in future betray the king. I don't think I shall ever return to Iran again. I will leave what there is left of my life, finances permitting, away from the world of politics. . . . You must stay and preserve the family name."[40]

On September 2, 1963, General Zahedi died in Montreux. He had been sick for some time. Friends who visited him shortly before his death described his loneliness and his deteriorating mood and condition. His grieving son, Ardeshir, arranged for the body of his father to be returned to Iran after a short pilgrimage to Karbala and Najaf. He was buried near Tehran, after a state funeral reserved for prime ministers.

Parts of this profile were published earlier in Abbas Milani's *Eminent Persians: The Men and Women Who Made Modern Iran, 1941–1979,* 2 Volumes, (Syracuse, NY: Syracuse University Press, 2008), 495–505.

NOTES

1. Ardeshir Zahedi, *Khaterat-e Ardeshir Zahedi* [Memoirs of Ardeshir Zahedi] (Bethesda, 2005), 345.

2. Ardeshir Zahedi, *Khaterat*, 338.

3 Ardeshir Zahedi, interview with author, Montreux, Oct. 20, 2002.

4. Jalal Andarzamani, "Zahedi dar Takapuye godrat" [Zahedi in search of power], *Tarikhe Moaser-e Iran* (Winter 1399/1988): 126.

5. General Hassan Alavi-Kia, interview with author, Apr. 12, 2004.

6. *Ardeshir Zahedi be Ravayat-e Asnad SAVAK* [Zahedi according to SAVAK documents] (Tehran: Markaz Baresiye Asnade Tarikhiye Vezarate Etela'at, 1378/1999).

7. Ardeshir Zahedi, *Khaterat*, 10.

8. Ibid.

9. Cosroe Chaqueri, *The Soviet Socialist Republic of Iran, 1920–1921* (Pittsburgh: Univ. of Pittsburgh Press, 1995).

10. Many sources, including Reza Shah's travel diaries of his Khuzestan journey, confirm Zahedi's role in the arrest. See Reza Shah Kabir, *Safer-Nameye Khuzestan* [Khuzestan travel diaries] (Tehran, n.d.). 243.

11. In my *Eminent Persians*, there are chapters on Saba, Amirani, Egbal, and Behrouz. For Zahedi's relationship with Egbal Ashtiyani, see Abbas Milani, "Daneshkadeh and the Question of Modernity in Iran," *Iranshenasi* 12, no. 2 (Summer 2005).

12. Ardeshir Zahedi, *Khaterat*, 28.

13. Andarzamani, "Zahedi dar Takapuye godrat," 125

14. Ardeshir Zahedi, *Khaterat*, 34

15. British Legation to War Office, Nov. 11, 1941, Public Records Office, London, FO 371/31387.

16. British Consulate to British Embassy, Tehran, Oct. 16, 1942, Public Records Office, London, FO 248/1411.

17. Foreign Office to Tehran Legation, Dec. 13, 1942, Public Records Office, London, FO 371/31587.

18. Tehran to Foreign Office, Dec. 8, 1942, Public Records Office, London, FO 371/31387.

19. Fitzroy Mclean, *Eastern Approaches* (London: Jonathan Cape, 1949).

20. Ardeshir Zahedi, *Khaterat*, 63.

21. Ibid., 53.

22. Nasser Ghashgai, Harvard University Oral History Project, Cambridge, MA, Jan. 31, 1983. Interview conducted by Habib Lajevardi. Nasser Khan talks about his relations with the general and about how, in his view, Zahedi was very faithful to the shah and never conspired against him—though the opportunity arose on more than one occasion.

23. Ardeshir Zahedi, *Khaterat*, 68.

24. US Embassy in Tehran to State Dept., July 31, 1952, in US Dept. of State, *Foreign Relations of the United States*, vol. 10, *Iran, 1952–1954* (Washington, DC: GPO, 1989), 427

25. "Memorandum Prepared in the Office of National Estimates, Central Intelligence Agency," Mar. 1, 1953, in ibid., 691.

26. US Embassy in Tehran to State Department, February 22, 1952, in ibid., 674.

27. US Embassy in Tehran to State Department, February 1953, in ibid., 681.

28. US Embassy in Tehran to State Department, March 31, 1953, in ibid., 721

29. US Embassy in Tehran to State Department, May 30, 1953, in ibid., 730–32.

30. In my book *The Shah*, I have discussed at some length the events of this period. See chapters 1, 9, and 10 in *The Shah* (New York: St. Martin's Press, 2011).

31. Ardeshir Zahedi, interview with author, Montreux, Switzerland, Oct. 28, 2009.

32. US Embassy in Tehran to State Department, Aug. 27, 1953, in US Dept. of State, *Foreign Relations of the United States*, vol. 10, *Iran, 1952–1954*, 769.

33. British Embassy to Foreign Office, April 5, 1955, Public Records Office, London, FO371/114810.

34. Ibid. 2.

35. "US Embassy in Tehran to State Department, April 8, 1955," in US Dept. of State, *Foreign Relations of the United States, 1955–1957, Near East Region, Iran: Iraq* (Washington, DC: GPO, 1991), 727.

36. Andarzamani, "Zahedi dar Takapuye godrat," 142.

37. Ibid., 146.

38. Ibid., 144.

39. *Ardeshir Zahedi be Ravayat-e Asnad SAVAK*, n.p.

40. Ibid.

ARDESHIR ZAHEDI: A PROFILE

Figure 9
Ardeshir Zahedi

Ardeshir Zahedi, whose remarkable papers constitute the bulk of the Zahedi Archives at the Hoover Institution, was at the center of Iran's politics for much of the second half of the twentieth century. As the son of the much-decorated general; as a diplomat serving as ambassador in London and Washington;as a foreign minister in the mid-1960s as Iran was mapping a more assertive and independent foreign policy; as a member of Iran's royal family through marriage to the shah's daughter, Princess Shahnaz; and finally as one of the shah's closest confidants, he was certainly "present at the creation."

Iran's last king was his father-in-law. Egypt's last king was his mother-in-law's elder brother. A third king was his maternal grandfather; his own father might have become a king in August 1953 but instead opted for the role of kingmaker. He personally knew nine American presidents—Truman, Eisenhower, Kennedy, Johnson, Nixon, Ford, Carter, Bush senior, and Reagan. The Ardeshir Zahedi Papers, whose arrival at Hoover we here celebrate with a small selection, is replete with correspondence between him and many of these leaders.

Zahedi's home in exile, the Villa les Roses in the picturesque lakeside town of Montreux, Switzerland, is itself a treasure house of his past vocations, present avocations, and the nostalgia of exile. It is replete with reminders of Persia—rugs and photographs in the house, jasmine and roses in the garden. Pictures of kings and presidents sit side by side with those of family and friends.

The largest image at Villa les Roses is of his father—an oil painting of General Fazlollah Zahedi in full military regalia. It was the general who purchased the villa in the late 1950s, some four years after he had been forced out of Iran. On entering, visitors to the house encounter a simple glass case filled with the medals and honors his son has received. They range from an oversize red medal from the Soviet Union to the soft blue Taj, the highest honor of the Pahlavi era.

When I first visited there, all around the house, even in its handsome stone-finished cellar, were documents and newspaper clippings, some neatly filed, others stacked in orderly piles. Zahedi, like his father, is something of an archivist. Beneath the facade of exile, retired from the fury of politics, there thrives a serious, disciplined retired diplomat with a penchant for politics, a thirst to learn and communicate the lessons of Iran's modern history, a clear understanding of the weaknesses and strengths of his "beloved monarch,"[1] an unbending resolution not to openly criticize him, and yet a refreshing willingness to look back not in nostalgia or thirst for a return to power but with a desire to find out what went wrong. His dedication to preserving the papers and his decision to donate them to a major research university, as well as his decision to create an endowment at Stanford University to allow future scholars to visit the university to study these papers, are all rooted in his love of Iran and of history.

Ardeshir Zahedi was born in Tehran in October 1927 (1307) or 1928 (1308). His maternal grandfather, Motamenol-Mulk

Figure 10 In the Bersabeh elementary school–Tehran. Ardeshir Zahedi sixth person (*third row, from below*); he is sitting on Ms. Bersabeh's lap.

Pirnia, was one of his generation's most venerable statesmen and an unseasonably modern man.[2] He sent his daughters—including Ardeshir's mother, Khadijeh—to Europe for their education. That was where Khadijeh learned the piano.[3]

On his paternal side, Zahedi's family, as we can see in the profile of his father, were landlords in the city of Hamadan. He was already famous as a flamboyant and bon vivant officer when he married Ardeshir's fiercely independent mother, Khadijeh—making for a potentially fragile marriage. The fact that the general was often away on military missions made the marriage more fraught. During one of these absences Ardeshir was born. It was a complicated birth, which threatened the life of the mother, but mother and child both survived. Three years later, Ardeshir's younger sister, Homa, was born.

Their father was stern but kind, a disciplinarian but averse to physical punishment. A mere angry look was all it took to silence the children. He was also keen on teaching his son the "manly arts." No sooner could Ardeshir get on a horse than he was taught to ride; every morning he would be awakened at four o'clock for lessons in riding and hunting.

Ardeshir was only about seven years old when his parents decided to divorce. He lived the next few years in his parents' joint custody, spending time alternately with his mother and father. While his mother's house offered the serenity and security of doting and deeply cultured grandparents, his father lived a more eventful life and became, before long, "the true hero" of the young boy's life.

Shortly after the beginning of the Second World War in Europe, Ardeshir's father, by then the commander of an Iranian army division stationed in the vicinity of Isfahan, was arrested by the British military, which was—along with the Soviet Red Army—occupying Iran. General Zahedi's outline for a memoir of his time in a British prison is included in this book.

In 1942, with his father in prison, Ardeshir and Homa were sent to Tehran, where they spent the next three years. No sooner was Ardeshir registered at the Adab School than he began agitating against the British.[4] In 1945, he was sent to Beirut to continue his education. He enrolled in Eslamiye High School, and there he organized a political protest against the Soviet occupation of parts of Iran. By 1946, he had set out for the United States, where he ended up at Utah State University. He received a bachelor's degree in agricultural engineering (the origin of his often-used title of Muhandess, or engineer).[5] His grades were mediocre, but the experience was formative. During the summers, he traveled around the United States, venturing all the way to Alaska and often working at menial jobs—from factory labor at canneries to busing at restaurants.[6] To his father's dismay, by then another of Ardeshir's character traits had become clear: he was a spendthrift, and generous to a fault.

Ardeshir's stay in the United States had another, crucial consequence. In 1949, when the shah traveled to the United States, he visited Utah; Ardeshir for the first time spent some time with the monarch. It was the beginning of an enduring relationship, one that would last until the final days of the shah's life. In 1950, Zahedi returned to Iran and soon began to work for the Point Four Program, an American aid initiative that was helping Iran develop its infrastructure. A year later, Dr. Mohammad Mossadegh became prime minister and was soon embroiled in a bitter battle with the shah and his supporters, particularly Ardeshir's father, General Zahedi. In a clear attempt to put pressure on General Zahedi, Mossadegh met with William Warne, the head of Point Four—with the US ambassador to Iran also present—and demanded that since Ardeshir, in the prime minister's words, "had been engaged in activities incompatible with his duties at Point Four . . . he should be separated from that organization."[7] Soon after this meeting, Ardeshir resigned from his job, and shortly afterward, he was arrested in the middle of the night on the charge of conspiring against the government.

After spending a few eventful weeks in prison, Ardeshir succeeded in escaping. During his prison days, he had been tortured—handcuffs tightened his arms awkwardly behind his back, and a guard struck him with a rifle. The aftereffects of that incident, which left him with a damaged disc, continue to afflict him today.[8]

The conflict between the shah and Mossadegh turned into a direct confrontation in August 1953: on August 12, at the strong urging of the American and British governments, the shah used Mossadegh's closure of Parliament as a pretext to issue two recess orders (*firmans*), one dismissing Mossadegh as prime minister and the other appointing General Zahedi as his successor. This event catapulted Ardeshir to the center of Iranian politics. By August 19, after four days of tumult in many cities, particularly Tehran—and though the shah had fled Iran on August 16—General Zahedi assumed power and declared himself the legal prime minister. Some of the hundreds of historic pictures included in the Zahedi Archives record those events, and a couple have been included in this book.

Beginning with his memoir of those fateful August days, *Five Days of Crisis*, published soon after those events, and continuing with books, articles, interviews, and opinion pieces, most written from exile, Ardeshir Zahedi has offered a detailed account of the August 1953 events as he witnessed and participated in them.[9]

In the contested accounts of what happened on those days, it is clear that by the end of the day on August 18, both the American and British governments had decided that the attempt to overthrow Mossadegh had failed. The two governments must, they said, "take a whole new look at the Iranian situation" and would "probably have to snuggle up to Mossadeq if we are going to have anything there."[10]

But General Zahedi and his allies had not given up. On August 19, the tide turned. As Ardeshir has never tired of emphasizing, what happened on that morning was nothing less than a heroic national uprising in support of the shah and General Zahedi. The opposition, on the other hand, has always maintained that the American and British governments played a key role. What is clear is that by the end of the night, General Zahedi was the new prime minister, and Ardeshir was his father's indefatigable aide-de-camp, adviser, and emissary.

When the shah returned six days later, Ardeshir acted as a trusted courier between his father and the monarch. Each day, often more than once, he traveled between the court and the offices where his father was established, taking some of the more sensitive messages between the shah and his prime minister.[11] He also acted as his father's translator when the general was meeting with important English-speaking diplomats or dignitaries.[12] He was eventually named special adviser to the prime minister and civil adjutant to the shah.

Zahedi's allegiance to his father and his growing closeness to the shah came into heart-wrenching conflict in 1955, when the shah forced his father to resign and leave the country. He contemplated leaving Iran with his father but eventually, partially at the urging of his father, decided to remain and work with the shah. Ardeshir began to work, initially ad hoc, on the problem of helping the growing number of Iranian students studying abroad. Those years also witnessed a major change in his life: he married the shah's daughter, Princess Shahnaz. The two had first met when the shah traveled to Europe in 1955. Before long, they were in love and had decided to marry. But love in courts is never just a matter of hearts. There were many around the shah and in the royal family who adamantly opposed this union. In the tense weeks after the young couple announced their intention, a roadside bomb almost killed Zahedi, who came to believe that it was someone from the inner circle of the court opposed to the marriage who had organized or paid for the plot.[13] Zahedi considered the shah's twin sister, Princess Ashraf, to be the principal suspect. As we can see in one of the documents included in this book, Ashraf tried to mend fences with Zahedi's father by writing to him that she had no role in court machinations. Eventually all objections were overcome—according to Zahedi, in no small measure because the shah's mother, a powerful presence in the court, strongly favored the marriage. Images documenting the marriage can be seen in this collection. In October 1957, in a relatively simple ceremony, Zahedi and Princess Shahnaz were married.

During the first years of their marriage, one point of contention concerned where the newlyweds would reside. Some in the court wanted them to occupy a palace. Zahedi, however, insisted on taking his wife to Hesarak, his family's sprawling compound overlooking Tehran. Moreover, soon a comment by Princess Shahnaz raised eyebrows in the court and put Zahedi in line to be the father of Iran's future king. She claimed that absent a son for the shah—the shah's then wife, Queen Soraya, was known to be incapable of bearing a child—should she have a boy, he would be the legitimate heir to the Pahlavi throne. The US State Department concurred, suggesting that "with the betrothal of Princess Shahnaz to Ardeshir Zahedi, it is now considered likely that any son of theirs would be the most promising claimant to the throne."[14]

When the shah, desperate to have a male heir to the throne, divorced Soraya, Zahedi and his wife played a crucial role in finding a new queen for Iran. They introduced a tall, young Iranian girl, then studying architecture in Paris, to the shah. Her name was Farah. The first meeting between the shah and his future queen took place in Zahedi's home.[15]

In 1959, Zahedi was named Iran's ambassador to the United States. This would be the first of the two terms he served in Washington. Ever since Richard Nixon's trip to Iran in 1953, the shah, as well as Zahedi, had had close ties to the then vice president. Zahedi's tenure in Washington was tumultuous and controversial. On the one hand, a rumor began that haunted him and the shah for the next two decades. It was said the shah illegally made a substantial contribution to the 1960 Nixon presidential campaign. Asadollah Alam, the shah's trusted court minister, refers to these payments more than once in his published diaries.[16] Zahedi, on the other hand, has repeatedly and emphatically denied any such contributions to any of the three Nixon presidential campaigns.

But there were other reasons that Zahedi's first tenure in Washington was relatively brief and troubled. The Kennedy brothers, particularly Robert, did not like the shah, and this was more than enough to become a source of tension between the fiercely nationalist and monarchist Zahedi and the new administration in the United States. Eventually these tensions, as well as changes in Iran, led Zahedi to return home.

Before long, Zahedi had his next ambassadorial appointment. He was given a choice between Rome and London. He chose England, though his wife had wanted to go to Rome, preferring its sunny climate to London's dark, damp weather. But London was, along with Washington, the most important ambassadorial post in Iran's foreign service. Furthermore, Zahedi had set himself the task of healing the personal and political wounds that continued to cast a shadow on his and the shah's relationship with Great Britain. It was, after all, the British who had in 1941 forced the abdication of the shah's father and soon thereafter arrested Zahedi's father on the charge of conspiring with Nazi Germany. Exacerbating the history of mistrust was the looming question of Bahrain, where an intensely pro-British ruler, Sheikh Issa, was, with the help of the British, trying to declare independence. At that time Iran continued to claim sovereignty over Bahrain. Moreover, Sheikh Issa refused to countenance the Shiite majority's demands for voting rights.[17]

Arriving in London, Zahedi set out to quickly "open a new chapter of cordiality between Britain and Iran."[18] He opened the Iranian embassy in London to a wide array of political, cultural, and social figures. He paved the way for British firms—producing everything from heavy tanks to automobiles—to return to Iran and expand the British share of the Iranian market. The British Foreign Office found his work in London surprisingly successful: "He did a remarkable job in London in his fashion. Inexperienced, not a profound thinker, and apt to be impetuous, his strictly professional performance at times left something to be desired. But he entertained incessantly and lavishly, was extremely generous, and had a remarkably wide circle of friends and acquaintances. He was better known in London than any of his predecessors. . . . He did a lot single-handed towards putting Iran on the map."[19]

Zahedi's success as an ambassador came at a heavy price: his marriage to Shahnaz soon came to an end. Much has been written, from gossip columns to embassy reports, about the reasons for the breakup. But the truth has yet to be discovered; neither Ardeshir nor his estranged wife have ever provided details. For a while, evidence indicates, the shah tried to bring about a reconciliation. When his efforts failed, coinciding with a period of "dangerous living" by Princess Shahnaz, he grew angry and more or less declared her persona non grata at the court.[20]

It was a measure of Zahedi's political resilience that his power grew, rather than diminished, after the divorce. After three years in London, he received a call from the shah, who told him that he would soon have a new job.

Zahedi showed his true mettle when he was appointed Iran's foreign minister on January 5, 1967. To some, it was an occasion "to live down the playboy reputation of his youth and the 'glittering' reputation gained as ambassador to the United States between 1960 and 1962."[21] A report of the US embassy in Tehran praised him for introducing "a completely new style, a new spirit of activism, and even flamboyance into the conduct of the foreign ministry. . . . During the first few weeks of his tenure . . . [he] spent not only his days, but most of his nights there. . . . [His] metallic blue Rolls Royce is still seen parked in front of the ministry at two o'clock or even later in the morning."[22] His only daughter, Princess Mahnaz, then nine years old, lived with him, yet, as he once explained, "his only opportunity to be with his . . . daughter [was] at breakfast at 7 o'clock."[23]

The British, on the other hand, offered a starkly different assessment of Zahedi's first ministerial portfolio. They wrote that "since becoming Foreign Minister his inexperience and impetuosity added to his growing nationalism have made for difficulties in our dealings with the Iranians. In recent months his extreme nationalism particularly on Persian Gulf affairs have at moments seemed likely to do considerable harm to the Anglo-Iranian relations."[24]

Zahedi brought about a number of policy changes in the Foreign Ministry. "He instituted a system of night duty officers," requiring every "division to take turns at the vigils." For the first time, he required that "note takers [be] present during talks with foreign diplomats."[25] The Zahedi Archives provide a rich testament to his diligence in preparing such notes and preserving them for posterity. A few of these memos are included in this collection. Hundreds are available in the Zahedi Archives.

Of course, not all was smooth sailing. His relationship with the prime minister, Amir-Abbas Hoveyda—who occupied that post for almost fourteen consecutive years during the sixties and seventies—was marked by tension bordering on animosity. From his first day as foreign minister, Zahedi had made it clear that he would not take part in cabinet meetings, "as nothing important ever happens there." Instead he regularly sent his undersecretary. Zahedi also quarreled with Hoveyda over the budget for the foreign ministry. When Hoveyda refused a request for more funds, Zahedi "won hands-down by appealing to the Shah over the head of the prime minister."[26]

Another facet of Zahedi's tenure as foreign minister was his investment in attractive buildings for Iran's embassies abroad. He understood that architecture denotes power, and he used his personal influence with the shah to secure the requisite budget for these new symbols of Iran's power and importance. In Tehran, he built a luxurious social club for the ministry, as well as a housing complex for employees.

Those who worked with him in those years and took part in meetings describe his "unfailing pride" and his "no nonsense" attitude in his dealings with diplomats from other countries. "He was never intimidated." He was known to eschew the decorous rules of diplomatic discourse when he was angry. After one meeting with Zahedi, the British foreign secretary, George Brown, recorded that "he had been much disturbed by the tone of some of [Zahedi's] remarks yesterday."[27] On another occasion, Zahedi received the ruler of a newly founded sheikhdom that had claimed ownership of one of three small islands to which Iran also laid claim. With ceremony, the new "sheikh" formally presented his written claim to Zahedi. "I will wipe my ass with this paper," Zahedi responded, "and then flush it down the toilet."[28] Iran eventually established its sovereignty over the three islands of the Greater and Lesser Tunbs and Abu Musa. They are

Figure 11

Pro-Shah demonstrators, supported by the military, on August 19, 1953, when the government of Mossadegh was toppled.

Figure 12

Another scene of pro-Shah demonstrations on August 19, 1953.

indispensable for strategic control of the Persian Gulf and the Strait of Hormoz.

Zahedi was particularly critical of British policy in the Persian Gulf. The "extreme nationalist" position he took on the question of Bahrain led to some confrontations between Iran and England. On March 12, 1968, for example, in the episode with George Brown, Zahedi had angrily complained of an incident in which British planes had flown threateningly close to Iranian ships in the Persian Gulf, stating that the next time Iranian ships would shoot down any threatening planes. Brown responded that "he understood the position that [Iran had a] historic claim [over Bahrain] which was on the table. He would however be surprised and disappointed if Iran thought of going to war to enforce her claim. If she did, many consequences would follow." The British position that Brown emphasized "was that so long as our treaties remained in force and our forces were in the area, we would fulfill our obligations."[29] Some of the documents collected in this volume show Zahedi's often defiant discourse in defending what he perceived to be Iran's interests or standing up to any gesture he saw as a slight to Iran's dignity as a nation. Zahedi, for example, would walk out of official ceremonies—once even when Queen Elizabeth was present—as soon as any British official referred to the "Gulf" instead of the Persian Gulf. On one occasion, he declared the British ambassador to Iran, Sir Denis Wright, persona non grata at the Foreign Ministry for what Zahedi saw as a slight.[30]

Zahedi repeatedly complained to the Americans about the behavior of the British, as evidenced during a trip to Washington in March 1968, shortly after his heated encounter with Brown. In a meeting with Secretary of State Dean Rusk, he asserted that "Iran [is] hurt by UK's recent actions. . . . He then mentioned formation of FAA [Federation of Arab Emirates, consisting of nine Persian Gulf ministates, including Bahrain, Qatar, Dubai, and Fujairah] accusing the British of double-cross."[31] Rusk was taken off guard by the vehemence of Zahedi's attacks and "hesitated to give off-the-cuff-response to such serious and far-reaching problems," but the Americans commented that they "would be disturbed if Iran and UK at odds."[32] Zahedi would also quarrel with American officials if they referred to the Persian Gulf as "the Gulf."

While insisting on a nationalist approach to the question of Bahrain and the name of the Persian Gulf, Zahedi pushed for a more moderate policy toward Egypt and the rest of the Arab world. He often insisted, in both private pronouncements and public statements, that in the context of Arab-Israeli relations, Iran should be less identified with Israel. Indeed, the Israeli embassy in Tehran at the time considered Zahedi one of the chief opponents of full diplomatic relations between Iran and Israel.[33]

In March 1968, Tehran was awash with rumors of Zahedi's imminent appointment as the prime minister. A report from the British embassy claimed they had "heard from a reliable source that Ardeshir Zahedi had let it be known to at least two prominent Iranians that he was going to become Prime Minister in the near future. Needless to say, we were thunder-struck by this item of information and could only speculate that—if it were really true—the Shah had decided on a thoroughly hard line on the Persian Gulf (which he could later jettison, together with Zahedi, if it proved a failure)."[34]

The rumors were false. Zahedi's continuing clashes with Hoveyda and occasional confrontations with Asadollah Alam finally led in 1971 to his forced resignation. He had, on more than one occasion, written tartly worded letters to the prime minister, who had in turn shown them to the shah. But the break came over a particularly harsh letter Zahedi wrote to Hoveyda. When he refused to take back the letter, he was forced to resign. Immediately after tendering his resignation, he left for his villa in Switzerland. As evident in some of the documents in this

Figure 13
Ardeshir Zahedi with his soon-to-be wife, Princess Shahnaz (at the time the Shah's only child).

Figure 14
Princess Mahnaz, the only daughter of Ardeshir Zahedi and Princess Shahnaz, pointing to a portrait of her grandfather, the Shah.

Figure 15 Ardeshir Zahedi during his first tenure as Iran's ambassador to the United States (1959–62)

Figure 16

The Shah on one of his many vistis to the United States. Ardeshir Zahedi stands right behind Nixon.

Figure 17

The Shah after attending the funeral services of President Eisenhower during Nixon's presidency and Ardeshir Zahedi's tenure as Iran's ambassador to the United States.

volume and many more in the archive, more than once Zahedi offered his resignation when he thought he had roused the ire of the shah, or when he found a policy incongruent with his own views.

But the shah arguably tolerated more from Zahedi than from anyone else. Zahedi's outbursts, his many letters of resignation, and his repeated angry and defiant journeys to Switzerland never terminated his career. The only exception to this tradition of royal tolerance can be seen in the shah's *Answer to History*, where he claims, "I was ill-served by Ardeshir Zahedi's inaccurate reporting. He had been in Washington too long and was closely identified with the Nixon and Ford administration. He pretended to have access to the highest authorities [in the Ford and Carter administrations] but his reports could never be confirmed. His outgoing temperament was unsuited to the straight-laced Carter White House and I should have replaced him."[35] Hundreds of documents in his archive, some included here, amply show Zahedi's truly impressive array of friends and acquaintances at the highest echelons of power not just in the United States and Britain but around the world.

But in 1971, more evidence of his special relations with the shah came when, a few months after his resignation as foreign minister, Zahedi was for the second time named Iran's ambassador to the United States.[36]

Zahedi, using his private access to the shah, succeeded in increasing the "special budget" of the embassy, allowing him to throw parties that became famous in Washington for the splendor of their hospitality—particularly their Beluga caviar—and the glamour of their star-studded guest lists. At the same time, Zahedi and the embassy were locked in an increasingly fierce battle with the growing ranks of Iranian students studying in the United States who were opposed to the shah. Again the documents in the archive, including at least one collected in this volume, underscore the seriousness of this ongoing fight.

Nixon's fall and the 1976 US presidential elections posed a particularly difficult challenge for Zahedi and the embassy. Ever since the Kennedy years, the shah had been distrustful of the Democrats. Furthermore, Carter had made several inflammatory remarks about Iran and abuses of human rights in his election campaign. His victory and his appointment of William Sullivan as America's new ambassador to Iran made the shah nervous. Sullivan had a reputation, as Zahedi saw it, of going to hot spots in Indochina and fomenting trouble. Zahedi suggested to the shah that Iran should refuse to accept the Sullivan appointment, but the shah did not heed his advice.[37]

Beginning in 1978, amid early signs of turmoil in Tehran, Zahedi was once again back at the center of Iranian domestic politics. As the shah became increasingly dependent on signs of support from the United States, Zahedi's role in Washington took on more crucial dimensions. At the same time, he was needed in Iran to give the shah confidence. When the situation deteriorated late in 1978, Zahedi made a now famous trip back to Iran. He met with the despondent shah, trying unsuccessfully to bolster the king's courage.

It was then that Zahedi learned for the first time that the shah was undergoing treatment for cancer. He insisted that the shah immediately tell the nation about his illness. "Iranian people are decent and forgiving," he said. He also met with key officers in the armed forces and some of the shah's most trusted guards, saying to them, "The country needs you; are you ready to sacrifice for the country?" The officers all indicated their willingness even to die and lamented the utter "lack of leadership."[38] Zahedi took notes in these meetings and prepared detailed talking points; all of those documents are now part of this indispensable archive.

Zahedi was apparently contemplating a pro-shah coup—a repeat of the 1953 events. At the same time, Zahedi met with various political figures and tried to form some

Figure 18

Ardeshir Zahedi and his father General Zahedi when the latter is the Prime Minister.

Figure 19

General Zahedi at his son's wedding, welcoming the bride, Princess Shahnaz.

kind of coalition to save the crown. When the Carter administration, without even informing the shah and the government of Iran, sent General Robert Huyser to Tehran to dissuade the Iranian military from trying to organize a military coup in favor of the shah, Zahedi recommended that the general be arrested and put on a plane out of Iran. He also recommended that the British and American embassies, "as hotbeds of incitement," be closed. The shah dismissed all these ideas as "naive and childish."[39]

Zahedi's effort came to naught. He left Tehran for the last time in January 1979. When the Iranian embassy in Washington was taken over in early February by new representatives of the Islamic regime, Zahedi quietly slipped away to his favorite hideaway in Montreux. He spent the next few months shuttling between Villa les Roses and wherever the exiled shah happened to be. He visited him in Egypt, Morocco, the Bahamas, Mexico, Panama, and then Egypt again. He used his extensive contacts around the world to find an entry visa for the shah and his family to some safe country.

After the death of the shah, Zahedi had his last big row with members of the royal family, particularly the queen. It came immediately after the death of the shah. The queen, as she readily admits in *An Enduring Love*, wrote down what she called "the King's deepest thoughts" and offered the resulting manuscript to the press as the king's "last wish."[40] Zahedi was adamantly opposed to publishing such a document and even threatened to go to court. The court challenge never came; Zahedi was convinced of its futility. He returned to Montreux to tend to his gardens and begin a life of exile.

Since then, he has dedicated a considerable part of his life to bringing order to his rich archive and writing his memoirs—two volumes of a four-volume project have now been published in Persian, English, and French—as well as granting interviews and writing books not just on modern Iranian history but also on current events. If ever he feels a politician—from Senator John McCain to Secretary of State Mike Pompeo—has said something wrong about Iran as a nation, he writes a response and has it published in major newspapers. His collection of documents on Yemen, tellingly titled *Yemen: 1000 Days of a Disgracing War, a Carnage We Can Neither Forget nor Forgive and That History Will Recall with Shame*, speaks to his passion for humanity and his willingness to speak out.[41] He is now working on the third and fourth volumes of his memoirs.

Parts of this profile were published earlier in Abbas Milani's *Eminent Persians: The Men and Women Who Made Modern Iran, 1941–1979*, 2 Volumes (Syracuse, NY: Syracuse University Press, 2008), 327–40.

NOTES

1. In talking about the shah, Ardeshir Zahedi often refers to him as "my beloved monarch."

2. For an account of Pirnia's life and times, see Bastani Parizi, *Dar Talashe Azadi* [The struggle for freedom] (Tehran: Amir Kabir, 1355/1976).

3. Ardeshir Zahedi, interviewed by author, Montreux, June 20, 2002.

4. Ibid.

5. *Ardeshir Zahedi Be Ravayat Asnade SAVAK* [Ardeshir Zahedi according to SAVAK documents] (Tehran: Markaz Baresiye Asnade Tarikhiye Vezarate Etela'at, 1378/1999), 108.

6. Ardeshir Zahedi, interviewed by author, Montreux, June 7, 2004.

7. US Dept. of State, *Foreign Relations of the United States, 1952–1954, Iran: 1951–1954* (Washington, DC: GPO, 2017), 389–91.

8. Both in his memoirs and in many interviews with me, he has described these prison ordeals.

9. Ardeshir Zahedi, *Panj Roozer Bohrani* [Five days of crisis]. This book was first published as a series of articles in a weekly journal, which have since reappeared in a different formats. One full version has been published online at https://ketabnak.com/book/80633/.

10. US Dept. of State, *Foreign Relations of the United States*, vol. 10, *1952–1954* (Washington, DC: GPO, 1989), 738.

11. Ardeshir Zahedi, interviewed by author, Montreux, August 18, 2003.

12. US Embassy to State Dept., Jan. 8, 1954, in *Foreign Relations of the United States of America*, vol. 10, *1952–1954* (Washington, DC: GPO, 1989), 894. The report indicates that Ardeshir was acting as translator in the meeting between his father, the prime minister, and Henderson, the US ambassador. The subject was the upcoming elections.

13. Ardeshir Zahedi, interviewed by author, Montreux, June 7, 2004.

14. "The Shah of Iran: A Revised Study," in US Dept. of State, *Foreign Relations of the United States, 1955–1957*, vol. 12, *Near East Region, Iraq and Iran* (Washington, DC: GPO, 1991), 917.

15. I had heard the story from Zahedi, and the queen confirms the story—in broad outlines, without going into too much detail about the role of Zahedi—in her memoirs. See Farah Pahlavi, *An Enduring Love: My Life with the Shah* (New York: Hyperion, 2004).

16. Asadollah Alam, *Yadashthaye Roozaneh* (Diaries). 7 volumes (Bethesda, MD: Iranbooks/Ibex Publishers, 1992–2014)

17. Sir Elden Griffith, interviewed by author, Los Angeles, May 12, 2004.

18. Ibid.

19. "Zahedi, Ardeshir, Engineer (Muhandess)," Public Records Office, London, FCO 17/373.

20. The most detailed account of these simmering tensions between the shah and his eldest daughter can be found in Alam's *Diaries*. He was in charge of attending to her problems and needs.

21. Dept. of State, Oct. 22, 1968, National Archives.

22. US Embassy, Tehran, Iran, "Style of the New Foreign Minister," Feb. 13, 1967, A-431. National Security Archive, George Washington Univ., Washington, DC.

23. Ibid., 2.

24. "Zahedi, Ardeshir, Engineer (Muhandess)."

25. Ibid., 3.

26. Ibid.

27. "Record of Conversation, between Foreign Secretary and the Iranian Foreign Minister, 12 March 1968," Public Records Office, London, FCO 17/1372.

28. Fereydoon Zandfar, *Iran Dar Jahani Por Talatom* [Iran in a tumultuous world] (Tehran: Shirazeh, 1379/2000), 94–101.

29. "Record of Conversation."

30. Sir Denis Wright, interviewed by author, London, Aug. 11, 2004. The episode is also described in his unpublished memoirs, to which he kindly gave me access. The papers have been donated to Oxford University, UK.

31. Dept. of State to US Embassy in Iran, Mar. 16, 1968, in US Dept. of State, *Foreign Relations of the United States of America*, vol. 22, *1964–1968* (Washington, DC: GPO, 1999), 482–83.

32. Ibid., 483.

33. Moir Ezri, *Yadnameh* (Jerusalem: n.p., 2000). Ezri was, for many years, Israel's ambassador to Iran.

34. "Iranian Internal Politics," British embassy in Tehran to Foreign Office, Mar. 28, 1968, Public Relations Office, London, FO 248/1646.

35. Mohammad Reza Shah Pahlavi, *Answer to History* (Toronto: Clarke, Irwin, 1980), 165.

36. Ibid., 191.

37. Ardeshir Zahedi, interviewed by author, Montreux, August 18, 2003.

38. Colonel Cyrus Khiltash, interviewed by author, Washington, DC, June 5, 2004. He was present at the meeting and had been for many years one of the shah's bodyguards.

39. Ardeshir Zahedi, interviewed by author, Montreux, July 10, 2003; and Ardeshir Zahedi, Harvard University Iranian Oral History Project, Cambridge, MA, January 15, 1992. Though the interview is sealed until after his death, he kindly gave me access to it.

40. Farah Pahlavi, *An Enduring Love*, 391. I have also interviewed Mr. Ali Rezai, who took part in preparing the document, and Ardeshir Zahedi, who was present at its creation.

41. Ardeshir Zahedi, *Yemen: 1000 Days of a Disgracing War, a Carnage We Can Neither Forget nor Forgive and That History Will Recall* (Bethesda, MD: Ibex Publishers, 2018). At his own expense he has made the book available to many schools and colleges and even more important made it available for purchase for a very reasonable price—far below cost.

Selected Documents

SELECTED DOCUMENTS

The documents included in this volume were selected by Abbas Milani, in consultation with Eric Wakin. The documents were translated by Arman Saify.

Document 1
1922–1924
1.1–1.15 Sheikh Khazal of Kurzestan: Despot or King without a Crown.

Document 2
23 November 1935
2.1 State permission for installation of concert radio receiver in the home of Brigadier General Zahedi

Document 3
23 August 1953
3.1 Confidential advice to Zahedi from "Hirad" in regard to Hossein Makki's note to the shah

3.2 Note from Hossein Makki to the shah of Iran regarding Mohammad Mossadegh

Document 4
9 September 1953
4.1–4.2 Letter from Hassan Taqizadeh to General Zahedi

Document 5
15 September 1953
5.1 Letter to General Zahedi from a professor at the university

Document 6
6 October 1953
6.1–6.5 Correspondence from Great Britain seeking to resume diplomatic relations with Iran following the overthrow of Mossadegh government

Document 7
16 January 1954
7.1 Report of Anoushiravan Sepahbodi to A. Zahedi

Document 8
17 February 1954
8.1 Letter of Nasser Ghashghaei to Ardeshir Zahedi

Document 9
13 December 1954
9.1 Memorandum from Prime Minister to Mr. Abtin in re orders of Dr. Mofakham

Document 10
3 December 1955
10.1–10.2 Letter of Ali Asghar Hekmat to Ardeshir Zahedi

Document 11
1953–1955
11.1 Detailed account of gifts

Document 12
1954–1955
12.1–12.8 Outline of General Zahedi's career prepared in anticipation of his personal memoirs

Document 13
1953–1955
13.1–13.11 More of the outline General Zahedi prepared in anticipation of his personal memoirs

Document 14
1 April 1956
14.1 Letter to Ardeshir Zahedi from a cleric who had worked to overthrow Mossadegh

Document 15
19 August 1955
15.1 Letter from Shaban Jafari to Ardeshir Zahedi

Document 16
12 October 1955
16.1 Letter from Hassan Ma'assar

Document 17
Around 1957–1958
17.1–17.2 Letter from Princess Ashraf to Ardeshir Zahedi

Document 18
17 February 1959
18.1–18.2 Ali Asghar Hekmat to General Zahedi

Document 19
13 June 1959
19.1 Letter of General Teymour Bakhtiar to General Zahedi

Document 20
30 January 1967
20.1–20.2 Letter from Ardeshir Zahedi as foreign minister to the shah reporting on foreign policy

Document 21
3 February 1967
21.1–21.4 Correspondence between Ardeshir Zahedi and the shah.

Document 22
Approximately March 1967
22.1 Letter of Ardeshir Zahedi to shah of matters revolving around influence of Kermit Roosevelt

Document 23
11 June 1967
23.1–23.6 Digest of the shah's meeting with the Soviet ambassador regarding Soviet breech of bilateral agreement to use of Iranian air space

Document 24
Around 1967
24.1–24.6 Correspondence between Ardeshir Zahedi as foreign minister and Armin Meyer, US ambassador to Iran

Document 25
13 November 1968
25.1–25.14 Minutes of a meeting between the shah of Iran and the Saudi monarch, King Faisal

Document 26
25 January 1969
26.1–26.4 Zahedi reporting in minute detail his conversations with the Soviet ambassador

Document 27
10 February 1969
27.1–27.5 Letter from Ardeshir Zahedi, then foreign minister, to the shah of Iran

Document 28
28 July 1969
28.1 Letter in English from King Hussein of Jordan to Mohammad Reza Pahlavi, shah of Iran

Document 29
10 February 1970
29.1–29.5 Ardeshir Zahedi report to the shah of Iran

Document 30
2 March 1970
30.1–30.8 Ardeshir Zahedi report to the shah of Iran

Document 31
19 February 1974
31.1–31.2 Telegram to US Ambassador in Tehran requesting prevention of broadcasting *60 Minutes* interview

Document 32
9 July 1974
32.1 Letter to Ardeshir Zahedi from US Senator Edward Wm. Brooke

Document 33
6 May 1976
33.1–33.2 Letters of Assadollah Alam (former prime minister of Iran) to the shah

Document 34
20 December 1976
34.1–34.2 Documentation of gifts of caviar

Document 35
11 January 1977
35.1 Letter of thanks from US Representative James Wright to Ardeshir Zahedi

Document 36
22 January 1977
36.1 Letter of thanks from Kirk Douglas

36.2 Letter of thanks from *Washington Post* columnist Art Buchwald

Document 37
26 January 1977
37.1–37.2 Letter to Ardeshir Zahedi, ambassador of Iran to US, from Sylvan M. Marshall, giving a legal opinion

37.3–37.7 Letter from Ardeshir Zahedi to David Susskind, US television producer, objecting to allegations made by Reza Baraheni

37.8 Letter to Ardeshir Zahedi from David Rockefeller

Document 38
27 January 1977
38.1 Letter to Ardeshir Zahedi from Rose Mary Woods, secretary to President Richard Nixon

Document 39
16 March 1977
39.1 Letter to Ardeshir Zahedi from US Senator Barry Goldwater

Document 40
16 March 1977
40.1 Letter to Ardeshir Zahedi from Mrs. Arthur Hays Sulzberger

40.2 Letter to Ardeshir Zahedi from Katharine Graham of the *Washington Post*

Document 41
18 March 1977
41.1 Letter of gratitude to Ardeshir Zahedi from John R. Silber, president of Boston University

Document 42
7 November 1977
42.1 Letter of gratitude to Ardeshir Zahedi from US Senator Hubert Humphrey

Document 43
5 January 1978
43.1 Letter of gratitude to Ardeshir Zahedi from Claudia A. "Lady Bird" Johnson

43.2 Telegram to Ardeshir Zahedi from Mrs. Ronald Reagan (Nancy)

43.3 Letter to Ardeshir Zahedi from Mrs. Ronald Reagan

43.4 Handwritten note of thanks to Ardeshir Zahedi from Mrs. Ronald Wilson Reagan

Document 44
30 January 1978
44.1 Letter to Ardeshir Zahidi from Lord Hartley William Shawcross

Document 45
25 September 1978
45.1 Letter to Ardeshir Zahedi from Douglas Fairbanks in regard to Tabas earthquake

45.2 Response to Douglas Fairbanks

Document 46
9 January 1979
46.1 Letter of concern from Nelson A. Rockefeller

Document 47
22 January 1979
47.1 Letter from Ronald Reagan to Ardeshir Zahedi

Document 48
January 1979
48.1 Telegram from William Rogers

Document 1
1922–1924

Sheikh Khazal (1863–1936) was one of the most notorious "allies" of the British in Iran in the first two decades of the twentieth century. With clear encouragement from the British, he treated Iran's oil-rich province of Khuzestan as his virtual private fiefdom (Sheikdom of Mohammerah). General Zahedi was instrumental in the central government's eventual decision to arrest the sheikh and bring him to Tehran. The events unfolded during the early months of the rule of Reza Shah (1878–1944, reigned 1925–41). These are Zahedi's handwritten records of these remarkable historical events.

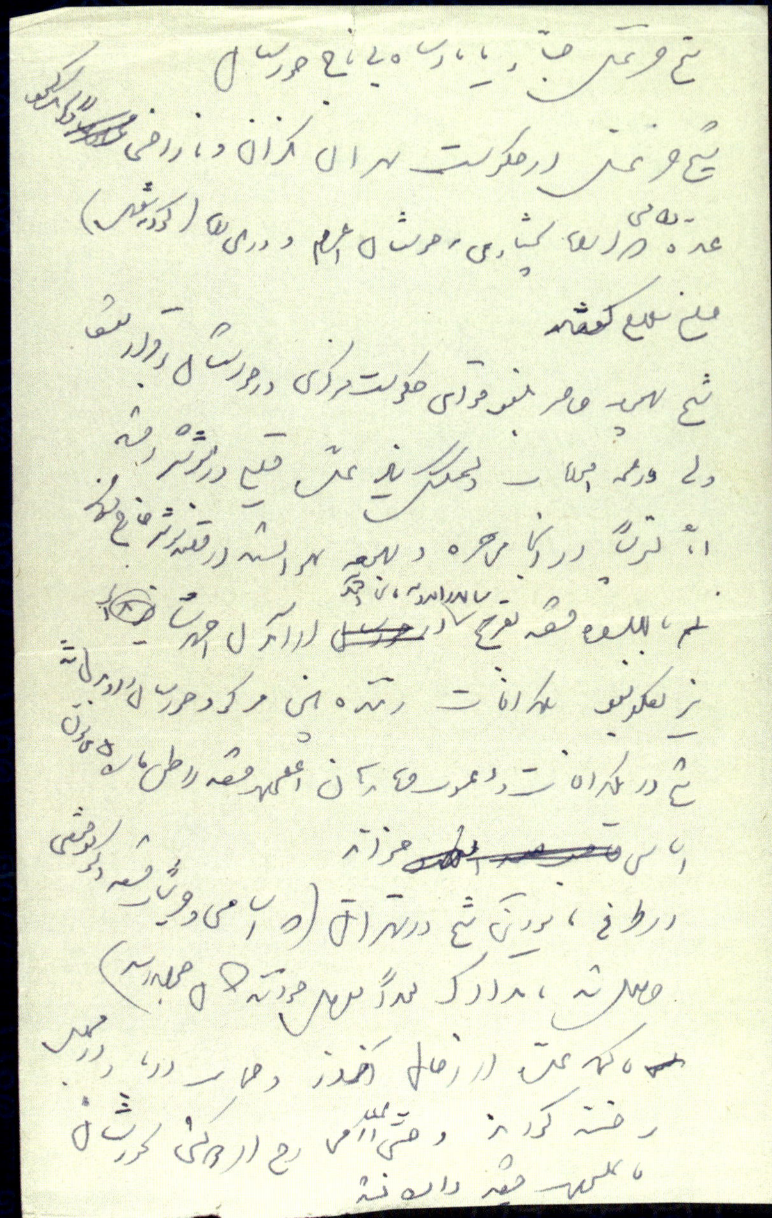

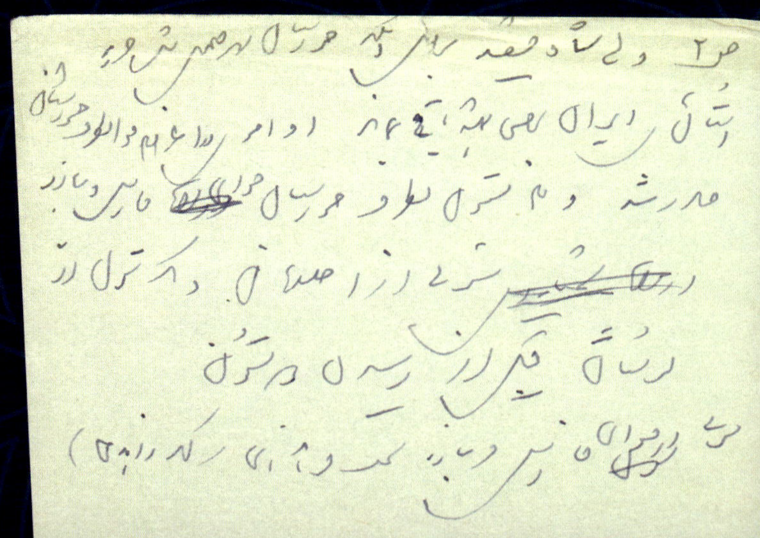

1.1 Sheikh Khazal of Kurzestan, Despot or King without a Crown

Sheikh Khazal was worried about the government in Tehran and was discontent and complained

A detachment composed of Bakhtiari tribesmen was sent to Khuzestan and dispersed among them to disarm them

Sheikh was not ready under any circumstance to allow central government forces to be posted in Khuzestan

But amid all happenings and many skirmishes a small group went to Shooshtar but were almost surrounded and were not able to get out of Shooshtar Fort

___, Salaroldowleh's retelling of the story of Ahmad Shah's visit about which a number of harsh telegrams were exchanged between the Center and Khuzestan

At a public event the Sheikh called His Majesty a usurper based on Clause 5 of the Constitution.

Moreover, the Sheikh's agents in Tehran (their names and details of their actions were received, and the documents will be provided for the information of readers of newspapers)

With the help of some of the dignitaries of those days and support of the Court they managed to penetrate the Majlis and as a result not even the expenses of the military expedition to Khuzestan were given to His Late Majesty

1.2 But in order for Khuzestan to remain one of Iran's provinces at any cost forever the late King issued orders for dispatching troops to Khuzestan and three columns [were dispatched] toward Khuzestan Fars forces and fighting forces from Esfahan and one column from Lurestan before arrival of two columns from Fars Forces under the command of General Zahedi

شیخ خزعل [illegible] در تاریخ خوزستان

پس از چندی [illegible] حکومت مرکزی [illegible] قطع شد [illegible]

[illegible] خوزستان [illegible]

[illegible]

[illegible]

حکومت مرکزی [illegible] شد [illegible]

[illegible] شیخ [illegible]

[illegible]

[illegible] شیخ [illegible]

[illegible]

[illegible] شیخ [illegible]

~~[illegible]~~

~~[illegible]~~

~~[illegible]~~

[illegible]

[illegible]

[illegible]

حکومت [illegible] خوزستان [illegible]

[illegible]

[illegible] شیخ [illegible]

[illegible]

1.3 Sheikh Khazal of Khuzestan: Despot or King without a Crown

After relations were cut between Khazal and the Central Government Salaroldowleh came to Khuzestan and there were discussions about Ahmad Shah's visit to Khuzestan (later the details and minutiae of the roots of the insurgency with documentation will be brought to the attention of media) Telegrams were exchanged between the Sheikh and the Central Government The armed forces disarmed him in _______

Basing it on Clause 5 of the Constitution, Sheikh Khazal called His Late Majesty an usurper and furthermore the Majlis did not approve any funds for the military expedition to Khuzestan because Sheikh Khazal had agents in Tehran and in the Majlis because the Late King wanted Khuzestan province to remain part of Iran, he was compelled to send some columns to suppress Sheikh Khazal

and as a result, Sheikh Khazal's forces were defeated at Rendoon (near Behbahan)

Second Fars Division Command

Khuzestan's military Command and local government were established

1.4 Fars Expedition and campaign headed and commanded by General Zahedi to Behbahan and

مرد ما باید آنکه [illegible] مست و سرشار [illegible]

امروز [illegible] دیدار [illegible] عشق [illegible]

و همه [illegible] در شور [illegible] زاده و [illegible]

[illegible] طعمه [illegible] و [illegible]

در سال [illegible] هر [illegible]

[illegible] کس [illegible] پاره پاره

[illegible] شکوه [illegible] رسید

و [illegible] و [illegible] آن [illegible]

[illegible]

[illegible]

[illegible] شد [illegible]

[illegible]

[illegible]

1.5 The order was issued to detain the Sheikh and his sons An armed group and the Sheikh's slaves were in the corridor of the living room on the ground floor and the Sheikh and his elder son in the room upstairs They were detained for the resolution of the problem and at this same time a reliable person accompanied by General Mostafa Khan Shokooh arrived without notice and entered the Sheikh's ship moored at Karkheh and its personnel who were all Majlesi tribe were arrested were aiming at the ship

But the Sheikh's slaves and personnel were caught by surprise and imagined that they were surrounded by an armed group and saw no alternative but to surrender and proceeded to do so

[illegible] دوررشه [illegible]

درلش [illegible]

[illegible]

[illegible]

[illegible] ۵ [illegible]

[illegible]

[illegible]

[illegible]

[illegible]

[illegible]

[illegible]

[illegible]

[illegible] ۱۵ [illegible]

[illegible]

[illegible]

[illegible]

1.6 (it was decided on the ship for him)

In his ship Sheikh Khazal and his sons and son-in-law and some of his armed guards and slaves want to entertain the Commandant and military ruler of Khuzestan and incidentally a few .... and musicians had come from Basrah

Colonel Majd was summoned to the salon and the Commander issued orders that tonight Sheikh Khazal and his sons had to be detained orders were obeyed

Lieutenant Zarghami the head of the escort was told if he does not cooperate to use weapons

They must secure and close the ship's stairs with a few men and if he does not surrender and the need to use weapons arises they should obey orders

at this time Colonel Ebtekar arrived with one ______ and a detachment of 10 military personnel

because local musicians were present around the ship the Sheikh's armed guards themselves ....

[illegible] این [illegible] را [illegible]

[illegible]

[illegible]

[illegible]

[illegible]

[illegible]

[illegible] ...

[illegible]

[illegible]

[illegible]

[illegible]

[illegible]

[illegible]

[illegible]

[illegible]

[illegible]

[illegible]

1.7 I will recount this report in brief from Shiraz to the Sheikh's arrest and dispatch from Khuzestan to Tehran for the dear readers and then we will deal in detail with all the required documents that I have compiled

....

The dispatched Column from Fars moved toward the _______ Command that is located in _____ today from Shiraz with experienced _____ and a group of famous people Khans and tribal leaders of Fars upon their request accompanied the Commandant to Khuzestan and in the Mamasani [tribal region] Brigadier Zarghamoldowleh, Assad Khan Navi and some of the Khans of Boveyr Ahmad tribes joined the Column and in Behbahan Sardar Ahmad Behbahani and that region's khans joined in

After the Forces were deployed in Behbahan, the Sheikh's demands and telegrams were answered in the negative The Fars Command engagement with the Arabs took place next to Ramoo Rendoon

The result of the two-day battle was

[illegible]

[illegible]

[illegible]

[illegible]

[illegible]

[illegible]

[illegible]

[illegible]

حکومت نظامی در تهران [illegible]

[illegible]

[illegible]

حکومت نظامی [illegible]

سلطنت [illegible]

[illegible]

[illegible]

1.8 Arab forces that were many times the size of our military forces were defeated and our military forces captured _____ and ______ villages at this time His Late Majesty traveled from Tehran to Esfahan and then to Shiraz and by way of ______ to Bandar Deylam and then inspected the victorious Iranian Forces The Sheikh's men surrendered at the village of ______ and the Sheikh surrendered himself to his Majesty in Ahvaz and was pardoned _____ our financial and human _____

The responsibility for Martial Law and Commander of the Forces in Khuzestan was given to _______

His Late Majesty returned to Tehran via Beynol Nahrain [Iraq]

The military government resided in the ship moored on the river in front of the Customs

During this time all Arab tribal chiefs who were discontent with the Sheikh met with the Commander and the local Governor

سپس سردار [illegible] حکم [illegible]

[illegible]

[illegible] محمد [illegible]

~~[illegible]~~

[illegible]

[illegible]

[illegible] سردار [illegible]

[illegible]

[illegible]

~~[illegible]~~

[illegible]

[illegible]

[illegible]

[illegible] عراق [illegible]

ایران [illegible]

1.9 who then came to Ahvaz and took over the governorship Martial Law was extended to Shooshtar and the surrounding areas The Sheikh was not happy with the presence of a few troops at the Muhammareh barracks and the Sheikh's agents were among the Ka'ab and other tribes to do something in the vicinity of Shooshtar and Dezful, military barracks had been set up Sheikh constantly expressed his concern he left for Basrah and started his provocation there and sought assistance from Majlesi tribe that is his own tribe and other tribal chiefs and in Basrah bought land near his palace here with the help of other Arab tribal chiefs started some activities against our military forces at this time the government of Iraq had been recognized by the government of Iran

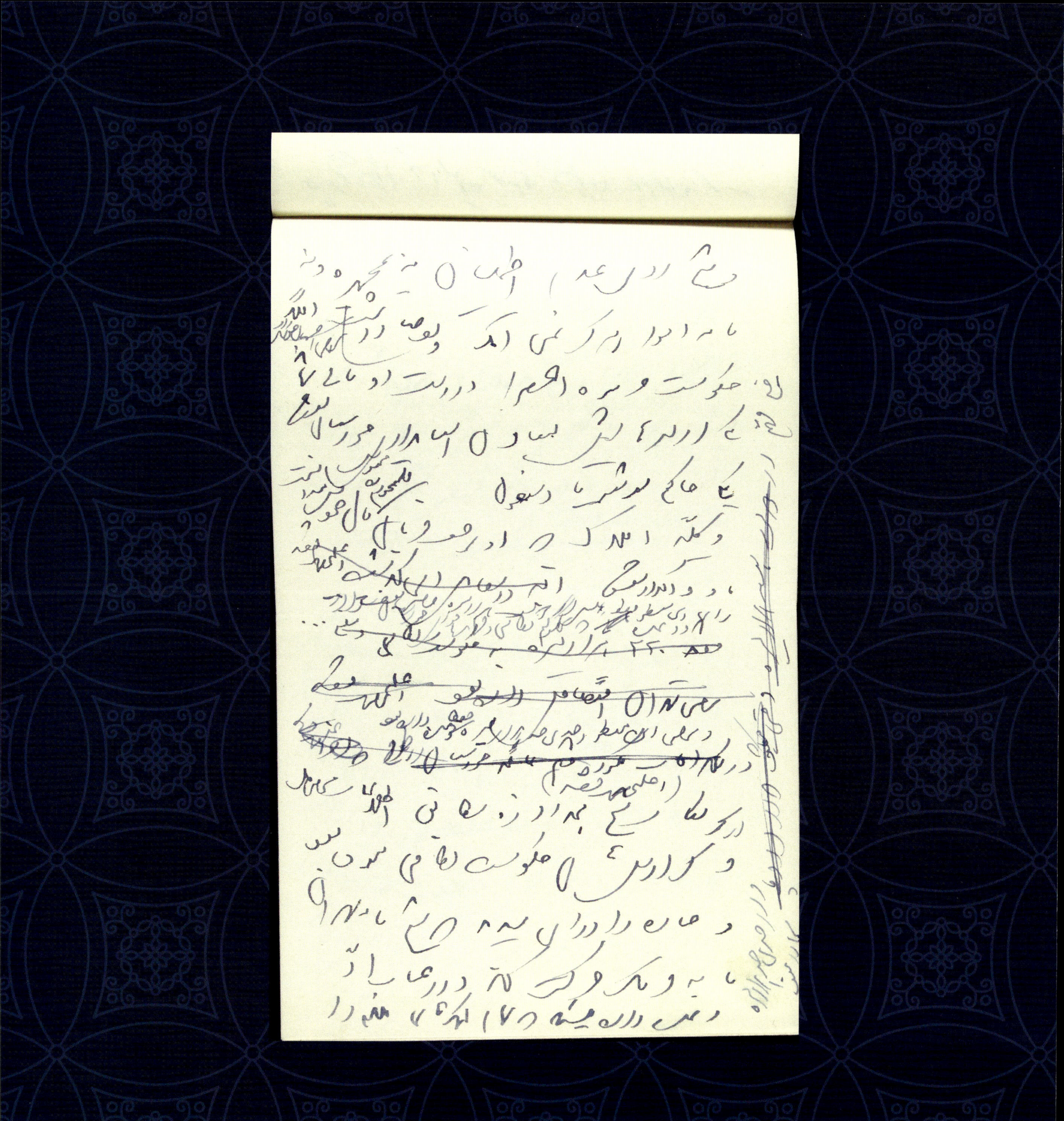

1.10 Because of his distrust, the Sheikh would never come to Muhammareh or to Ahvaz and stated that the government should remain in his hands and one of his sons should become Deputy Governor of Khuzestan, and another the ruler of Shooshtar or Dezful and believed all property owned by him that was seized by royal decree should be returned to him.

[*Crossed-out lines, and writing in between not legible*]

Daily special reports of the Sheikh's intrigues reached the martial law government, which saw the only solution in sending the Sheikh to Tehran or abroad and he was promised that all important Divisions

[illegible] شیخ [illegible] در [illegible]

[illegible]

[illegible] شده

ولی شیخ [illegible] X [illegible]

ولی ای در قضیه [illegible]

[illegible]

[illegible] ولی [illegible]

و [illegible] قضیه [illegible]

[illegible]

[illegible] ولی شیخ [illegible]

[illegible]

[illegible]

[illegible] قضیه [illegible]

[illegible] شیخ را [illegible]

1.11 would be removed and even the return of the Sheikh's properties would be proposed to the Majlis

But the Sheikh in all stubbornness stayed with his slaves and relatives in Basra sometime and other times in his Fort where his palace was located near the Iran-Iraq border

And His Majesty continued to send telegrams issuing orders that the Sheikh must be convinced to go either to Tehran or to Europe

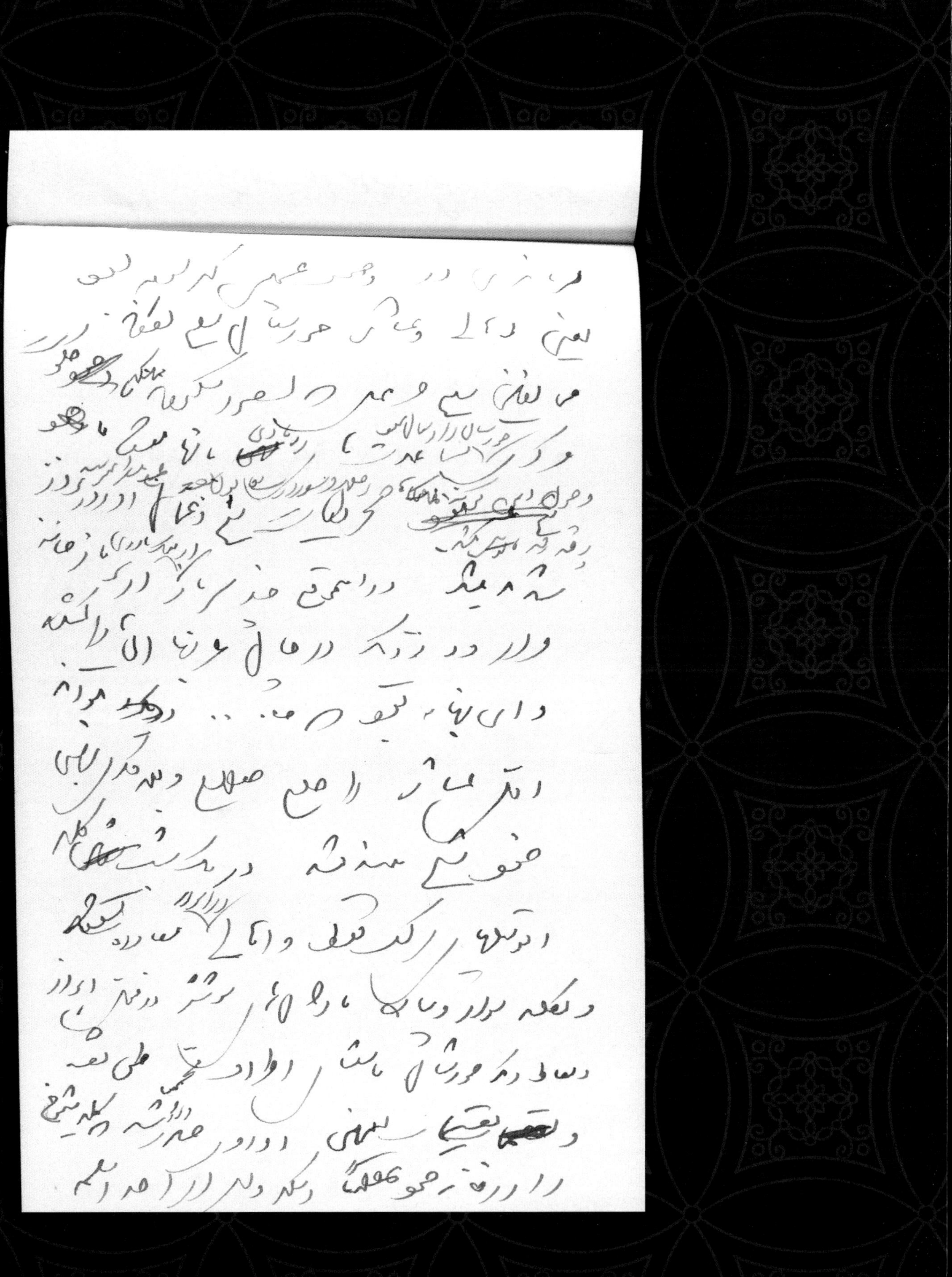

1.12 but the Commandant was caught in difficult position, meaning the tribes and people of Khuzestan were armed, Khazal's opponents and those who thought the possibility was there that the Central Government would provide a lot of aid to them

and because these types of instigations by the Sheikh and his agents continued to increase day by day at this time a few soldiers from Naderi regiment ran away (AWOL) and were murdered nearby in the Arab neighborhood and this became the excuse that enabled our forces to disarm the tribes and clans and then think of what to do about the Sheikh himself.

One night they confiscated all local automobiles in Ahvaz and distributed them according to the national maps to all cavalry and mounted garrisons of Shooshtar, Dezful, Ahvaz, and other points in Khuzestan with the exception of the vicinity of Mohammareh Orders were issued to detain all Sheikhs in their homes and after disarming them

1.13 to release them and set them free without bringing any harm or discomfort to them This action eased the mind of the Commandant to a certain extent but still faced with the continued instigations and activities of the Sheikh, total confidence was lacking And one of the problems was the Sheikh's refusal to come to Mohammareh or Ahvaz and the presence of enough armed personnel in his palaces in the fort And no orders were received from Central [command] for ending the Khuzestan rebellion

A telegram about this situation is sent by the Military Governor to His Late Majesty that the Sheikh is keeping out of Khuzestan on purpose (To convince the Sheikh to go to Tehran, I set out for Mohammareh) The Sheikh's sons and their riverboat were on the River Karoun (during the time when their automobiles had been confiscated they stayed there). Moving orders came, and on behalf of the Sheikh we were requested to be the Sheikh's guests at the Fort we.

1.14 Some of Khazal's people Military commander of Mohammareh and the head of tribal affairs, the then head of Khuzestan Telegraph a few senior officers six personnel were escorts of the Commandant * [**Right margin*: The ship had to wait a few hours in Mohammareh]

The following orders were issued the presence of the Sheikh's men in the Ship _______ because it was agreed that the reception would be on the ship (ethnic)

<u>Commandants Orders</u> Khorramshahr garrison after 8 pm Military Forces traffic person with weapon and suspicious persons must not cross

Custom's agents must prevent _______ and Karjis from crossing

Military Government of Mohammareh that confiscated automobiles

[illegible] دهلی از [illegible]

[illegible]

[illegible]

[illegible] از اهواز [illegible] دولت و [illegible]

[illegible] است در [illegible]

[illegible] از اهواز [illegible]

[illegible]

[illegible]

[illegible] از اهواز [illegible]

[illegible]

[illegible]

[illegible] از اهواز [illegible]

[illegible] اهواز [illegible]

[illegible]

1.15 and continue to be held and this is the secondary order

General Lotfi and his detail are on the Khuzestan ship today and will be setting off for Ahvaz around 6 o'clock and another order that is sealed was given to the secretary at 7 o'clock

Commander of Ahvaz Garrison confiscated all automobiles in the city and surroundings that belong to the people or companies and sent them to Khorramshahr immediately and as soon as possible

Interior Deputy ______ for Ahvaz a group of cars parked in Dezful on the right bank of Karoun River should be sent toward Ahvaz along with the cavalry regiment with enough personnel

Colonel Afshar aide-de-camp of the Commandant and a unit have been assigned to Abadan

At 8:30 wo ships were ready

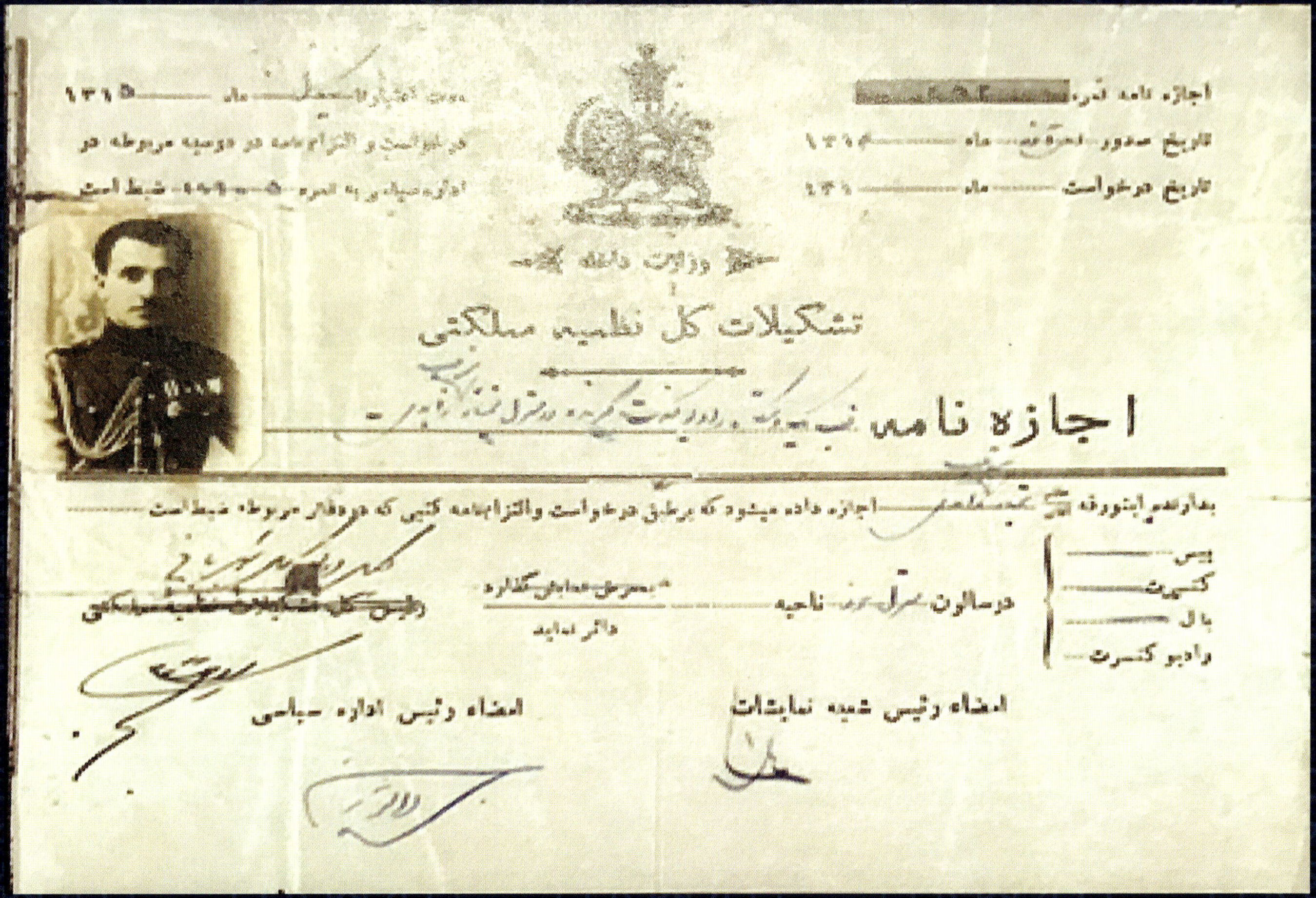

وزارت داخله

تشکیلات کل نظمیه مملکتی

اجازه نامه

امضاء رئیس اداره سیاسی

امضاء رئیس شعبه نمایشات

Document 2
23 November 1935

The document included here is partly intended to give the reader a sense of the depth and kinds of documents found in the archive. The content speaks for itself about the nature of control in that era and fear of foreign conspiracies—a staple of modern Iranian politics.

2.1

Validity To: One Year 1936 Application and letter of guarantee filed in Political Division and archived under Number 169-5 Photo of General Zahedi	Imperial Lion and Sun Emblem Interior Ministry General Directorate of National Police PERMIT Installation of one concert radio receiver in the house of Brigadier General Zahedi	Permit Number 252 Date of Issue: 23 November 1935 Date Applied For:

The holder of this sheet Mr. Brigadier General Zahedi is given permission that according to his written application and letter of guarantee that have been archived in the relevant files .....

Piece ...... lined through............
Concert .... lined through .... } To be set up in the family room of his house
Ball .... lined through ....
Concert Radio ....

Signed: Acting Commandant of Police
Signature of Head of the Political Division
Signature of Head of Exhibitions Branch

Document 3
1953

The author of this note, Hossein Makki (1911–99, member of Parliament 1947–53) had once been a fierce ally of Mohammad Mossadegh (prime minister 1952–53). Like many others in Mossadegh's ranks, by early 1953, he had become a no less fierce critic. In this letter to the shah, who had just returned to Iran, from his temporary exile in the eventful days of August 1953, Makki invites the monarch to treat Mossadegh in accordance with the strict confines of existing law and to resist the temptation to take revenge. The suggestion was not taken to heart. Mossadegh spent the rest of his life in prison or under house arrest. General Zahedi was, according to his son, opposed to this treatment.

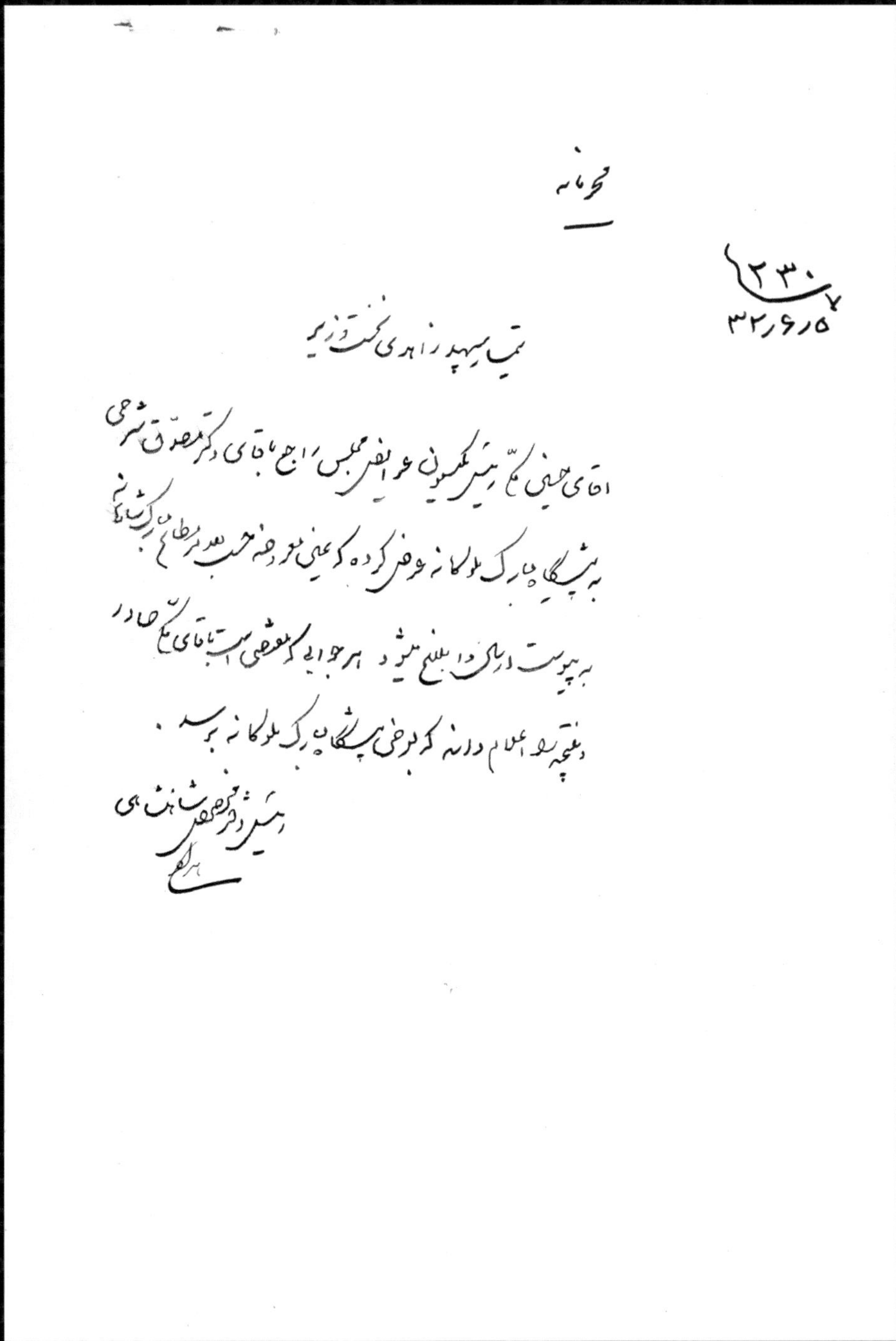

محرمانه

۲۳۰
۳۲/۶/۵

تیمسار سپهبد زاهدی نخست وزیر

آقای حسین مکی رئیس کمیسیون عرایض مجلس راجع به آقای دکتر مصدق شرحی به پیشگاه مبارک ملوکانه عرض کرده که عین عریضه حسب الامر مطاع مبارک شاهانه به پیوست ارسال و ابلاغ میشود هر جوابی که مقتضی است به آقای مکی صادر و نتیجه را اعلام دارند که بعرض پیشگاه مبارک ملوکانه برسد.

رئیس دفتر مخصوص شاهنشاهی

3.1 Confidential

230
27 August 1953

General Zahedi Prime Minister

Mr. Hossein Makki Chairman of the Petitions Committee of the Majlis submitted a report about Dr. Mossadegh to his August Majesty that the actual submittal is attached and is being communicated to you by the auspicious orders of his Majesty. Whatever response deemed appropriate should be conveyed to Mr. Makki and the result reported back so that it is brought to the attention of his Auspicious Majesty.

Head of the Imperial Private Office

Hirad

(نمونه ۷۴)

شماره: مستقیم

پیوست

مجلس شورای ملی

اداره

تاریخ: اول شهریور ۱۳۳۲

پیشگاه مبارک اعلیحضرت همایون شاهنشاهی

در این موقع که بعون الله تعالی بمیهن عزیز مراجعت فرموده اند با عرض خیر مقدم و تبریک وتهنیت و امیدواری بدوام وبقاء سلطنت مشروطه ایران واحترام قانون اساسی واجراء کامل مقررات آن از نظر کمال علاقه واعتقاد ذات شاهانه بحفظ اصول قانون اساسی واجراء کلیه قوانین مصوبه مجلس شورای ملی مقتضی دانست باستحضار ذات شاهانه برساند که .

طبق قانون اساسی و قانون محاکمه وزراء مصوب ۱۶ تیرماه ۱۳۰۷ تعقیب و محاکمه وزراء باید با استحضار و رای مجلس شورای ملی باشد و از قراریکه اطلاع حاصل شده جناب آقای دکتر محمد مصدق را دستگیر و زندانی نموده اند و مسلم است این جریان برخلاف منویات ذات شاهانه ومخالف با اصول ومقررات قانون اساسی وقانون محاکمه وزراء میباشد والبته قصد وغرض از این تذکار همانا رعایت واجراء کامل قوانین است وبااینکه جناب ایشان مرا که نماینده ملت ودارای مصونیت قانونی هستم برخلاف قانون دستگیر وبازداشت نمودند ولی عمل خلاف قانون ایشان نباید مجوز عمل خلاف قانون دیگری درمورد خود ایشان باشد واصلح آنستکه مادام که طبق قانون محاکمه وزراء موضوع درمجلس مطرح نشده ومنتهی بتصمیم نهائی قانونی نگردیده مصلحت ومقتضای قانون چنین ایجاب مینماید تا موقع انعقاد جلسات علنی مجلس شورای ملی وطرح موضوع در مجلس امر ومقرر گردد هیئت دولت با توجه بمقررات قانونی جناب آقای دکتر محمد مصدق را باحمد آباد (ملک شخصی خودشان) یا بیک نقطه امن دیگری که خود ایشان بخواهند انتقال دهند و برای رعایت احتیاط و پیش بینی اینکه مبادا آسیب وگزندی با یشان وارد آید همانطوریکه اعلیحضرت همایونی هم از رم تلگرافی دستور اکید دراین موضوع بهیئت دولت صادر فرمودند عده مامور حفظ جان ایشان باشند تا پس از تشکیل جلسات مجلس شورای ملی طبق مقررات قانون تعیین تکلیف بعمل آید .

البته با این ترتیب هم موجبات تامین عده علاقمندان بحفظ واجراء اصول قانونی فراهم شده وهم اینکه سابقه برخلاف قانون را مسجل باقی نگذارده باشند .

حسین مکی - رئیس کمیسیون عرایض مجلس شورای ملی

۲۳۰
۳۲/۶/۵

3.2 Office
Attachment ....
Date First of Shahrivar 1332: 23 August 1953

Emblem
National Consultative Assembly [Majlis}
Number
Direct

May It Please His Imperial Majesty King of Kings

At this time that by the grace of the great God he has returned to the beloved country, with expressions of welcome and congratulations and salutations and with the hope of the continuation and survival of the Iranian Constitutional Monarchy and respect for the Constitution and enforcement of all its regulations, with view to the Royal interest and conviction for preservation of the Constitution and execution of all ratified laws by the Majlis we saw it appropriate to bring to the Royal attention that:

According to the Constitution and the law for prosecuting ministers ratified on 16 Tir 1307 [7 July 1928] arraignment and prosecution of ministers must be with the knowledge and vote of the Majlis and as it was learned that the Honorable Dr. Mohammad Mossadegh has been arrested and imprisoned and it is certain that this occurrence is against your Royal convictions and against the principles and regulations of the Constitution and the Law for prosecution of ministers and of course the reason for this reminder is only the total observance and execution of the Constitution, and although his Honor arrested and imprisoned me illegally while I was a representative of the people and had legal immunity, his illegal action should not become the license for illegal action by others to use against him and it is prudent that as long as the issue has not been considered by the Majlis in accordance with the Law for prosecution of ministers, and has not culminated in a final legal decision, it is prudent and advisable in accordance with the Law that as long as the Majlis has not convened in a public session and the matter has not been considered, the Government Council be ordered, in consideration of legal regulations, that Dr. Mohammad Mossadegh be transferred to Ahmadabad (his personal property) or to another safe location of his choosing and as a safety measure and to make sure that no harm or injury befall him just as His Imperial Majesty issued strict orders on this subject that he telegraphed to the government from Rome, that a group of guards be assigned to protect his life so that after the Majlis convenes, the matter be decided in accordance with legal regulations. Of course in this manner the Shahanshah's interest in the preservation and execution of legal principles will be promulgated and no precedence of action against the Constitution will remain.

Hossein Makki—Chairman of the Petitions Committee of the Majlis

Document 4
8 September 1953

Hassan Taqizadeh (1878–1970, president of the Senate 1957–60), the author of this letter to General Zahedi, is one of modern Iran's most influential intellectuals. He was an active proponent of Iran's constitutional revolution (1905–7) and an advocate of the view that Iran must modernize, and in this effort, it must completely emulate the West. By the time he wrote this letter, after having held numerous influential ministerial portfolios, he had been appointed a member of the parliament, a senator appointed by the shah. As a prime minister, Mossadegh had dissolved the senate. General Zahedi was about to reconvene it.

سید حسن
تقی‌زاده

۱۸ شهریور ماه سنه ۱۳۳۲ هجری شمسی

دوست عزیز محترم   برخود لازم میدانم که از مهمان‌نوازی مکرر
عالی که با همه گرفتاری بی‌اندازه که دارید درک فیض صحبت و تجدید مراتب مودت
فیمابین در ضمن آنها نصیب مخلص شد تشکر صمیمی و قلبی عرض کنم و یقین دارم
که نظر بمعرفتی که بحال و صفات اینجانب دارید میدانید که این ابراز امتنان
و مسرت قلبی بی‌ریا است   ضمناً خیلی خوشوقتم که اصلاحات و اقداماتی
که بسرعت و رشادت و جد مخصوص بآنها دست زده اید موجب قدردانی
مردمان سلیم و بیغرض این مملکت و عامه شده و خواهد شد   از تأخیری
که در اظهار این تشکر روی داد اعتذار دارم
خاتمهٔ صحبت روز پنجشنبه ۱۲ شهریور ماه بالخصوص برای مخلص موجب
سعادت و خوشوقتی عظیم بود و باعث تشکر قلبی و فراموش نشدنی است.
ترتیبی که برای انعقاد جلسات مجلس سنا پیشنهاد فرمودید البته بهترین
شقوق بود و با اعتماد کامل بقبول و وعدهٔ شرافتمندانهٔ عالی

4.1 Seyed Hassan Taqizadeh

18 Shahrivar 1332 Hegira Solar [8 September 1953]

Dear Honorable Friend,

I feel obliged to offer my heartfelt and sincere gratitude for your repeated hospitality with all the immense problems that you have, this devotee appreciates the good fortune and blessing of conversing [with you] and renewal of mutual friendship. And I am sure that with your knowledge of my principles and traits you know that this declaration of gratitude is from the happiness of my heart and non-hypocritical. Meanwhile I am very glad that the reforms and actions you have undertaken with speed and courage and special zeal are appreciated by the public and the humble and unbiased people of this country, and will be appreciated. I apologize for the lateness of this thank-you note.

The conclusion of our conversation of Thursday 12 Sharivar [2 September] was for [this] devotee particularly satisfying and joyous and caused me heartfelt and unforgettable gratitude. Your proposal of the plan for convening the Senate was the best choice, and with full trust in your honorable promises

منتظر انجام آن امر خواهم بود لکن باید عرض کنم که امید است قبلاً (یعنی اقلاً
ده روز قبل از ۱۴ مهر ماه آینده) برای فراهم آوردن مقدمات لازم امر
بنحو مطلوب توجه جدی خواهید فرمود که آن کار باین شکل بطور آبرومند
و شایسته انجام گیرد اگر از حصول مقدمات مزبور بموقع یعنی مثلاً
یک هفته یا چند روز قبل از موعد مخلص را مسبوق فرمائید موجب تشکر
جداگانه خواهد بود

بر حسب آنچه از نیات حسنه و عزم عالی در اصلاحات خیرخواهانه
مشهود اینجانب گردیده شکی ندارم که مجلس سنا بالاتفاق و یا با اکثریت عظیمه
پشتیبان ثابت حکومت حضرتعالی خواهد بود

راجع بموضوع تهیه مقدمات امر که عرض شد اگر اجازه بفرمائید مناسب
خواهد بود که از جناب آقای خواجه نوری خواهش کنم خدمت رسیده تدارکات
لازمه در این باب را حضوراً بعمل بیاورند زیاده عرضی نیست جز تجدید مراتب
ارادت صمیمی سید حسن تقی زاده

4.2 I shall await the fulfillment of that matter, but I have to say that I hope that prior (meaning at least 10 days prior to next 14 Mehr [6 October]), in order to make the necessary preparations for the desired results, you should pay serious attention so that the project is carried out in a respectable and competent manner. If you would apprise me of the attainment of the preparations in time, meaning one week or a few days in advance of the deadline, it will cause a separate expression of gratitude.

According to what I witnessed from your unequaled resolution and your high intentions for beneficial reforms, I have no doubt that the Senate will unanimously or with a great majority remain in firm support of your government.

About the subject of preliminary arrangements mentioned previously, it would be appropriate if you would permit me to ask Mr. Khajehnoori to meet with you in person for necessary discussions about this matter. I have no more to present except to renew my respect and sincere regards

Seyed Hassan Taqizadeh

Document 5
15 September 1953

During his tenure as a prime minister, General Zahedi was bombarded by many private pieces of news, gossip, and advice. Here, a professor at the university is obviously angling for an appointment and at the same time offering advice. What he knows to be exceptionally juicy and valuable gossip will, he hopes, be his ticket to an appointment. The archive thus documents both important acts of politics and diplomacy and occasionally a bit of gossip.

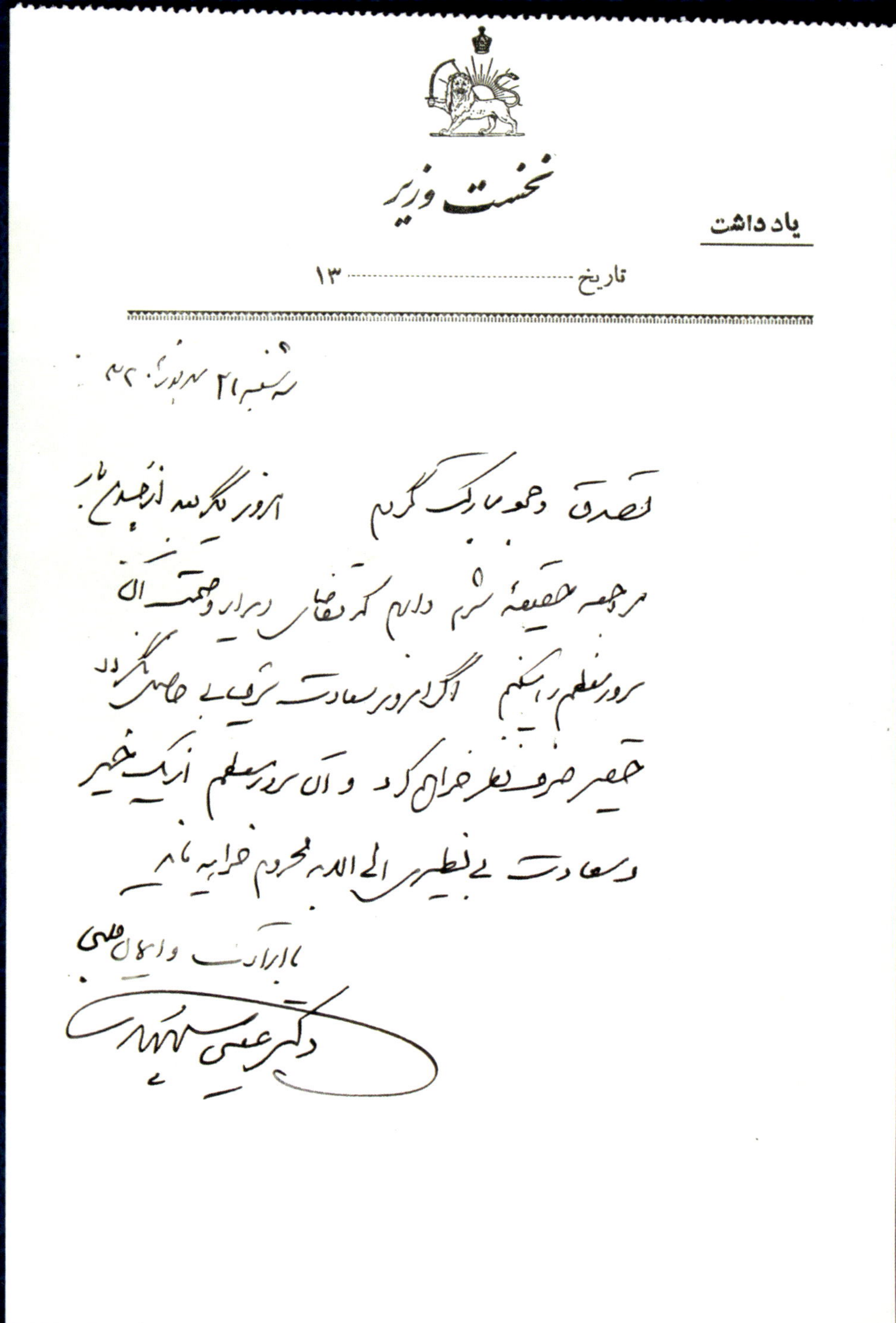

نخست وزیر

یادداشت

تاریخ ۱۳

5.1 Emblem

Prime Minister Memorandum

Tuesday 24 Shahrivar 32

May I be sacrificed for your blessed self

Today again after several failed attempts, I am really ashamed to be requesting a meeting with that great leader. If I don't have the good fortune of being received in audience, your humble servant will have to change my mind and that great leader will be deprived of an incredible benefit and good fortune until eternity.

With regard and heartfelt devotion

Dr. Issa Sepahbodi

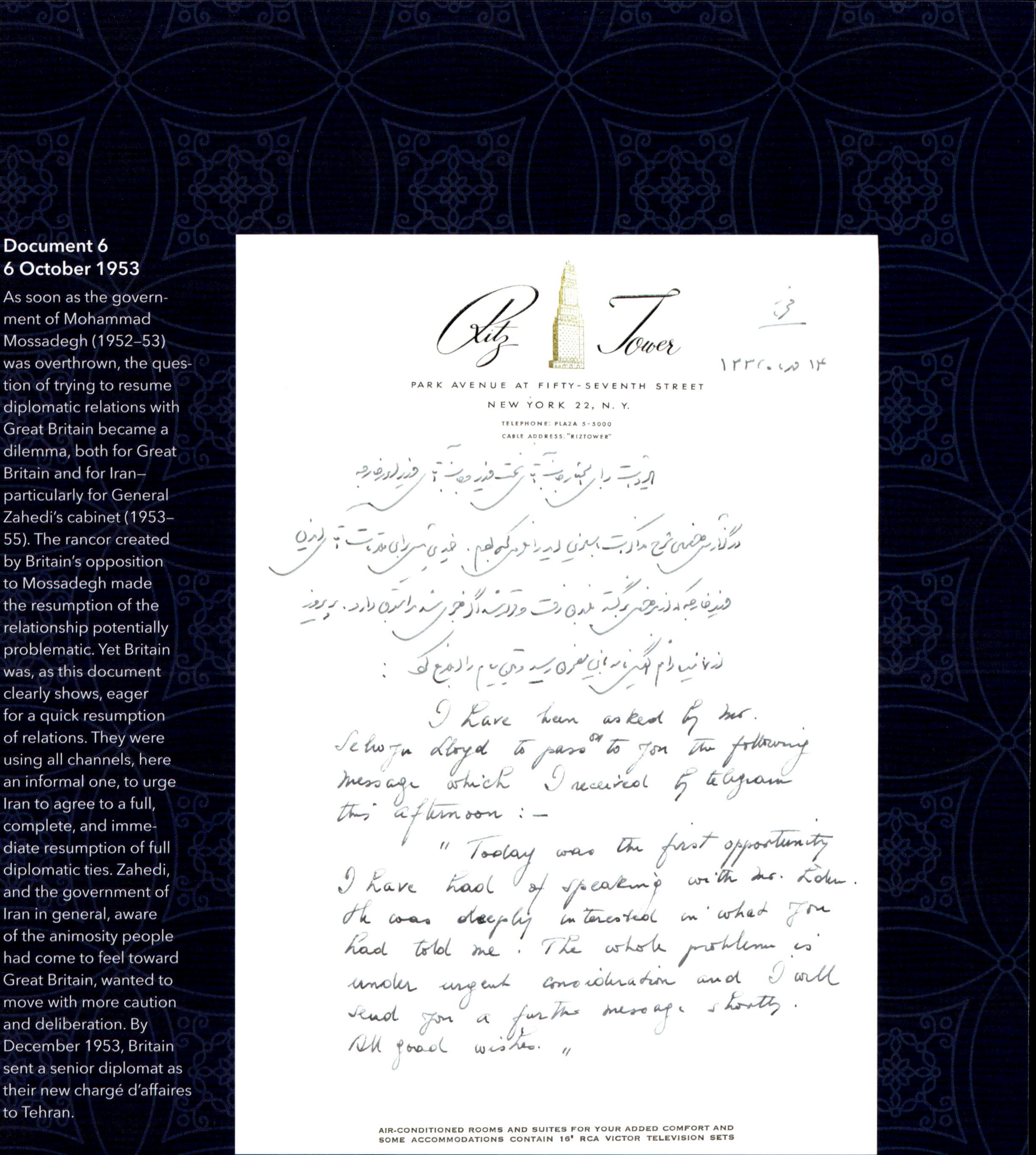

Document 6
6 October 1953

As soon as the government of Mohammad Mossadegh (1952–53) was overthrown, the question of trying to resume diplomatic relations with Great Britain became a dilemma, both for Great Britain and for Iran—particularly for General Zahedi's cabinet (1953–55). The rancor created by Britain's opposition to Mossadegh made the resumption of the relationship potentially problematic. Yet Britain was, as this document clearly shows, eager for a quick resumption of relations. They were using all channels, here an informal one, to urge Iran to agree to a full, complete, and immediate resumption of full diplomatic ties. Zahedi, and the government of Iran in general, aware of the animosity people had come to feel toward Great Britain, wanted to move with more caution and deliberation. By December 1953, Britain sent a senior diplomat as their new chargé d'affaires to Tehran.

Ritz Tower

PARK AVENUE AT FIFTY-SEVENTH STREET
NEW YORK 22, N. Y.
TELEPHONE: PLAZA 5-5000
CABLE ADDRESS: "RIZTOWER"

فوری

۱۴ مهر ۱۳۳۲

[illegible]

[illegible]

[illegible]

[illegible] :

I have been asked by Mr. Selwyn Lloyd to pass on to you the following message which I received by telegram this afternoon :—

" Today was the first opportunity I have had of speaking with Mr. Eden. He was deeply interested in what you had told me. The whole problem is under urgent consideration and I will send you a further message shortly. All good wishes. "

AIR-CONDITIONED ROOMS AND SUITES FOR YOUR ADDED COMFORT AND SOME ACCOMMODATIONS CONTAIN 16" RCA VICTOR TELEVISION SETS

6.1 Confidential

14 Mehr 1332 [6 October 1953]

Memorandum for the Honorable Mr. Prime Minister
the Honorable Mr. Minister of Foreign Affairs

I had brought to your attention the private report describing discussions with Selwyn Lloyd. A while ago he went to London to meet Mr. Eden the Foreign Minister, who had returned from vacation, and it was agreed that if there was news I would be informed. The day before yesterday a letter was received from the British Permanent Representative to this effect and communicated the following message:

I have been asked by Mr. Selwyn Lloyd to pass on to you the following message which I received by telegram this afternoon:

(The following is the original English text)

"Today was the first opportunity I have had of speaking with Mr. Eden. He was deeply interested in what you had told me. The whole problem is under urgent consideration and I will send you a further message shortly.

All good wishes"

ترجمه

لندن ۱۹۵۵

آقای ایدن وزیر امور خارجه انگلیس از من خواهش کرده‌اند پیغام ذیل را که دیروز عصر تلگرافاً رسید

به اطلاع برسانم : « به محض اینکه به وزارت امور خارجه برگشتم آقای وزیر مشاور صحبت شما

با ایشان را به اطلاع من رساند. آنچه در آنجا گفته بودید عمیقاً مرا متأثر نمود و قدردانی بفرمائید

قرار گرفته و امیدوارم که به نتیجه مطلوب برسیم. با درود فراوان »

امضاء ... آقای ... را خواهشمندم ... اعلیحضرت همایونی و آقای نخست وزیر ابلاغ نمائید

ترجمه

I have been asked by Mr. Eden to pass to you the following message which I received by telegram late last night :–

" As soon as I got back to the Foreign Office the Minister of State told me of your recent talk with him. Would you please convey to the Shah and the Prime Minister my thanks for this initiative. I feel

Translation

Mr. Selwyn Lloyd has requested that the following telegraphic message, which was received this afternoon, be brought to your attention: "Today I had the first opportunity to speak to Mr. Eden. He is extremely interested in the matter you had told me about and the subject is under immediate consideration and I hope to be sending you another message shortly. With sincere regards"

Today another letter was received from Gladwyn Jebb and he has forwarded Mr. Eden's telegraphic message

Now the content and translation

(The following is the original English text)

I have been asked by Mr. Eden to pass on to you the following message which I received by telegram late last night:

"As soon as I got back to the Foreign Office the Minister of State told me of your recent talk with him. Would you please convey to the Shah and the Prime Minister my thanks for this initiative. I feel that the best way to begin this new phase is for us to resume diplomatic relations. We are ready to do this and I am sure that everything will be easier when we are in direct touch. Perhaps you could ask your Government to consider this. Meanwhile either the Minister of State or, if he has not returned to New York, Sir Gladwyn Jebb, will be ready to discuss the matters further with you."

ترجمه

بعد از بند ۵

متن انگلیسی از نظر تفاهم کامل است. پیام وزیر را که ترتیب ترجمه وقت نگرانم

برای اطلاع شما :

در همینکه نمایندگان خارجه برگشتم وزیر خارجه در مذاکرات خود با [illegible] جهت اطلاع ارسال

خواهد شد. ... وزیر ... بنده

... بهترین طریق ... دوستی جدید را ... که روابط ...

... داریم همیشه ... هستیم ... برای ... خواهد بود.

that the best way to begin this new phase is for us to resume diplomatic relations. We are ready to also do this and I am sure that everything will be easier when we are in direct touch. Perhaps you could ask your Government to consider this. Meanwhile either the Minister of State or, if he has not returned to New York, Sir Gladwyn Jebb, will be ready to discuss the matter further with you."

Translation

Mr. Eden has requested me to inform you of the following message that was received late last night:

"As soon as I returned to the Foreign Ministry the Minister of State informed me of his discussions with you. Please convey my thanks for this initiative to His Majesty the Shah His Honor Mr. Prime Minister. I imagine the best way for us to examine the current situation is to establish diplomatic relations. I am certain as soon as direct contact is established everything will be easier.

شاید بتوانید از دست آن نجات یابید که این نظر را در مطالعه قرار دهند. در این فاصله آقای وزیر [illegible] در [illegible]

هم اگر ایشان به نیروی دیگر رفته باشند برگردانیدن چنین [illegible] که در [illegible] به حال

اثبات کند.»

در گزارش سابق توضیح داده بودم که وزیر [illegible] هم نظرش [illegible] است ولی [illegible] ارجاع به [illegible]

[illegible] در [illegible] صحیح نیست [illegible] تمام شده است. [illegible]

[illegible] این [illegible] دارم در صورتیکه [illegible]

ارجاع مطلب و نظر دیگری [illegible] این جانب را مطلع فرمایید.

آقای [illegible] هم [illegible] در [illegible] را [illegible] بعد [illegible] تهران [illegible]

[illegible] را در [illegible] [illegible] در این [illegible] است و [illegible] دارد و [illegible]

[illegible] در [illegible] باشد [illegible].

[illegible] این جانب [illegible] [illegible] است [illegible]

[illegible] این [illegible] [illegible] ندارد

[signature]

You may want to ask friends to take this opinion under consideration. Meanwhile Mr. Minister of State or if he has not returned to New York Sir Gladwyn Jebb is ready to resume discussions with you."

In the previous report I had explained that the Minister of State also had a similar view, but I told him my reasoning about the immediate resumption of diplomatic relations, that it was not advisable, and I think he was convinced. It seems they are insisting on this action again, therefore I request that you let me know if you think it necessary to engage them regarding this or other views.

Mr. Walter Levy is also waiting for me to inform him about the Government's view as to whether they want him to come to Tehran. Because you know that he is very busy and has to take care of his work and prepare for his trip I request that you make a decision on this subject and inform me.

Because my credentials have not arrived yet and have not been presented to the President of the United States no contacts have been made with the American authorities, therefore I have nothing worthwhile to add.

[*Illegible signature*]

Document 7
16 January 1954

Anoushiravan Sepahbodi (1888–1980) was a career Iranian diplomat and a seasoned politician. For a crucial time during Iran's occupation by Allied forces, he served as the country's foreign minister. He also served as an ambassador to a variety of capitals. His report here is fascinating, in that it clearly shows how General Zahedi as a prime minister was hoping to use a shared military past with the officers who had just overthrown the Egyptian monarch, King Farouk, the shah's former brother-in-law. Zahedi's effort eventually failed. Before long, Egypt, in the powerful hands of Nasser—one of the three officers who overthrew the monarchy (Free Officers Movement, 1952)—became a serious foe of Iran and a nemesis of the shah. The archive is replete with references to the shah's continuing concern about what Nasser was doing in Iran, the Persian Gulf, and the rest of the Middle East.

سفارت کبرای شاهنشاهی ایران
قاهره

حضور محترم حضرت آقای زاهدی نخست وزیر مشرف باد

امیدوارم که مزاج محترم در عین سلامت باشد. در رادیو شنیدم که بعد از مسافرت برامسر کسالت پیدا کرده اید انشاءالله تا کنون بکلی رفع شده است.

دو روز قبل نامه های خود را بحضرت رئیس جمهور تقدیم و در موقعیکه در اطاق جداگانه بطور خصوصی با هم صحبت میکردیم سلام دوستانه حضرتعالی را همانطورکه به بنده فرموده بودید باستحضار ایشان رسانیدم از اینکه فرموده بودید ما هر دو سرباز هستیم و بین ما دیپلماسی در کار نیست و هرچه میگوئیم عین حقیقت است خیلی متأثر و خوشحال دیدم از بنده خواست که سلام دوستانه او را بحضرتعالی تبلیغ نمایم گفتم با کمال خوشوقتی اینکار را خواهم کرد و گفت باید همینطور باشد و بین دو سرباز دیپلوماسی نیست.

ما از صمیم قلب عظمت و شوکت ایران بزرگ را خواهان و یقین دارم همقطار من بکشور خود خدمات بزرگ خواهد کرد.

بنده شخص جنرال نجیب را خیلی مرد آرام و محجوب دیدم و همینطور هم مشهور است و زیاده هم با همکاران خود یک عقیده نیست. و اختیار واقعی اینطورکه میگویند در دست سرهنگ دوم جمال عبدالناصر و چند نفر دیگر است منتها چون جنرال نجیب فوق العاده در قشون مجرب و در نزد مردم مصر عزیز است مجبور هستند که با او اطاعت نمایند.

زیاده براین جسارت نورزیده و عرایض خود م که مربوط بسفارت میشود بموقع دیگر محول میکنم سلامت و موفقیت حضرتعالی را خواهانم.

۲۶ دی
ارادتمند انوشیروان سپهبدی

7.1 Imperial Iranian Embassy
Cairo

The Honorable Mr. Zahedi Prime Minister May You Be Honored

I hope you are in good health. I heard on the radio that after your trip to Ramsar you came down with an illness that I hope has gone away completely.

Two days ago I presented my letters to His Excellency the President of the Republic and when we were having a private talk in a separate room I conveyed to him your friendly greetings exactly as you had instructed me to do. That you said we are both soldiers and between us there is no diplomacy and whatever we say is the exact truth, I felt impressed him very much and made him very happy he asked me to convey to you his friendly greetings I said I shall do that with pleasure and he said that is the way it should be and between two soldiers there is no diplomacy.

With heartfelt sincerity we are desirous of the grandeur and glory of the great Iran and I am certain that my fellow soldier will do great service for his country.

I saw General Nagib as a very calm and likable person and this is how he is known and he does not share the same beliefs with his colleagues very much. And it is said that real control is in the hands of Lieutenant Colonel Abdul Nasser and a few others but because of General Nagib's extraordinary experience in the army and he is loved by the people of Egypt they are obliged to obey him.

I will not continue this impertinence and will report embassy matters another time [I am] desirous of your honor's health and success.

26 Dey Sincerely Anoushiravan Sepahbodi

Document 8
17 February 1954

Nasser Ghashghaei (1906–83) and his nomadic tribe had been a fixture of Iranian politics, particularly in the second half of the twentieth century. Nasser was considered an ally of Mossadegh but also tried to keep close ties to the US embassy as well as members of the National Front. In this letter, written after Mossadegh's fall, he tried to mend fences with General Zahedi, who had been a close friend of the Ghashghaeis for many years. Indeed, the relationship between the Zahedi family and the Ghashghaeis, as well as the relationship between the shah's regime and the Ghashghaei brothers, has been complicated—sometimes acrimonious, occasionally cooperative. Eventually, after the revolution, while Nasser Khan became for a short while a prominent political figure on the national scene, the Islamic regime forced him into exile and executed his brother, Khosrow, on charges of espionage.

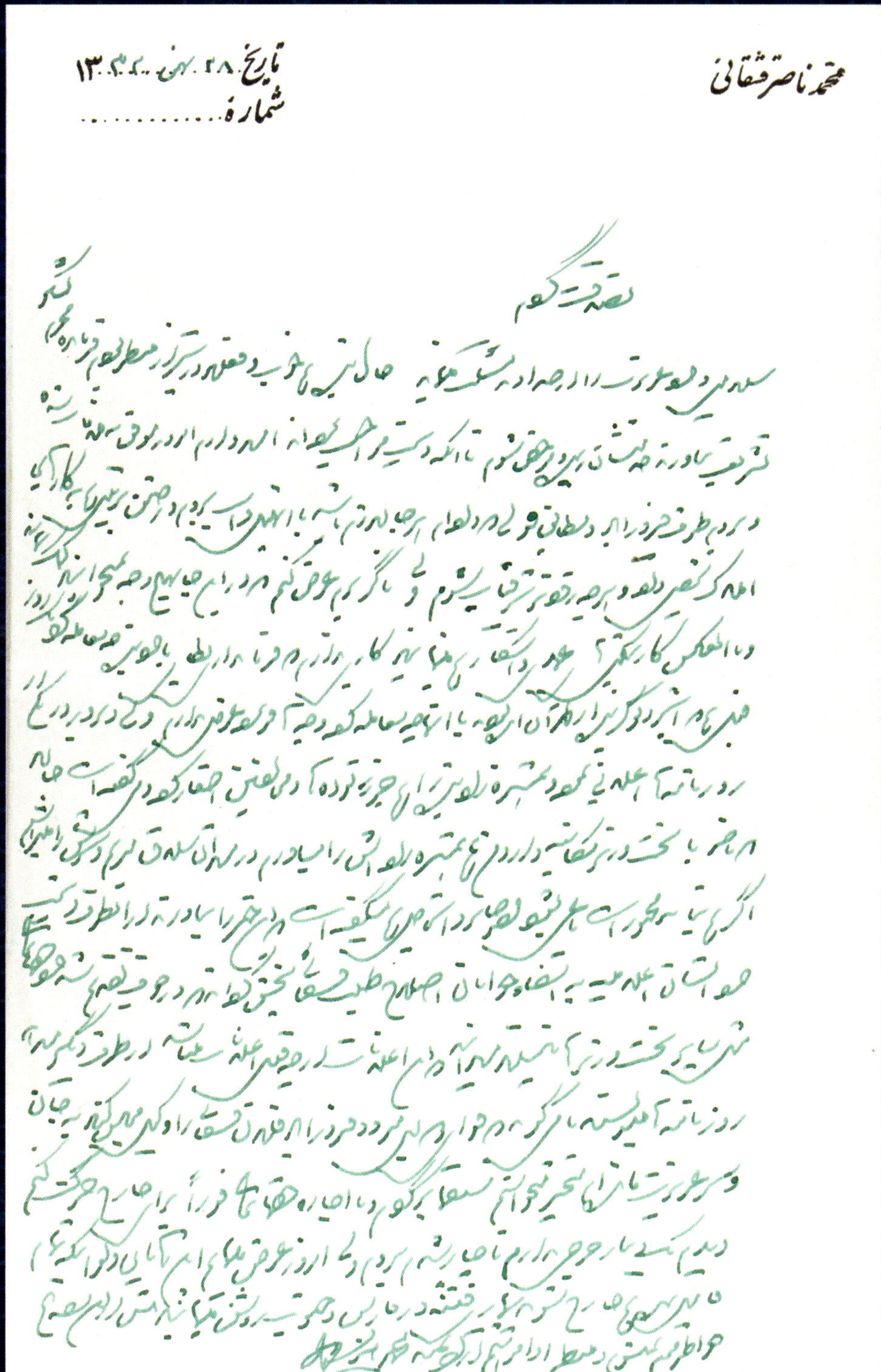
محمد ناصر قشقائی

تاریخ ۲۸ بهمن ۱۳۳۲

شماره ....

8.1 Mohammad Nasser Ghashghaei Date 28 Bahman 1332

May I be sacrificed for you

I ask God for your dear self's good health. I am also well and currently in Shiraz awaiting the arrival of the honorable Division Commander to meet with him and take my leave until he presses my hand I hope I will succeed in meeting him today and leave for Firoozabad and according to the promise I have made I will go wherever necessary by automobile or horse and also take care of my personal belongings and properties and have the honor of meeting as soon as possible. have no alternative but to say that here they don't want to help in any way, and on the contrary, they are publicly and openly obstructive. I won't say how the military administration treated me the day before my cook and servant arrived from Tehran how they were treated and what they did I won't say But yesterday in one of the newspapers it was announced that my nephew was part of the Tudeh and the opposition and she was summoned. He has said now that Nasser is in communication with the Prime Minister, I too will bring his niece to Tehran and whip her and shave her head and if she does not come she is forced to become an outlaw he had particularly said so in front of many people to bring the girl and he himself has distributed pamphlets with the forged signatures of young reformist Ghashghaeis, which I have attached. You are not like other Prime Ministers and know about these types of leaflets On the other hand newspapers write and say that Government forces are going to Firoozabad to elect so-and-so Ghashghaei as representative to the Majlis I swear upon your dear life and head that I am left dumbfounded. I wanted to return directly and with your honor's permission to go abroad immediately but noticed I did not have a dinar for expenses I had no alternative but not to go but today I say to you that even if all my family goes abroad these people will start trouble in Fars and the South I will not bother your good self and await your orders.

Sincerely
[*Illegible signature*]

Document 9
13 December 1954

As prime minister, General Zahedi insisted on maintaining virtually all the powers constitutionally granted to his office. His insistence on these powers in the face of the shah's newfound desire to increase the power of the crown, even to the detriment of the prime minister, was a source of constant tension between the shah and General Zahedi. Eventually, these tensions, in addition to other issues of contention, led to the acrimonious "resignation" of General Zahedi—a move masterminded by the shah.

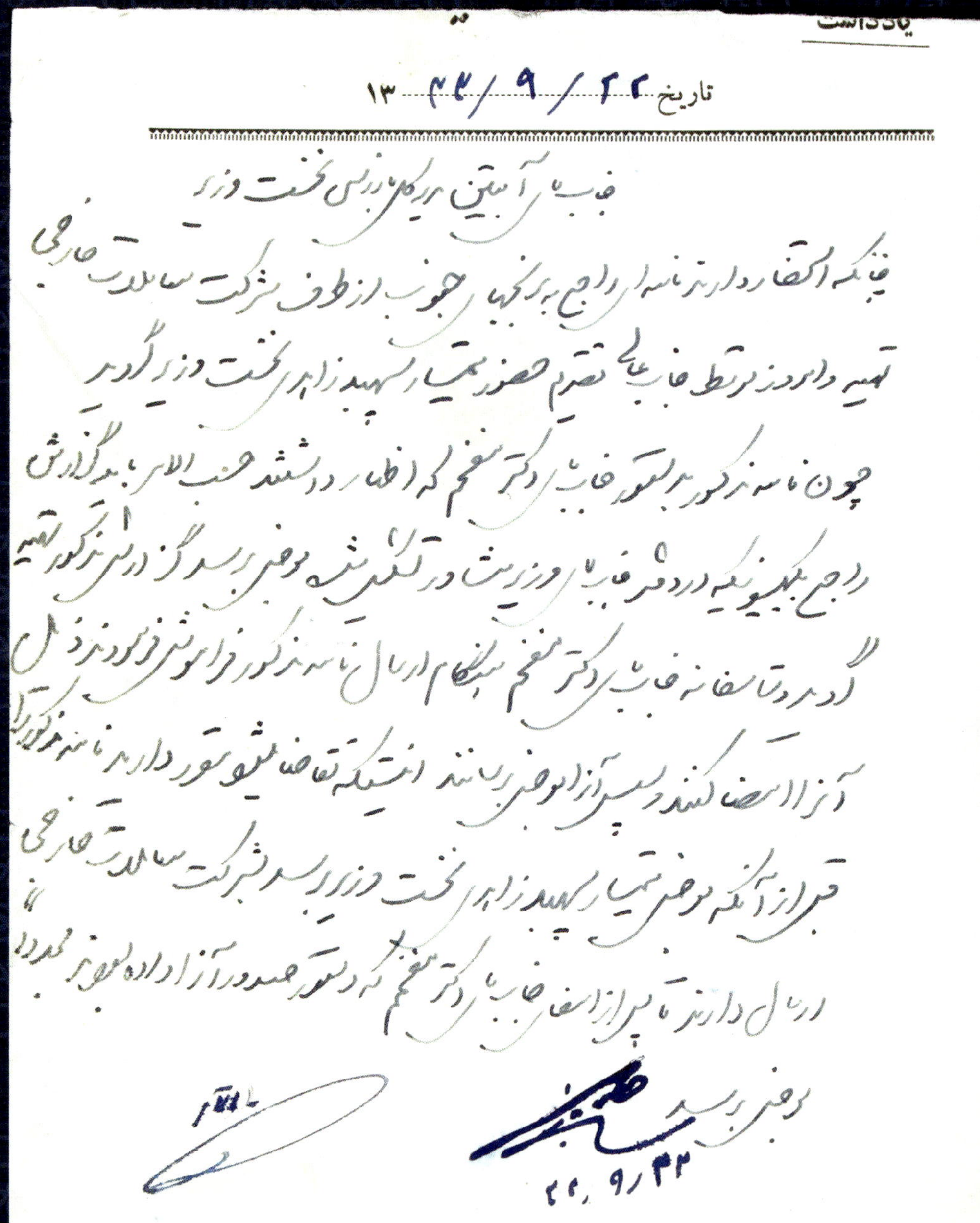

یادداشت

تاریخ ۲۲/۹/۳۳ ۱۳

۲۲/۹/۳۳

9.1 Memo

Date 22/9/1333

Honorable Mr. Abtin Director General of
Prime Minister's Inspection [Dept.]

As your Excellency is aware a letter about the rice in the South prepared by Foreign Trade Corporation was delivered by your honor to General Zahedi the Prime Minister

Because the said letter was prepared on the orders of Doctor Mofakham who had said that orders were that a report had to be presented about the committee [meeting] that was convened in the office of the Minister of State the said report was prepared but unfortunately Dr. Mofakham failed to sign the letter before it was brought to [his] attention therefore it is requested that [you] arrange that before it is presented to General Zahedi the Prime Minister the letter is returned to the Foreign Trade corporation to be signed by Dr. Mofakham who had ordered the issuance of the letter.

Signed 22/9/33

Document 10
3 December 1955

Here Ali Asghar Hekmat (1892–1980), one of Iran's most dedicated, respected, and erudite civil servants and diplomats, is reconnecting with his old friend General Zahedi. Hekmat had served in many cabinets, from minister of education to foreign minister. He is writing to General Zahedi hoping for a better job than ambassadorship to India.

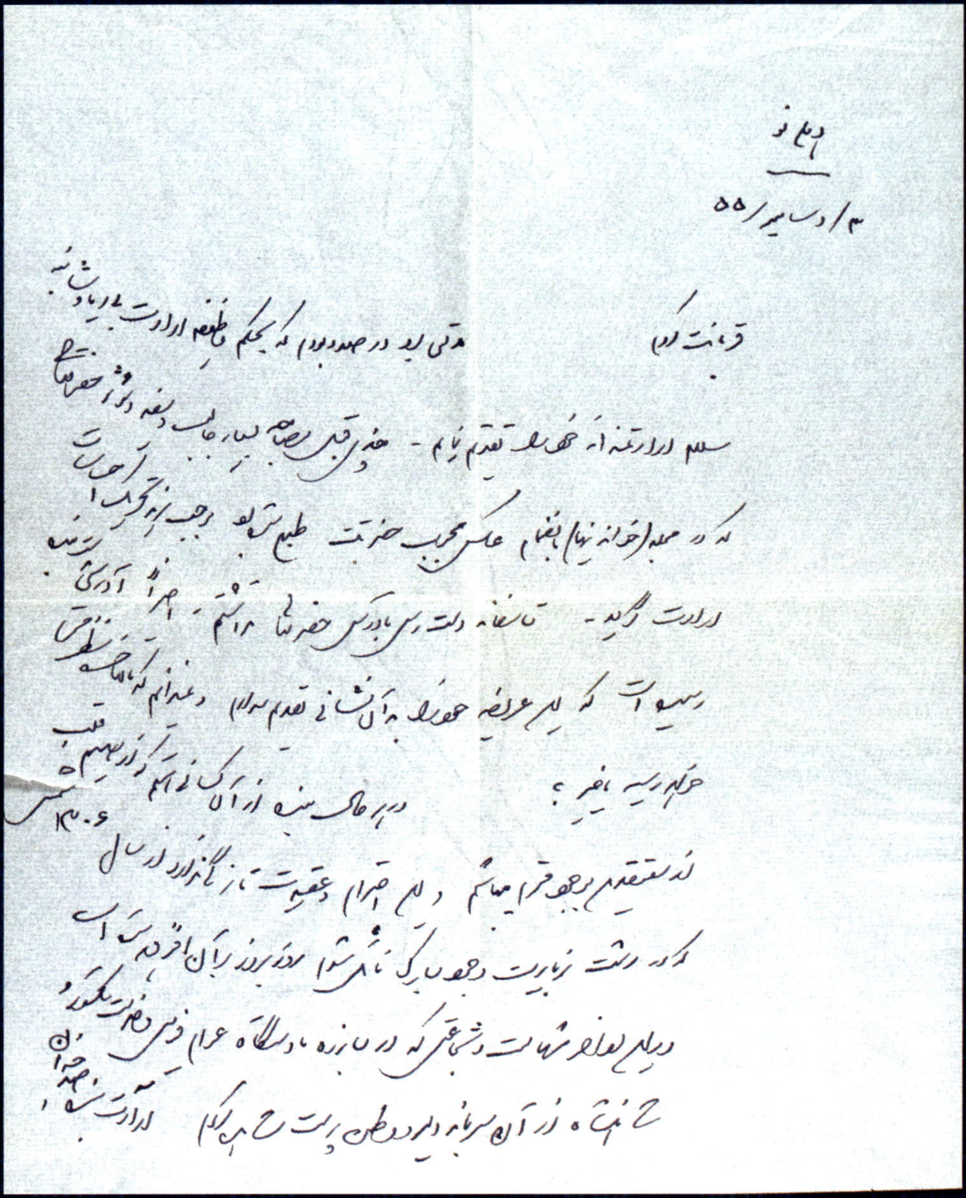

دهلی نو

۳/دسامبر/۵۵

قربانت گردم

10.1

New Delhi

3/December/55

May I be sacrificed for you I had intended for some time, as duty dictates, to present you my sincere, genuine and pure devotion, and my true greetings—A while ago your very interesting and useful interview, which included your Excellency's beloved photograph, was particularly effective because it was published in (Khandaniha) magazine, excited my feelings of devotion. Unfortunately I did not have access to your Excellency's address. Recently I received an address to which I am presenting this petition and do not know if it will reach you for your perusal.

Be that as it may, I am someone who from the bottom of my heart is a believer in your honorable person, and this respect and belief is not new and started in the solar year 1306 [1927] when I had the privilege of meeting your honor in Rasht and it has increased day by day.

Recently the courage and bravery shown in challenging organized demagoguery and the service to the country and the Shahanshah that I have witnessed from that nationalist soldier has increased my devotion a hundredfold

هم خداوند باشد. هر وقتی که محبت و الطاف بی‌پایان [illegible] در باب حقوق [illegible] فقط احساس نگرانی [illegible]

که تا چه حد با صداقت جوانمردانه و بصفات بزرگواری [illegible] آراسته است [illegible] ثابت

[illegible] در وقت حاضر - آنچه عرض میکنم ناشی از هیچ گونه غرض [illegible] احساس [illegible]

بلکه خدا گواه است که از احساسات صادقانه و [illegible] ناشی میشود.

امیدوارم خداوند وجود [illegible] را برای [illegible] نگهداری وطن عزیز و [illegible] محبوب حفظ [illegible]

[illegible] ارادتمند [illegible] در [illegible] رهبری و پیشوائی وجود شریف [illegible]

قدرت [illegible] نمایند.

اما [illegible] ارادتمند با [illegible] در گذشته [illegible] که حسب الامر [illegible] [illegible]

تا نقطه حال [illegible] چشم [illegible] در صدد [illegible] ایران [illegible]

و [illegible] باشم.

اگر [illegible] کامل [illegible] خاضعانه [illegible]

از [illegible] ارادتمند [illegible] شریف [illegible]

[illegible] العمر [illegible]

hundredfold. Whenever I remember the endless kindness and favors toward myself I get a sense of your principled chivalry and qualities of greatness that thank God you have been endowed with.

In any case, at this time what I am uttering is not induced by any old grudge or feeling or apprehension or hope, but as God be my witness, it is from true and sincere feelings.

I hope that God will protect your blessed self to serve our dear nation and the beloved Shahanshah and may He bring success to friends and devotees to serve the country under your honorable leadership.

But your devoted servant continues to serve per your order in the corner of India. Unfortunately I cannot say anything good about my health. My eye aches. I am planning on making a trip to Europe for medical treatment in a few months to improve my health.

If you have any commands for me here, I will be ready and it will be my honor and believe me that as long as I live, I am, and will be, one of your blessed self's true, sincere, and faithful devotees.

Your obedient servant

Ali Asghar Hekmat

Document 11
1953–1955

This is another example of the kind of the documents found in this archive, where detailed accounts of gifts, menus for receptions, and invitation lists are included. Here is a document prepared during General Zahedi's tenure as prime minister: a list of gifts.

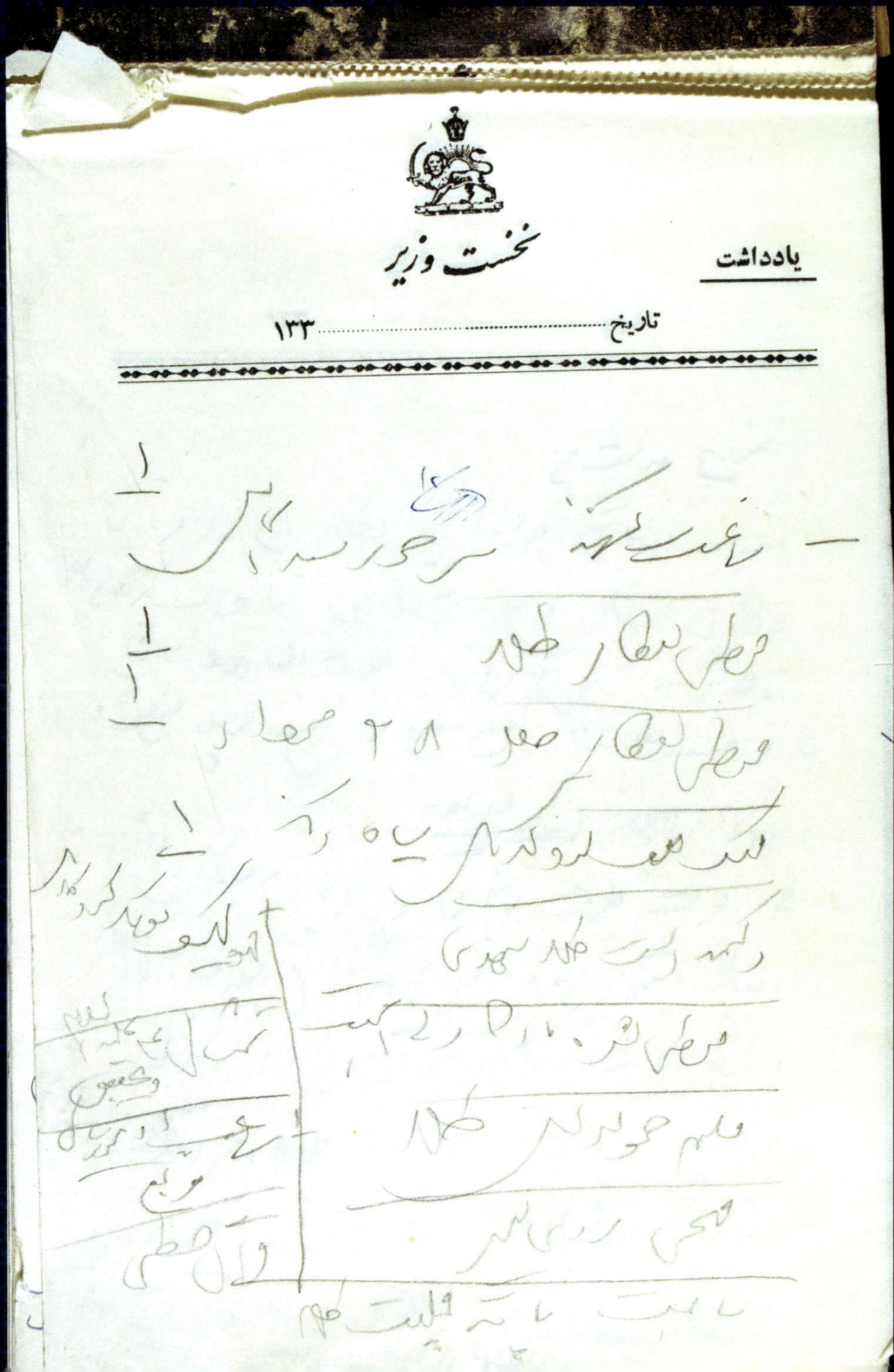
نخست وزیر

یادداشت

تاریخ ۱۳۳

11.1 Brown Crocodile Skin Bag

Image of Ali Peace Be Upon Him and agate

1 Square Universal Watch

Handwritten Koran

Old Clock Diamond Lion Head 1

Gold Cigarette Box 1

Gold 28-Cigarettes Box 1

Black Crocodile Skin Bag 1

Gold Cuff Links

Silver Box It is a memento

Gold Fountain Pen

______ table top

Gold Patek-Phillip watch

Document 12
1954–1955

During his tenure as prime minister, General Zahedi was clearly planning to write a memoir. The two sets of notes included in here are outlines of his envisioned narrative. His long career spanned nearly the entire course of the first half of the twentieth century in Iran, from his days as a decorated commander, his role fighting separatist forces in Iran in the early twentieth century, to his time as prime minister. According to Ardeshir Zahedi, several of his father's friends—historians and journalists in particular—had more than once encouraged him to write such a memoir. The project was unfortunately never completed. It is also General Zahedi's account of why he worked to overthrow Mossadegh.

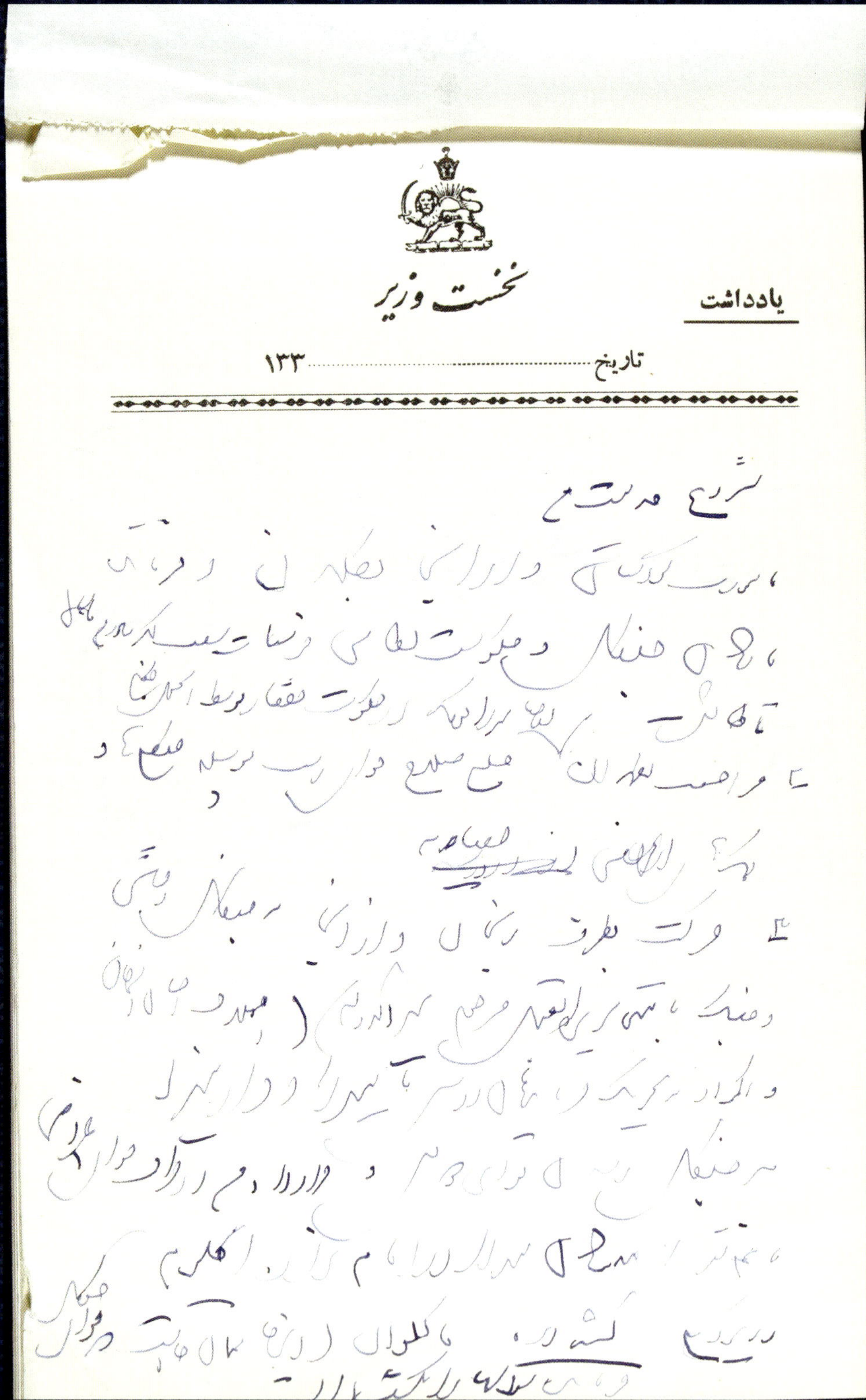

12.1

Center: Emblem

Prime Minister Memorandum

Date: ....133...

The start of my service

1. Assigned to Kurdestan and from there to Gilan as the Commander of the Forest Garrison and of Martial Law from Foomenat Rasht ______ Anzali to Talesh.

2. Return to Tehran Mirza Koochek's request from the Caucasian Government through the Jangali Society and the disarming of Rasht forces by the Jangalis and assistance from the Caucasus

3. Move toward Zanjan and from there to the Jangal and battle with _______ (murder of the late Moshiroldowleh) (Attacks by Ehsanollah Khan and the Kurds instigated by Russian commanders with Mirza and flight of Mirza to the forest arrival of Government Forces and my Agreement on behalf of the expeditionary forces with four persons at _____saray in Emamzadeh Akram near Maklavan (this is where the Jangali Forces defeated the Russian commander)

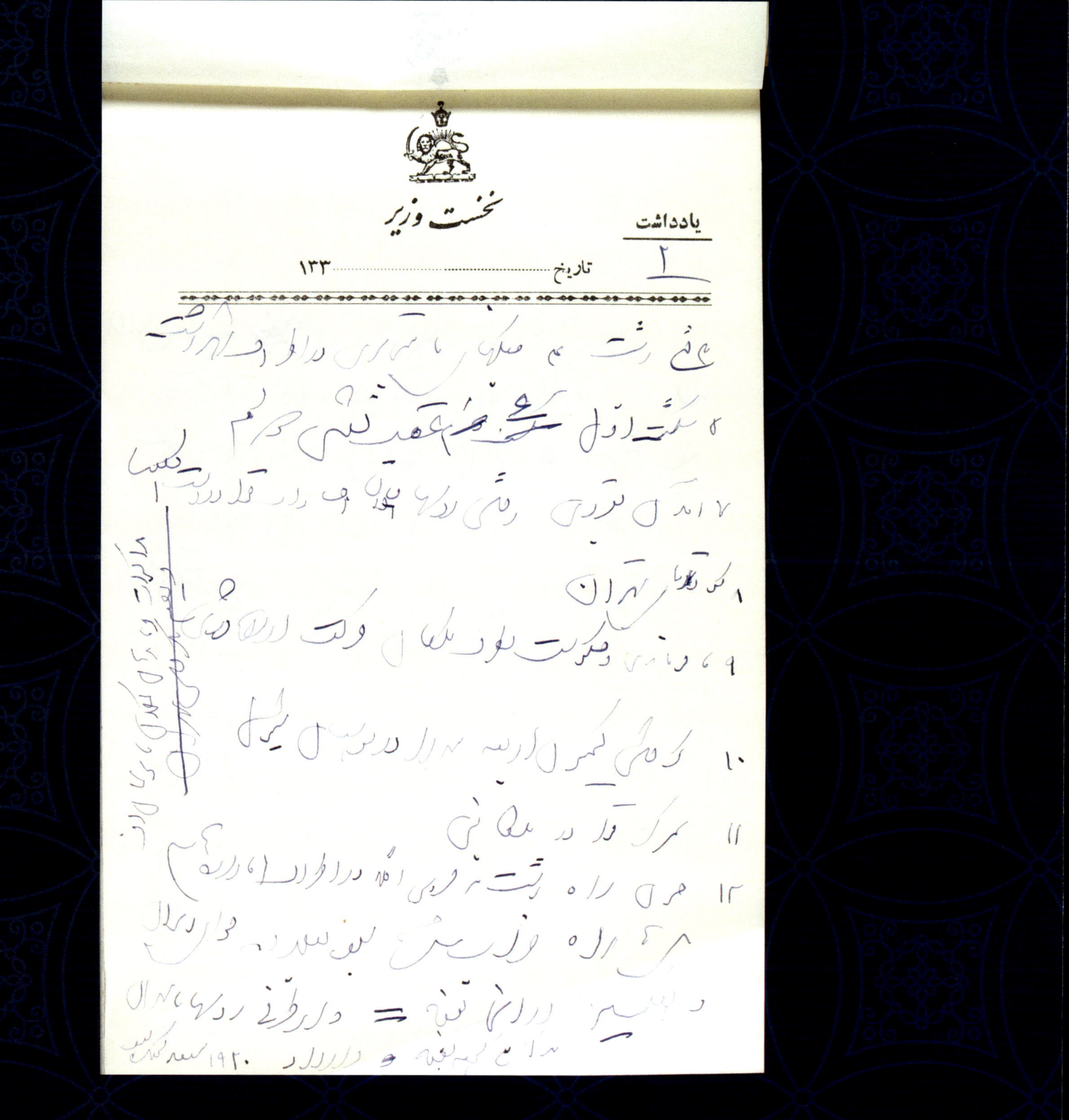

نخست وزیر

یادداشت

۲

تاریخ ۱۳۳

[illegible]

۵ [illegible]

۷ [illegible]

۸ [illegible]

۹ [illegible]

۱۰ [illegible]

۱۱ [illegible]

۱۲ [illegible]

[illegible]

12.2 4. Move to Rasht battles with insurgents around the city of Rasht

5. First defeat

6. We retreated

7. Coming to Ghazvin Departure of Russians Ivanof Forces in English hands

Left margin: negotiation of Gilan Commanders with Simanof??

8. Coup d'état in Tehran

9. With Commandant and government toward Gilan movement of forces ______

10. Capture of Urumieh comintern after ______

11. Centralization of forces in Tonkabon

12. Because the Rasht-Ghazvin road at least around Emamzadeh Hashem bridges and road had been destroyed Iranian and English forces stopped here == and on the other hand, the Russians had started negotiating with Tehran that produced the 1920 treaty

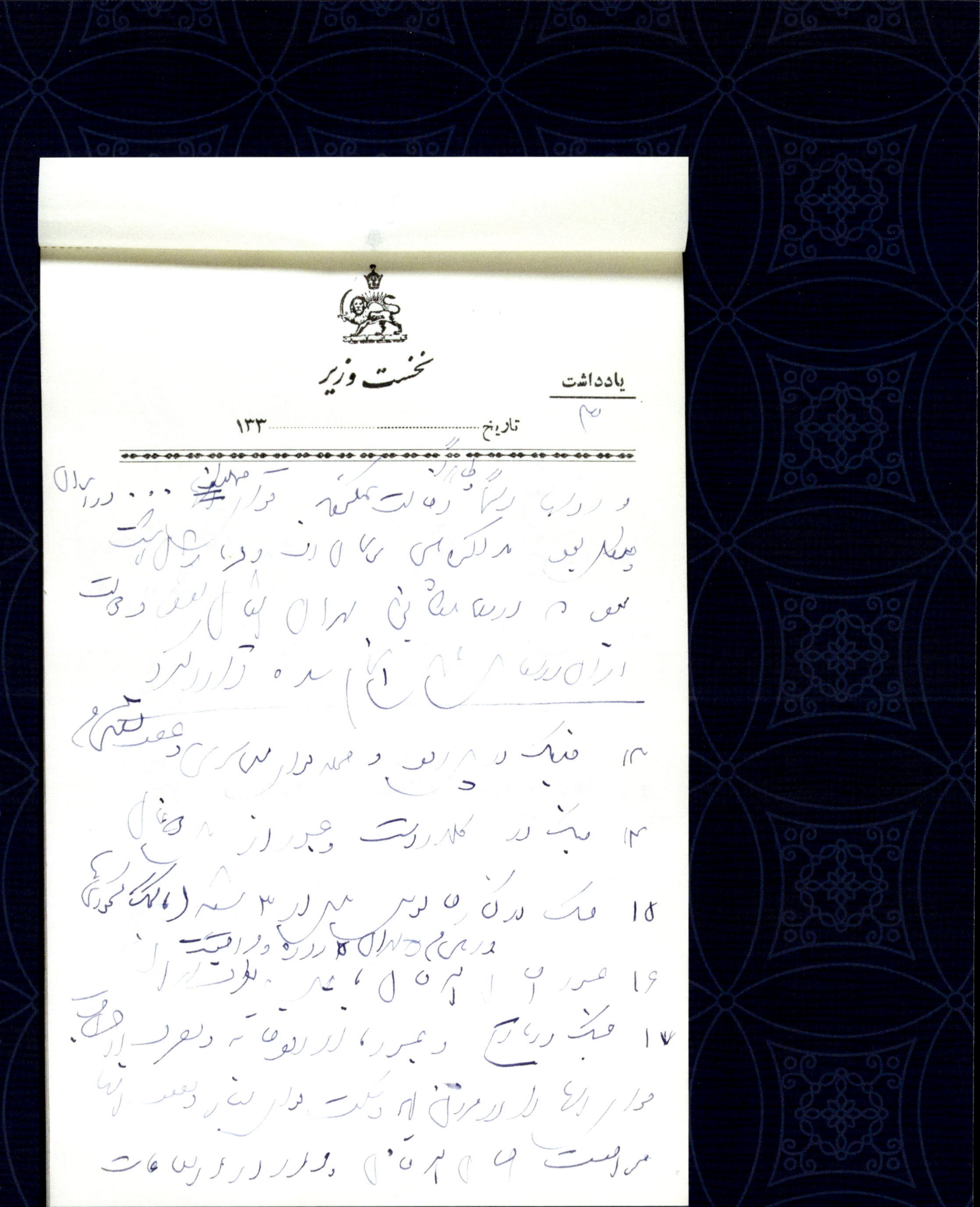

نخست وزیر

یادداشت

۳

تاریخ ۱۳۳

[illegible]

[illegible]

[illegible]

[illegible]

۱۳ [illegible]

۱۴ [illegible]

۱۵ [illegible]

[illegible]

۱۶ [illegible]

۱۷ [illegible]

[illegible]

[illegible]

12.3 According to which the Russians would never interfere officially and in appearance Melinkof's forces . . . were in Jangal in Iran Negotiation took place between Simanof and Rasht commanders that the Russians would occupy Tehran ahead of time so that the Government of Iran would face a fait accompli

13. Battle at Ramu Bridge and ______ locality and my retreat

14. Battle in Kalardasht and crossing of Doghal Bridge

15. Battle near Chalus more than three killed (with the help of Kojuris) and my departure for Tehran for five days and return

16. Passage of Ehsanollah Khan and his unit toward Tehran

17. Battle in Anzali and our crossing the river and occupying the heights Their Forces met in Ghazvin and their defeat and pursuit Return of Ehsanollah Khan and taking position in the elevations

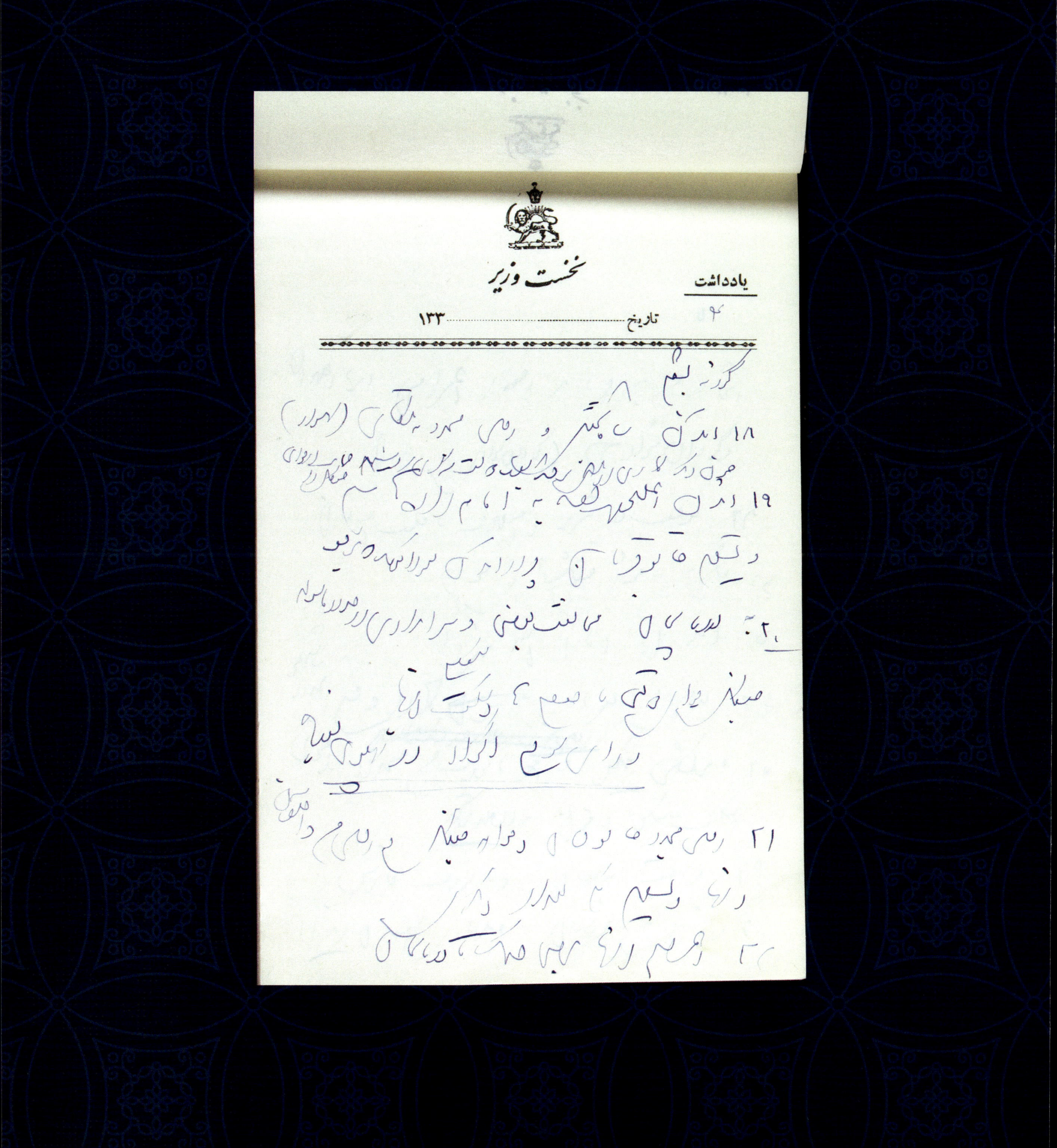

نخست وزیر

یادداشت ۴

تاریخ ۱۳۳

[illegible]

۱۸ [illegible]

[illegible]

۱۹ [illegible]

[illegible]

۲۰ [illegible]

[illegible]

[illegible]

۲۱ [illegible]

[illegible]

۲۲ [illegible]

12.4 18. Arrival of Shahbakhti and going to Tonkabon (Shahsavar) once again Because [they] were not able to succeed the Russian Central Government withdrew support from Jangal Forces

19. Arrival of His Late Majesty to Emamzadeh Hashem and surrender of Galoo Ghorban after arrival of Mirza Koochek

20. Azerbaijan Opposition of some and shots fired in the Masooleh region clash between Government Forces and Taleshis and their defeat

At this time the Kurds were in Pahlavi

21. Redeparture of ______ and the Jangal Forces and my departure and their transfer and general surrender of a number of others

22. Their dispatch for the battle in Azerbaijan

نخست وزیر

یادداشت

تاریخ ۱۳۳

[illegible]

[illegible]

۲۴ [illegible]

[illegible]

۲۵ [illegible]

۲۶ [illegible]

۲۷ [illegible]

[illegible]

۲۹ [illegible]

۳۰ [illegible]

12.5 My appointment as the Commander of the dispatched Forces and Moradi Battalian (Cavalry Battalion) orders from Tehran

23. Stopped in Tabriz and disagreement with Assad Khan

24. Went to Khoy Khoy Battles

25. Arrival of Amanollah Mirza

26. My appointment as the Commander of the Guard and _______

27. Constant inspection and my reassignment to Khoy

28. Sykes Pact and Turkish intervention

29. Returned to Tehran and assigned to Fars

30. From Fars to Khuzestan Behbahan prison murders

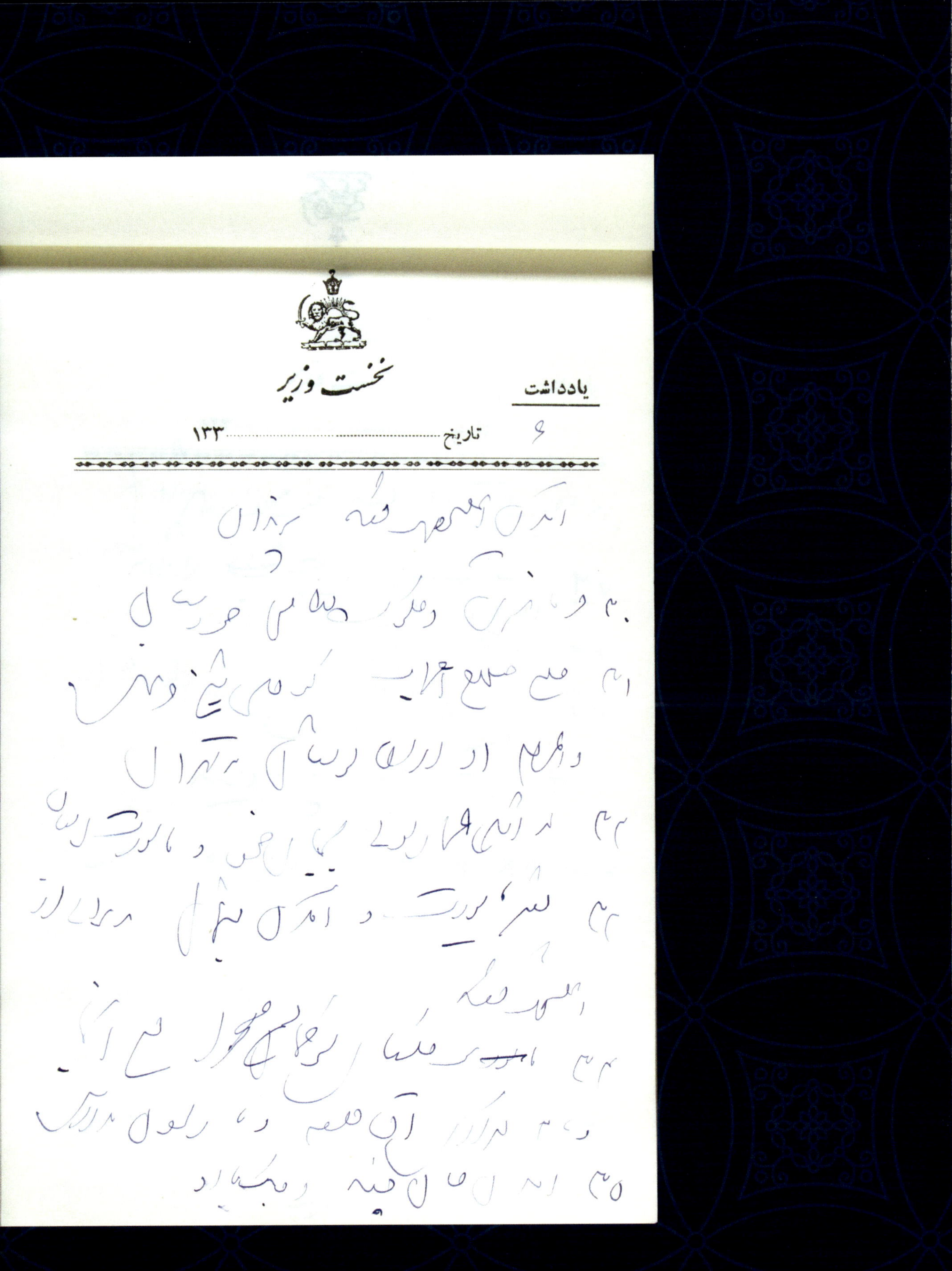

نخست وزیر

یادداشت

تاریخ ۶ .... ۱۳۳

[illegible]

[illegible]

[illegible]

[illegible]

[illegible]

[illegible]

[illegible]

[illegible]

[illegible]

[illegible]

12.6 Arrival of His Majesty

30. Commander and Martial Law Chief of Khuzestan

31. Disarming of Arabs arrest of Sheikh and his group and his transfer to Tehran via Lorestan

32. Placing ______ to take my place and [off to] Lorestan assignment

33. Change of assignment and coming to the north Reception for His Majesty

34. ____
and naming of that Agh Ghal'eh and resumption of schools

35. Arrival of _________ and battle with him

نخست وزیر

یادداشت ۸

تاریخ ۱۳۳

۳۶ مراجعت به تهران [illegible]

۳۷ [illegible] ریاست [illegible] را [illegible]

[illegible]

۳۸ ریاست [illegible]

۳۹ [illegible]

[illegible]

۴۰ [illegible]

۴۱ ریاست [illegible]

۴۲ [illegible]

۴۳ [illegible]

۴۴ مراجعت تهران [illegible]

[illegible]

12.7 36. Return to Tehran after various assignments in the North

37. Head of Gendarmerie Dismissal from the Armed Forces

38. Chief of Police

39. Trip to Paris Political studies in Officers University and 3 assignments to Europe and Russia

40. Start of World War Two escape _______ Palestine

41. Head of Gendarmerie

42. Commandant of Isfahan Division and Bakhtiari battles

43. Captive in Palestine

44. Return to Iran Commandant of Southern Forces battles with insurgents in the South

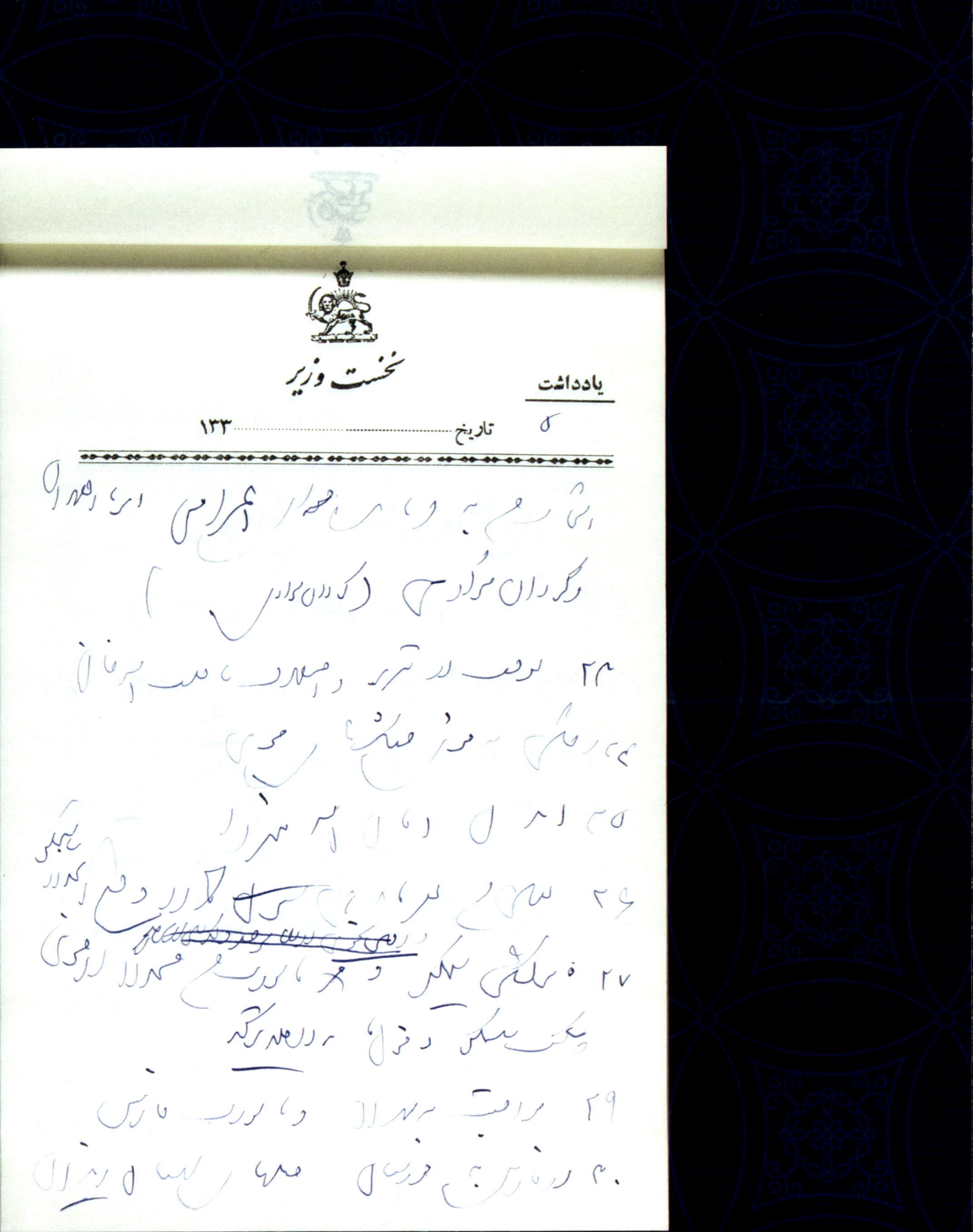

نخست وزیر

یادداشت

۵

تاریخ ۱۳۳

[illegible]

دیگران [illegible] (اگر لازم بود)

۲۴ [illegible]

[illegible]

۲۵ [illegible]

۲۶ [illegible]

۲۷ [illegible]

[illegible]

۲۹ [illegible]

۳۰ [illegible]

12.8 45. Our return and confirmation of the issue of the Senate

46. Chief of Police and squables with Razmara

47. My departure and disagreements between Mossadegh and his associates with Razmara

48. Minister of the Interior in Ala' Cabinet

49. Minister of the Interior in Mossadegh Cabinet with disagreements and resignation

50. Member of Parliament up to Fatemi's speech and my speech to the Senate

51. My detention by Mossadegh and the start of opposition

52. Going to the Senate till Mordad

53. My role and the 23 Mordad affairs

54. The day of 28 Mordad

55.

Document 13
1953–1955

This is yet another part of the outline General Zahedi prepared in anticipation of his memoir. Here the story begins with his arrest at the hands of the British, during their occupation of Iran in the early years of the Second World War. He was alleged of having pro-Nazi sympathies and thus spent much of the war as a British prisoner in Palestine (1942–45).

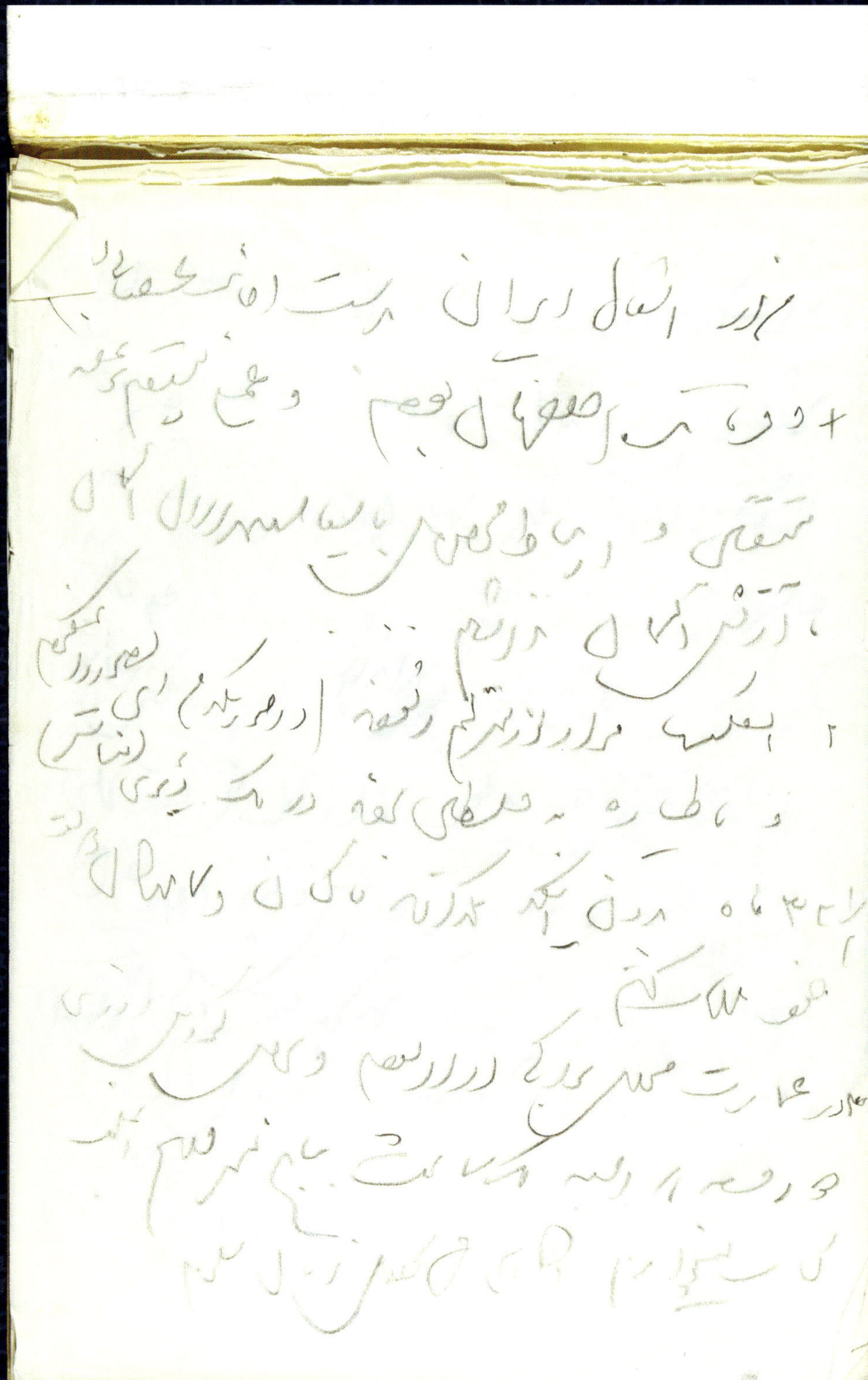

13.1 1. I am angry at the occupation of Iran today by foreigners and I was the Commandant in Esfahan and did not take special action against the Allies and did not have special relations with German politicians or the German military

2. The English kidnapped me from my house although I did not expect this and took me by airplane to Palestine in a monastery for thirty-two months without letting me meet my people or representatives of my government

3. I was given a big luxurious house and I went to the garden for a walk twice a day and every time for one hour I read books mostly and sometimes I studied language [English]

۵-۲ [illegible]

[illegible]

[illegible]

[illegible]

۱۶ [illegible] ۱۸ [illegible]

[illegible]

[illegible]

[illegible]

[illegible]

[illegible]

[illegible]

[illegible]

13.2 4–5. When Mozaffar Firooz went to Esfahan and imprisoned some Bakhtiari people and intended to arrest Ghashghaei people too they found out and fled and laid siege to Shiraz I was delegated the task of ending the rebellion of course at the time there were no more than sixteen gunners in the city this too was another new struggle all the tribes of Fars and Boveir Ahmad had united against the government of the time but I ended this struggle and the account of it is too detailed

6. Does not have answer

7. My travel to Europe was for treatment and also to get rid of fatigue

۱۱ [illegible]

[illegible]

[illegible]

۹ [illegible]

[illegible]

۱۰ [illegible]

[illegible]

۱۳ [illegible]

[illegible]

[illegible]

[illegible]

۱۲ [illegible]

[illegible]

13.3 8. His Imperial Majesty had resolved and through General Yazdanpanah wished me to accept the police assignment although I was a Senator and I obeyed

9. In the sixteenth round of elections complete impartiality was observed and this issue was also the view of His Majesty

10. They used my neutrality and power but at that time I had many supporters and many votes were cast

11. In action the Police on the principle of duty worked to maintain security and change the conditions of the police and prisons and finally procurement of buses, trucks, wireless, and other facilities and emphasis on schools and other works that were incomplete

12. In reality I was supposed to be the head of police temporarily additionally severe disagreement with then Chairman of the Staff resulted in my change

[illegible]

[illegible]

[illegible]

[illegible]

[illegible]

۱۴ [illegible]

[illegible]

۱۵ [illegible]

[illegible]

[illegible]

اختلاف نظر در کار [illegible] رسید بالاخره

[illegible]

13.4 13. The Ala Government was not aware of the times I did what I could and on behalf of Fadayan Eslam (Zealots of Islam) and other groups in Mr. Ala and Mossadegh's government previously two or three times there were assassination attempts on my life but they were not successful

14. When I was Minister of Interior in Mossadegh's government I served dutifully until disagreement occurred between us and progress in Mossadegh's government was due to my sincerity and service the details are extensive

15. I did not meet Harriman privately the reason why I separated from Mossadegh was calculated it was dangerous differences of views about the affairs and ultimately I was afraid that the trend would lead to worsening of the situation and was observing that there was a bad future in store for the country

آن یک شب [illegible] [illegible] [illegible] [illegible] کشته

و من [illegible] [illegible] [illegible] [illegible] [illegible] [illegible]

[illegible] قصد [illegible] [illegible] [illegible] [illegible]

[illegible] [illegible] [illegible] [illegible] [illegible]

~~[illegible] قصد [illegible] [illegible] [illegible] [illegible]~~

[illegible] [illegible] [illegible] [illegible] [illegible]

[illegible] [illegible] [illegible] [illegible] [illegible]

[illegible] [illegible] [illegible] [illegible]

[illegible] [illegible] [illegible] [illegible] [illegible]

[illegible] [illegible] [illegible] [illegible]

[illegible] [illegible] [illegible] [illegible]

[illegible] [illegible] [illegible] [illegible] [illegible]

13.5 15 to 20. Until one night the disagreements came to a fight and from there I went directly to the Police [Headquarters] and resigned immediately and after that did not plan on opposing him. In my view his actions were not in the best interests of the country plus he accused me and announced it and forced me

I issued a detailed statement against him and gave a detailed speech in the Senate and I warned about all the illegal actions and on that day at the Senate inevitably I said what I could and I said what I knew that resulted in dissolution of the Senate I never capitulated of course my presence in the Senate was because I wanted the lies that had been said about me to be investigated but the Senate was dissolved

21. Maybe Mossadegh intended to accuse me and damage my reputation but under no circumstance was it right to do so at that time

بعد از شش روز مهلتی که گفته بود ما [illegible] و [illegible]

در [illegible] [illegible] تصمیم [illegible] [illegible]

[illegible] در [illegible] [illegible] [illegible]

[illegible] [illegible] [illegible]

۲۴ [illegible] [illegible] [illegible] [illegible]

در [illegible] [illegible] [illegible] [illegible]

۲۴ در [illegible] [illegible] [illegible] [illegible]

[illegible] [illegible] نقطه [illegible] [illegible] [illegible]

[illegible] [illegible] [illegible] [illegible]

۲۵ [illegible] [illegible] [illegible] [illegible]

[illegible] [illegible] [illegible] [illegible]

[illegible] [illegible] [illegible] [illegible]

13.6 Mossadegh dissolved the Senate and the opposition was there with votes and _______ were present here and would not surrender to Mossadegh's views one hundred percent Additionally because of his enmity and personal [differences] with me he dissolved the Senate illegally

23. In the Majlis on account of the aforementioned points and pressure and having absolute majority Mossadegh's views won

24. I do not have information about this particular [subject] what I witnessed was that the American Government was inclined to accommodate any government that was in power and they did so too

25. When the Senate was shut down only that day the representatives of the Senate gathered at Mr. Nezamol Dowleh's house and issued a statement that the dissolution of the Senate and the decision of the Government were against the law they did not do anything else

۲۶ [illegible]

[illegible]

[illegible]

[illegible]

[illegible] مراجعه [illegible]

[illegible]

[illegible]

۲۷ [illegible]

[illegible]

[illegible]

۲۸ [illegible]

[illegible] ۳۰ [illegible]

۲۹ [illegible]

[illegible]

13.7 26. There were three groups in the Majlis one was the majority who were serious Mossadegh supporters the other those opposed that had been intimidated but did not dare oppose but were opposed and the third group (the minority in Majlis) that agreed with me and opposed Mossadegh in all fairness they made the ultimate sacrifice, which will be unforgettable for me

27. The reason for my success what I myself gather was [due to the fact that] His Majesty's move to Europe was averted without uproar this happened and that too [after] my arrest by the government

28. There was no such thing particularly because I opposed his departure and did not think it advisable

29. Mossadegh tried his best that I should die or to accuse me but because I had no sin except patriotism he did not find any evidence and could not

در صورتیکه [illegible]

۳۰ [illegible]

[illegible]

۳۱ [illegible]

[illegible]

۳۲ [illegible]

[illegible]

۳۳ [illegible]

[illegible]

13.8 While if he could do anything he would have

30. I myself am still unsure about Afshartoos' [an officer loyal to Mossadeq] murder that from what side it happened and those that were arrested were mostly opposed to the Mossadegh Government and in my Government the trials were carried out very carefully and the Judges issued the judgments that they did

31. I really went to the Majlis so that along with my friends and supporters I could freely enter the fight

32. With all friends and most of those who had [regard] for the country and the monarchy were [symbols] of patriotism that was reflected in their actions and services

33. No matter how many agents they put around the Majlis and instigated within the Majlis and a group in the Majlis

۲۰ جمعه ۲۳ [illegible] ملک المتکلمین [illegible]

[illegible]

صبح بعد [illegible] اتابک [illegible]

[illegible]

[illegible]

[illegible]

[illegible]

۳۵ [illegible]

[illegible]

۳۶ [illegible]

[illegible]

[illegible]

[illegible]

13.9 attacked us particularly on the day of the long meeting that they had I too had prepared enough connections and enough equipment with agents and supporters because I did not want to be caught off guard in Majlis that would cause delay in the works at the request of the then President of the Majlis and conferring with my close friends I exited the Majlis and was arrested

34.

It is very extensive it was in a book and can be viewed

35. Colonel Nasiri received the decree today ________

36. Colonel Nassiri was appointed by me to present the decree of Mossadegh's dismissal from office and my installation to Mossadegh but not only did Mossadegh not execute the order but arrested Nassiri and disarmed the Imperial Guard

۳۸ ۲ ۲ ۱ شنبه و همه کارهای [illegible] را

در [illegible] و لطف محمد [illegible]

[illegible]

~~[illegible]~~

۳۹ [illegible] دولت را با [illegible]

[illegible]

[illegible]

~~[illegible]~~

13.10 38. I recounted all of Mossadegh's mistakes and illegal works in my statement and speech to the Senate and it is available here and can be accessed

39. I did not choose the members of my government with the advice of anyone   only based on my past experience with them and introduced them to His Imperial Majesty after his return and then introduced them to the Majlis

شهاب

بدره‌ای ... صفا

دکتر شیبانی [illegible]

الهی

دکتر آیت [illegible]

ادیب [illegible]

دکتر صاحب‌قلم

[illegible]

صبح [illegible]

دکتر [illegible]

[illegible]

دکتر [illegible]

[illegible]

دکتر شروین [illegible]

محمد [illegible] جعفری

دکتر [illegible]

دکتر مسعود [illegible]

دکتر [illegible]

[illegible]

صادق چوبک

بزرگ علوی

جعفر شهری

دکتر [illegible]

دکتر [illegible]

[illegible]

13.11	Reza Afshar	Dr. Mojhdehi
	__________ Hosseini	___________
	Amir Moeeni Hawaie	Malek
	Elahi	Dr. Mansoorzadeh Kordestani
	Akbar __________	Ardeshir Kalani
	Dr. Saheb Ghalam	
	_____________ Afshar	through Rahmat Lashkari
	______________ Afshar	Sadegh Haji
	_________ Fooladvand	____________ Afsari Ghavami Shirazi
	Hassan Kashani	________________ Jafar Moshiri
	General Mostafavi	Dr. Pirnia
	Parsa Toviserkani	

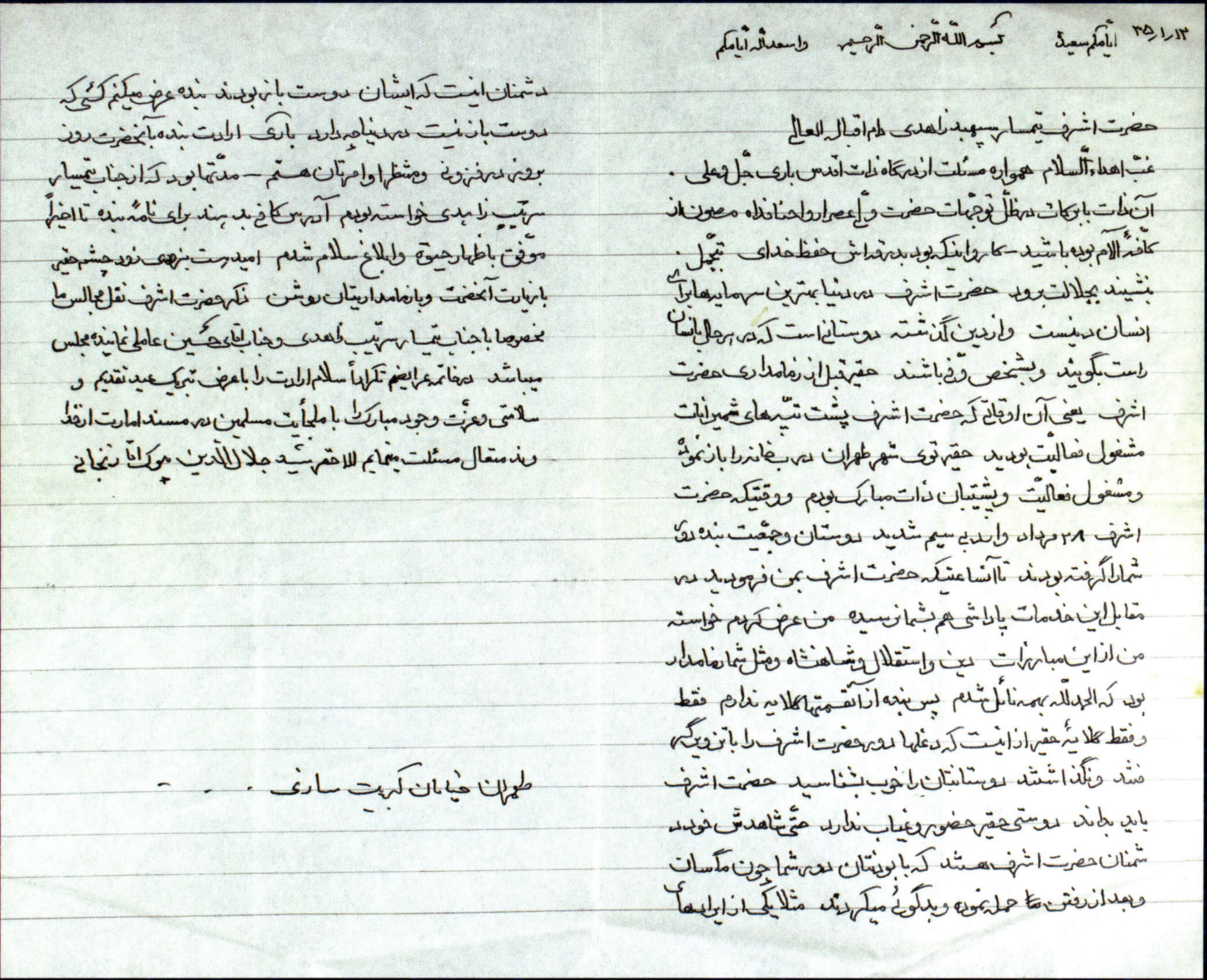

Document 14
1 April 1956

In the period of General Zahedi's premiership (1953–55), many letters were sent to him offering congratulations and sometimes gossip, and occasionally seeking a favor. Here is one from a cleric, who obviously helped overthrow Dr. Mossadegh, offering felicities and seeking some compensation for his services. Sometimes the notes are clues to the general's network of friends, sometimes changing allegiances, and sometimes

14.1

12/1/35 May your days be joyous In the name of the Charitable and Merciful God

Excellency General Zahedi May his good fortunes continue

After presenting greetings I continually besiege the Holy Spirit the Supreme Being to keep your generous self under the protection of the Guardian of Time [Imam Zaman, a reference to a sacred Iranian saint in Shiite faith] may our spirits be sacrificed for him and to keep you immune from the infidel—the caravan that was protected by God sat in luxury and went in grandeur Your Excellency the best capital for people in this world is religion and after religion friends who tell the truth under all circumstances and who are faithful your humble servant before your Excellency took the helm meaning those times when you were busy with your activities behind the Shemiranat hills your servant opened the door to his house in Tehran to activities in support of your auspicious self and when your Excellency entered the office on 28th of Mordad my group and friends were the ones surrounding you at that time your Excellency told me that for these services I had not been compensated I said that my desire from the outcome of these struggles was independence, the Shahanshah and a leader like yourself that thank God I achieved them all so I have no complaints from those quarters your servant's one and only complaint is that crafty and dishonest people have surrounded your Excellency and have kept you from getting to know your friends well your Excellency should know that my friendship has no presence or absence and witnesses are the enemies of your Excellency who surround you like flies and after leaving would attack and vilify you for example one of the objections

2

of the enemies is that he is obsessed with friends I say what does he who does not love to have many friends have in this world Anyhow my devotion to your Excellency grows from day to day and I await your orders—some time ago I had requested Brigadier General Zahedi to give me an adequate address for my letter until finally I was able to announce my existence and communicate my greetings it is hoped that your servant's eyes will be brightened by seeing your Excellency and your statesmanship very very soon talking about your Excellency particularly with Brigadier General Zahedi and Majlis Representative Mr. Hossein Ameli is like serving sweets at meetings in closing my comments I repeat my salutations and devotions and present you with my Eid [Persian new year ceremony] greetings and pray to the Almighty God for your good health and glory, and that of Moslems in leadership positions.

Your servant Seyed Jalaluddin Boyouk Agha Zanjani

Document 15
19 August 1955

Shaban Jafari (1921–2006), initially a street tough and eventually the owner of a club that specialized in traditional Iranian sports was one of the most controversial figures in the events surrounding the fall of Mohammad Mossadegh. Here he writes a letter of congratulations to General Zahedi. Jafari died in exile, and a lengthy interview with him, organized and published by an acclaimed journalist, Homa Sarshar (b. 1946, columnist for *Zan-e-Ruz* and *Kayhan* daily newspapers), allowed him to offer his version of his life and of his role in the fall of Mossadegh.

تهران ۲۸ مرداد ماه ۱۳۳۵

سلام و درود بی پایان ما به یگانه ناجی شرق و نجات دهنده ملت ایران جناب آقای سپهبد فضل اله زاهدی رهبر قیام ملی بیست و هشتم مرداد •

مدت سه سال تمام از قیام ملی و تاریخی بیست و هشتم مرداد میگذرد از همان روز یکه دشمنان کشور قصد داشتند ناموس و ملت ما را ملعبه دست خویش قرار دهند کشور مشروطه و شاه ازادیخواه را از ما بگیرند وحکومتی با صطلاح جمهوری دمکراتیک بوجود اورند • ولی خدا نخواست و از پس ابرهای تیره و تار سربازی را چون خورشید درخشنده برای نجات ملت ملتیکه کاملا در حیطهٔ اجانب بود برگزید و با خواست خدا کشوریرا که سقوطش حتمی بود با شجاعت و مردانگی و از خود گذشتگی نجات داد •

سرور ارجمندم جانثار افتخار دارد که بی آلایش ترین تبریکات را از طرف جمیعت جوانمردان جانباز بمناسبت گذشت سومین سال از قیام ملی بیست و هشتم مرداد عرض نموده توفیق و سلامت آن سرور ارجمند را از درگاه ایزد یکتا مسئلت نماید •

کسیکه هرگز نیکیها جوانمردانگی و بزرگواریهای شما را فراموش نمیکند •

جمیعت جوانمردان جانباز

شعبان جعفری

15.1 Tehran 28 Mordad 1335

Greetings and our endless salutations to the singular savior of the East and rescuer of the Iranian nation Excellency Mr. General Fazollah Zahedi leader of the 28th Mordad uprising.

A full three years have passed since the historic national resurgence of the 28th of Mordad the same day that the enemies of the country intended to make a game of our national honor to take away from us our constitutional country and our freedom-loving Shah and to create a so-called democratic republic. But God did not will it and he chose a soldier radiant as the sun to emerge from behind dark clouds to rescue the nation a nation that was totally under the influence of foreigners and as God willed it a country whose collapse was certain was rescued by his bravery, courage, and dedication.

My honorable Chief your liege has the honor to present you earnest felicitations on behalf of the Devoted Cavaliers Group on the occasion of the third anniversary of the national uprising of 28th Mordad and to pray to God Almighty for your success and good health.

The one who will never forget your courage and magnanimity.

Devoted Cavaliers Group

Shaban Jafari

Document 16
12 October 1955

While General Zahedi was at the time of this letter still the prime minister, a journalist named Hassan Ma'assar, who had in the past, in his own words, written eloquently about the many accomplishments of the general, feels he has been overlooked for proper advancement. Asking for a better position is a running theme in some of the private letters to both Ardeshir and General Zahedi.

حسن معاصر
تهران - میدان مخبرالدوله
تلفن دفتر ۳۸۷۰-۳
تلفن منزل ۷۵۵۳-۳

بتاریخ ۲۰ مهر ماه ۱۳۳۵

حضور محترم حضرت اجل عالی تیمسار سپهبد فضل‌الله زاهدی دامت شوکته

تصدق وجود مبارکت گردم پس از تقدیم سلام و عرض فدویت و احترام امیدوارم در نهایت صحت و سلامتی توام با آسایش خاطر روزگار ایام را بسر برده و همیشه در تمام امور موفق و کامیاب و سربلند باشید. در مسافرت اخیر دوست عزیز گرامی بنده آقای دکتر بهداد بایران با توجه بمراتب صمیمیت فوق‌العاده و احترامیکه نسبت به شخص حضرت اجل عالی دارند چون میدانستند که بنده هم در زمره اشخاصی هستم که از معتقدین و طرفداران حقیقی تیمسار هستند بمناسبتی با ایشان صحبت از این شد که در یک موقع در سوئیس ضمن مذاکرات متفرقه بنام‌های هم بنده و بعدم موفقیت در انتخابات دوره هیجدهم کرمان فرموده بودید. این پیش آمد موجب شد که بنده باصطلاح با «گشودن عقده دل خود» فرصتی یافته و یک موضوعی را برایشان شرح و عرضه نمایم که به بیان مصطلح ادبی «آموزنده» بوده و سزاوار است بآن لحظات توجه مخصوص بنمایند.
بنده در نظر داشتم شرح این موضوع و این عریضه را بوسیله آقای دکتر بهداد بحضور محترم عالی تقدیم دارم ولی چون ایشان فعلاً عازم مراجعت بسوئیس نیستند بدین جهت مستقیماً بعرض این معروضه مبادرت ورزیدم.
مقدمتاً بایستی عرض کنم چون بنده از مدتهای مدیدی پیش از این نسبت به شخص حضرت اجل عالی بدون تظاهر و تصنع و بدون احتیاج قلباً احترام و ارادت مخصوص داشته و حتی در سنوات ۲۷ تا ۲۹ که روزنامه هفتگی «دولت ایران» را انتشار میدادم کراراً مقالاتی (مخصوصاً در ایامی شهربانی کل و بعداً وزارت کشور را تصدی فرموده بودید) راجع به شخصیت و شایستگی و تهور و لیاقت مخصوص تیمسار برای انجام کارهای بزرگ مملکتی نوشتم و در اغلب مجالس و محافل هم هر وقت مناسبتی پیش آمد همیشه این اظهارات را بطور طبیعی و عاری از لحن ساختگی میکردم و چون مثل بسیاری اشخاص دیگر استفاده جو یا «کاسب» در معامله گر یا کلاش نبودم اظهاری هم در این باب نکردم ولی مطمئن بودم که حضرت اجل عالی هم نسبت به بنده نظر لطف و عنایت داشته و در موقع مقتضی از جهات معنوی از دستگیری و «جلو بردن» بنده مضایقه نخواهید فرمود

بر

16.1 Hassan Ma'aaser

Dated 20 Mehr 1335

Tehran—Mokhberoldowleh Circle
{ office 3-3870
Telephone{
{ Home 3-7552

His Excellency General Fazlollah Zahedi May You Be Ever Glorious

May I be given away as alms [as protection of] your blessed self After presenting greetings and conveying my devotion and respect, I hope you are in perfect health and spending your days with joy and peace of mind and that you will be successful and prideful in all your endeavors. In his latest trip to Iran, my dear and valued friend Mr. Dr. Behdad, considering his sincere and extraordinary regard for your Excellent person, because he knew that I too am among the true believers and supporters of his Excellency, there was an occasion when in our conversation the subject of talks in Switzerland came up that among other miscellaneous subjects, you had mentioned my lack of success in Kerman, in the 18th round of parliamentary elections—this incident has given me the occasion to, as they say, "get it off my chest," and to describe a subject for you that in colloquial terms is "educational," and is worthy of your full and special attention. I had intended to provide your Excellency this account through Mr. Dr. Behdad, but his sudden departure for Switzerland caused me to embark on providing these remarks directly.

As a prelude, I must say that because for a very long time I have had a heartfelt special respect and devotion to your Excellency without pretense and without needing to, even in the years 27 to 29, when I published the newsweekly Iranian Nation, I frequently wrote articles about your competence, your brave personality worthy of leadership to accomplish great national projects, and whenever the there was an occasion in meetings and assemblies, I would make these remarks naturally and not in an ostentatious tone, and because I was not like most others after my own self-interest or a "tradesman," or a haggler or a hustler, I would not make any mention of this subject, but I was sure that your Excellency had me in his good favors and graces and at the appropriate time, would not hold back from providing me intellectual support and assist my "advancement"

Document 17
Around 1957–1958

At the time of this note, Ardeshir Zahedi was married to the shah's then only child, a young girl named Shahnaz (b. 1940). Her mother was the shah's first wife, Queen Fawzia (1921–2013), herself the sister of Egypt's last ruling monarch (Farouk I of Egypt, 1936–52). There was, as is often the case, much court intrigue around the Ardeshir-Shahnaz wedding (10 October 1957). Zahedi believed that the shah's twin sister, Princess Ashraf (1919–2016), was behind the worst of these intrigues. In a letter to General Zahedi, Ashraf offers her version of the story. For much of the rest of his life in Iran, Ardeshir Zahedi's relation with Ashraf was sometimes tense.

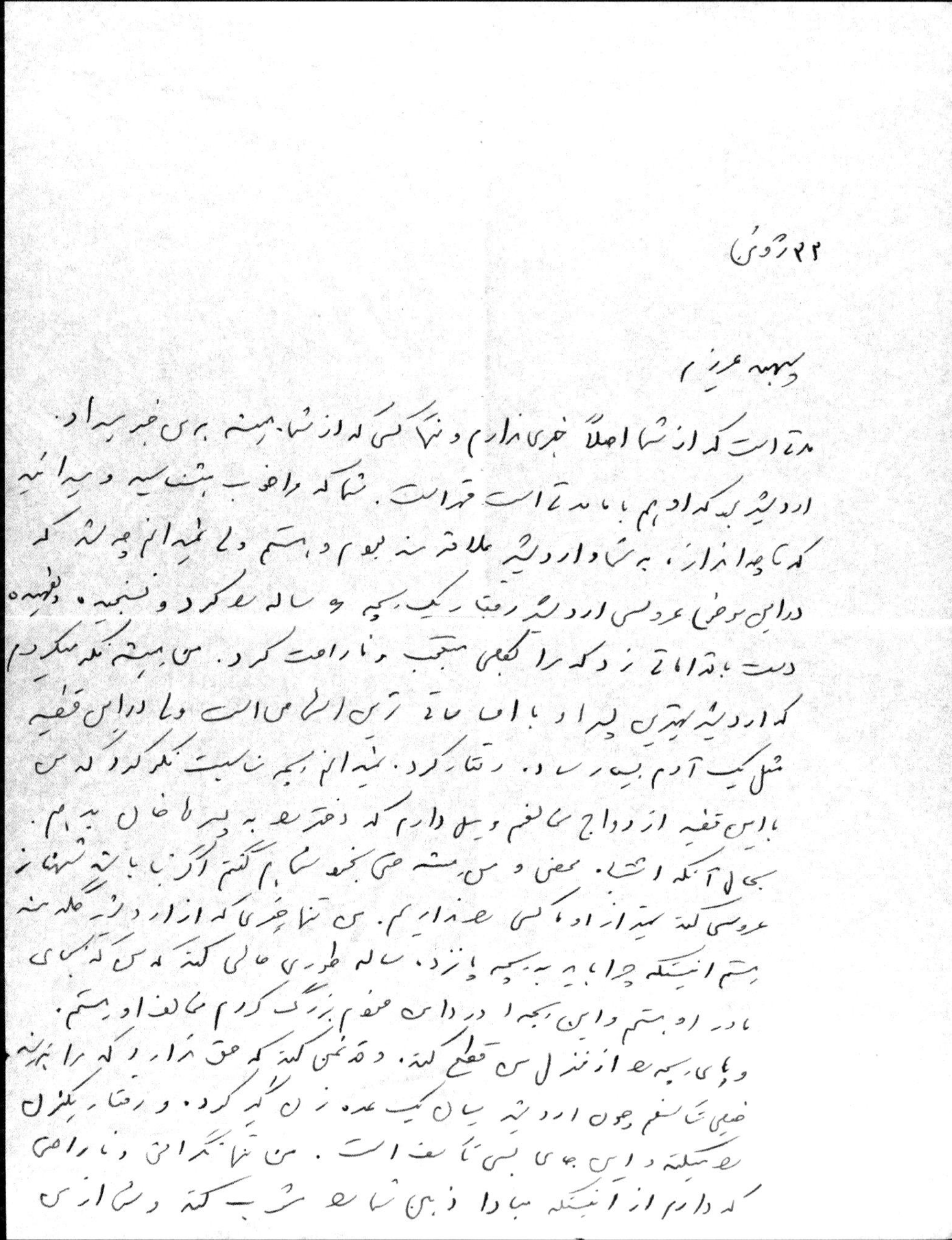

۲۲ ژوئن

سپهبد عزیزم

مدتی است که از شما اصلاً خبری ندارم و تنها کسی که از شما همیشه برای من خبر میداد
اردشیر بود که او هم با مادر مدتی است تهران است. شما که واقف به حسن نیت و میدانید
که تا چه اندازه به شما و اردشیر علاقمند بوده و هستم ولی نمیدانم چه شد که
در این موضوع عروسی اردشیر رفتار یک بچه ۱۷ ساله را کرد و نسنجیده
دست باقداماتی زد که مرا کمی متعجب و ناراحت کرد. من همیشه فکر میکردم
که اردشیر بهترین پسر و با احساسات‌ترین اشخاص است ولی در این قضیه
مثل یک آدم بی‌رسید رفتار کرد. نمیدانم بچه مناسبت فکر کرد که من
با این قضیه ازدواج مخالفم و میل دارم که دخترم به پسر فلان خان بدهم.
بجای آنکه اشتباه محض و من همیشه صحبت کرده‌ام گفتم اگر با شاه شهناز
عروسی کند بیشتر از او کسی را نداریم. من تنها چیزی که اظهار داشتم گله‌مند
هستم اینستکه چرا به بچه پانزده ساله طوری حالی کنند که من که بجای
مادر او هستم و این بچه را در دامن خودم بزرگ کردم مخالف او هستم.
و پای بچه را از منزل من قطع کنند. دشمن کند که حق ندارد که مرا بهانه
خیلی متأسفم چون اردشیر پیش یک عده زن گریه کرده و رفتار پلتیک
[illegible] این جوری کسی تأسف است. من تنها نگرانی و ناراحتی
که دارم از آنستکه مبادا ذهن شما را مشوب کنند و شما از من

17.1

22 June

My Dear General

I have had absolutely no news from you for some time and the only one who used to always give me news about you was Ardeshir and he too has not been on talking terms with me for some time. You know me well and know how much affection I had and have for you and Ardeshir but I don't know what happened about this wedding that Ardeshir started to act like a six-year-old child and thoughtlessly and without understanding took actions that surprised me and made me uncomfortable. I always thought of Ardeshir as the best son and a sensitive person but he acted like a naive person in this case. I don't know why he thought I was against the subject of marriage and wanted to give the girl to the Agha Khan's son. Anyhow it is a total mistake and I have always even told you that if Shahnaz is to get married we don't have a better person than him. My only complaint about Ardeshir is why he had to convince a fifteen-year-old girl whom I had raised in my own bosom that I was against her. And prevent the child from visiting my home. And forbade her from seeing me. I'm very sorry because Ardeshir was caught between a bunch of women. And he behaves like a woman and that is very regretful. The only thing that worries and bothers me is lest he taints your mind and you get

برنجید چون همه میدانند که من نسبت به دوستانم چطور هستم. دلم میخواهد که برای
من همیشه یک دوست بسیار خوب باشید و از من نرنجید و خاطر جمع باشید.
والا اردشیر و غیره برای من اهمیتی ندارند. آنها برای بچه‌های
من خوب میشوند و میشود آنها را ببخشید. در هر حال شما و فقط شخص
شما را که من در ته قلب همیشه اردشیر را دوست دارم و جز
خوشبختی و سعادت او و شهناز عزیزم چیز دیگری نمیخواهم. و اگر هم بعضی
از طرف من به اردشیر گفته ام دردم عشق است. [illegible] نمیتوانم این
مسائل را برای شما بنویسم چون بعضی از مطالب است که بهتر است خاموش
باشد. و از شما میخواهم که به دوستی من اطمینان داشته باشید و بدانید
که من به دوستان صمیمی خیانت نمیکنم و شما همیشه برای من بهترین دوست
من خواهید بود. حساب ما را [illegible] از حساب آنان جدا کنید. آنها اکثریت
[illegible] ما هستند تا بفهمند دنیا چه خبر است. کم کم خواهند فهمید و از کرده
خودشان پشیمان خواهند شد. از شما خواهشمندم از این مطلب و نامه
من با اردشیر صحبتی نکنید چون من از او گله و شکایتی ندارم و از حالت که
بر حالت [illegible] امیدوارم که امسال اگر به جنوب فرانسه رفتید با لطف
که قرار بود از خانه محقر و کوچک من استفاده کنید. من قبلاً به جا [illegible]
دادم و شما حتماً [illegible] کنید و [illegible] خانم و
شما را از دور میبوسم و امیدوارم که بزودی فیض دیدار دست دهد
و بار دیگر من شما را ببینم.   دوستدار شما اشرف

17.2 2

upset with me because everyone knows how I treat my friends. And you who have always been a good friend to me become upset with me. Otherwise Ardeshir and others are not important to me. They can be counted as my children and they can be forgiven. Anyhow you and only you should know that I love Ardeshir from the bottom of my heart and wish nothing but happiness and prosperity for my dear Shahnaz and him. And if they have told Ardeshir anything on my part, it is utterly false. Unfortunately I don't know anything more to write to you about because there are subjects that best remain untold. And I ask you to trust my friendship and know that I do not betray my friends and you will always be a best friend for me. Separate your account from that of the others. They are children and have a long way to finding out how the real world works. They will understand gradually and will come to regret their actions. I request that you not speak of this subject and my letter to Ardeshir because I have no complaints against him and [as the poem says] "it is from us, unto us." I hope that if you go to southern France this year you will use my small and modest house as planned. I had previously instructed Jahangiri and all you have to do is to call him and ask for the key. I kiss you and your wife from afar and hope that I will be blessed with seeing you again soon.

Affectionately

Ashraf

Document 18
17 February 1959

Ali Asghar Hekmat, then Iran's foreign minister (1948–49 and 1958–59) and, as is evident from other letters included in this collection, an old friend of General Zahedi, writes to him about an issue that is, in light of that friendship, obviously hard for him to articulate. The letter is fascinating in that it shows Hekmat's honesty and the firm bonds of amity between him and the general. Other letters between them show the continued depth of their friendship. Eventually, the matter was resolved in a letter from the general. In another letter included in this archive, we hear from Hekmat about the resolution of the matter and his conclusion that no impropriety had taken place.

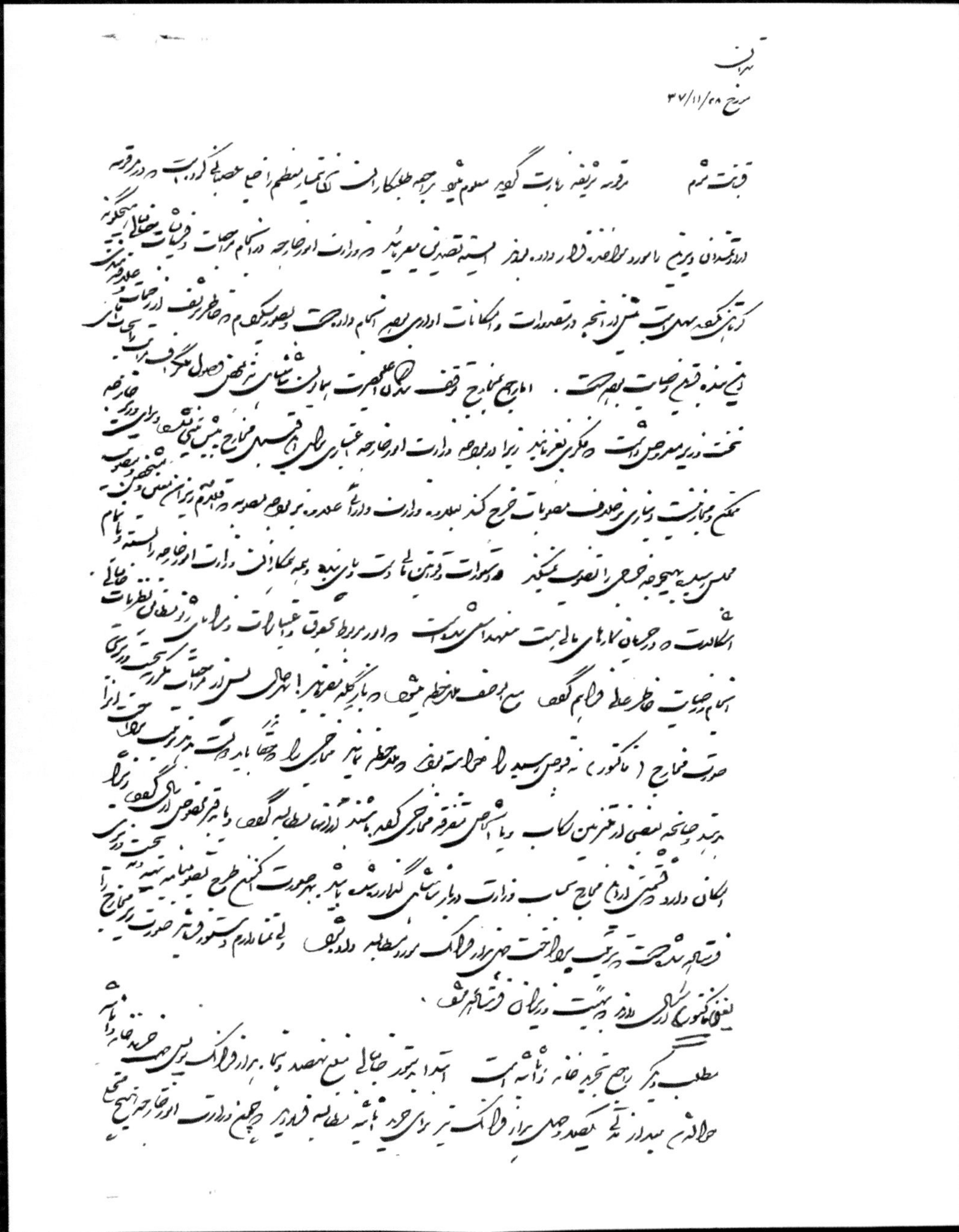

تهران

مورخ ۳۷/۱۱/۲۸

18.1

Tehran

Dated 28/11/37

May I be sacrificed for you   Your honorable letter was viewed it is apparent that approach of creditors has made the great General very angry that in his letter he reprimanded his longtime devotee Indeed you acknowledge that the Ministry of Foreign Affairs has never neglected fulfilling any of your honor's orders but has performed above and beyond its administrative abilities and capabilities and I had presumed that your honor would be completely satisfied with this servant's labors and regards for you.   But regarding the expenses of His Imperial Majesty's stopover, as soon as I received the telegram I notified accounting of the Office of the Prime Minister for their consideration because no credit was forecast for such expenses in the budget of the Ministry of Foreign Affairs, and the Minister of Foreign Affairs is not permitted to spend a penny contrary to what was ratified additionally the Ministry of Treasury will not ratify any expenditure beyond the components that were stated, defined and ratified by the Majlis   Directives and financial laws have bound the hands and feet of myself and all my colleagues in the Ministry of Foreign Affairs and all the problems relating to finances have prevented us from carrying out the issue relating to salaries and credits and fringe benefits of Geneva to be carried out in accordance with your Honor's views and to your Honor's satisfaction   Nevertheless it is observed that you complain again! In any event after several contacts with the Office of the Prime Minister the expense sheet (invoice)   they had not demanded receipts so that the expenses that should rightly be paid can be determined and processed for payment because some of the members of the entourage or miscellaneous persons may have had expenses that should be recovered or be charged to the Special Office because it is possible that part of these expenses have been allocated to the Ministry of Imperial Court. In any event, a draft of a resolution for forty thousand franks owed has been prepared and sent to the Office of the Prime Minister for processing and payment   but I beg you to order them to send their detailed expense sheet (invoice) to the Ministerial Committee.

The other issue regards the purchase of a house and furniture   Initially per your order the sum of nine hundred and fifty thousand Swiss franks was transferred for the purchase of the house and after a while one hundred and forty thousand franks for purchase of furniture was demanded that because the Ministry of Foreign Affairs had no credit allocation

برای برداشت این وجه از اعتبارات خود داشت دیگر پیدا کردن را جلب بفرمائید و دستورات لازم بحساب آقای ... داده

البته بعرض برسانید.

در ضمن ما چاکرم روی ارادت و خلوص قلب و از نظر خیالی دارم مطالبی را ببعضی از مغرضین در افواه میگویند باستحضار عالی برسانم

و نظر بعلاقه خاصی که بوجود معظم دارم اجتماع این شایعات حقیقت ندارد. راجع به تأثر و ملول کرده است از جمله میگویند خانه بنام دولت خریداری

شده است اگر حقیقت دارد بهتر این بود که خانه را بنام دولت معامله بفرمائید در باعث این بود تعبیر نشود که منظور بابت مخارج گرفتن

در جهت خرید اثاثیه صرف شده است مغرضین و دشمنان انتقاداتی میکنند شهادت میدهم تحت محرم بنده بنام و احترام مقام شماره معظم له علاقه‌مندیم

وجود مبارک را یکی از ذخایر مملکت میدانم و امیدوارم در آتیه مانند گذشته خدمات برجسته بمملکت بفرمائید بعلاوه قلم ... دشمنان

مغرضان سخنی نگویند در سفیدی حیثیت حضرتعالی نباشد در صورت همانطور که عرض کردم از فرط علاقه و ارادت است بعرض حضرت ... میرسانم

امیدوارم حمل بر بی ادبی نفرمائید ارادتمند نهایت کوشش را دارم در حال حضرتعالی از هر جهت آسوده کنم ولی استدعا دارم حضرتعالی هم در فکر ما

باشید و از نظر مبارک ضعف ما را در نظر بگیرید در عبارات نامحدود در اختیار داریم و عسرت مالی ... هم مخصوصاً در اواخر سال

بحد اعلا رسیده است و چاره ای جز محدود نمودن و جلوگیری از مخارج زائد و غیر لازم نیست.

ضمناً همانطور در امر ... حساب آقای ... در مشکلات وزارت امور خارجه که ما علاقه‌مند هستند ترتیب اعزام گردیدند تا ...

و لطف حضرتعالی در وضع خانه و اثاثیه رسیدگی و ترتیب صحیح بدهید در بعدها تولید سخن‌گوئی و گفتگو ننماید و بزرگان مردم استحضار خاطر عالی

عرض میکنم که ... در بودجه دولت داشت در جلسه ... دولت ... اعضا تمام وزارتخانه‌ها و موسسات دولت از جمله

وزارت امور خارجه حذف و بودجه سال ۱۳۳۸ مطابق سال ۱۳۳۷ تصویب کردند و دولت ... سال ۱۳۳۸ ... کرده‌اند

چه بنویسم که ... حاضر است. در خاتمه مراتب ... خلوص خود را تکرار میکنم ... سلامت وجود عزیز را از خداوند متعال خواستارم

و در خاتمه ... یک بار دیگر با کمال ... سعادت ... هستم.

ارادتمند [illegible]

for the amount we thought of finding a solution and issued the required orders to Mr. Atabaki that of course you have been apprised of.

In the meantime because of my fifty years of loyalty and devotion to you I would like to bring to your attention what spiteful people are saying and considering the special affection that I have for your honorable self, listening to these words has truly touched and disturbed me among other things they say the house was not purchased for the government if this is true it would have been better for the house to have been bought for the government so that it would not cause such misinterpretation the same way about the excessive expense for purchase of the furniture the spiteful and the enemies make criticisms I have heartfelt affection for the name and respectful position of the great General and consider his auspicious self to be a national treasure and hope that in the future as in the past you will do significant service for the country consequently the pen will not consent to what the enemies and the spiteful say, which is not appropriate to your stature anyhow as I said it is because of intense affection that I am being forthright and impertinent, and I hope you do not consider it disrespectful your devotee is trying my best to put your mind at ease in every respect but I beg of you to consider us and our problems and do not keep our situation far from your auspicious mind because our budget is limited and we do not have authority and the financial problems of the government have reached their zenith particularly in this time of year and have no alternative except to limit and prevent superfluous and unnecessary expenditures.

Incidentally, as you had directed, Mr. Atabaki, who is well aware of the difficulties of the Ministry of Foreign Affairs, was dispatched to Geneva so that with your Excellency's assistance and favor he can tend to the affairs of the house and furniture and set them right so that there will not be any talk or misinterpretation in the future and to bring to your Excellency's esteemed attention I submit that because of the obscene budget deficit at yesterday's cabinet meeting the government deleted all extra allocations of the ministries and government institutions including the Ministry of Foreign Affairs, and the 1338 [1959] budget corresponding to the 1337 [1958] budget was passed and bound our hands completely in 1338. What can be done we must acclimate ourselves to current conditions In closing, I reiterate my sincere and cordial .... And ask God almighty for the good health of your dear self and once again ask your pardon with deep embarrassment for my frankness and impertinence.

Ali Asghar Hekmat

Document 19
13 June 1959

During and in the aftermath of the fall of Mossadegh, General Teymour Bakhtiar (1914–70) was a key figure in the fight against communists and supporters of Mossadegh. In the mid-1950s, when Iran, with the help of the United States and Britain, created its first security police—known by its Persian acronym SAVAK (Organization of National intelligence and Security)—Bakhtiar was named its first director (1957–62). Here, as a powerful SAVAK director, he is writing to his one-time commander, General Zahedi, by then forced to resign his role as the prime minister and living in virtual forced exile in Switzerland.

۲۳ خرداد ۱۳۳۸

تیمسار فرمانده عزیز   فدایت شوم

پیوسته تندرستی وجود گرامی تیمسار محبوب را از خداوند خواهانم. از حال
بنده خواسته باشید مشغول انجام وظیفه میباشم و مراقب کامل اوضاع
هستم و آنچه به وظیفه خود باشد در خدمتگذاری به اعلیحضرت اول شخصیت.
کوتاهی نکنم و جای نگرانی هم نیست زیرا مراقبت کامل میشود
چون رهبر حقیقی عازم شرفیابی حضور مبارک بود لازم دانستم
به تقدیم این عریضه عرض ارادت نموده باشم. مقدار ناچیزی هم
برنج و خاویار برای مصرف آشپزخانه تیمسار تقدیم گردید.
همیشه مترصد اوامر و فرمایشات میباشم.

ارادتمند سرلشکر بختیار

19.1 22 Khordad 1338 [13 May 1959]

Dear Commandant

I perpetually besiege God for your good health and happiness. If you want to know about me, I am busy fulfilling my duties and keeping close watch over the situation and I will not shirk in any of my duties in the service of His Imperial Majesty the Shahanshah and there is no need for worry because there is total vigilance

Because Colonel Haghighi was on his way to an audience with your auspicious self, I felt compelled to send you this note to convey my regards. A paltry amount of rice and caviar for use in the General's kitchen was also presented.

I vigilantly await your assignments and orders.

Regards Lieutenant General Bakhtiar

Document 20
30 January 1967

The document belongs to the early days of Ardeshir Zahedi's tenure as foreign minister. While it is far from hyperbole to say that Zahedi was the most powerful foreign minister of the shah's last twenty-five years of rule, the note is interesting in showing the detailed kind of reporting the shah received in matters relating to foreign policy. It is important to add that in these, and other official reports, Zahedi uses commonly used Persian honorifics. Their literal translation into English renders them strange. In all such cases, Zahedi uses virtually exactly the same words. We chose to eliminate all such references and replace it with a simpler note. The shah wrote his comments in the right margin of this document.

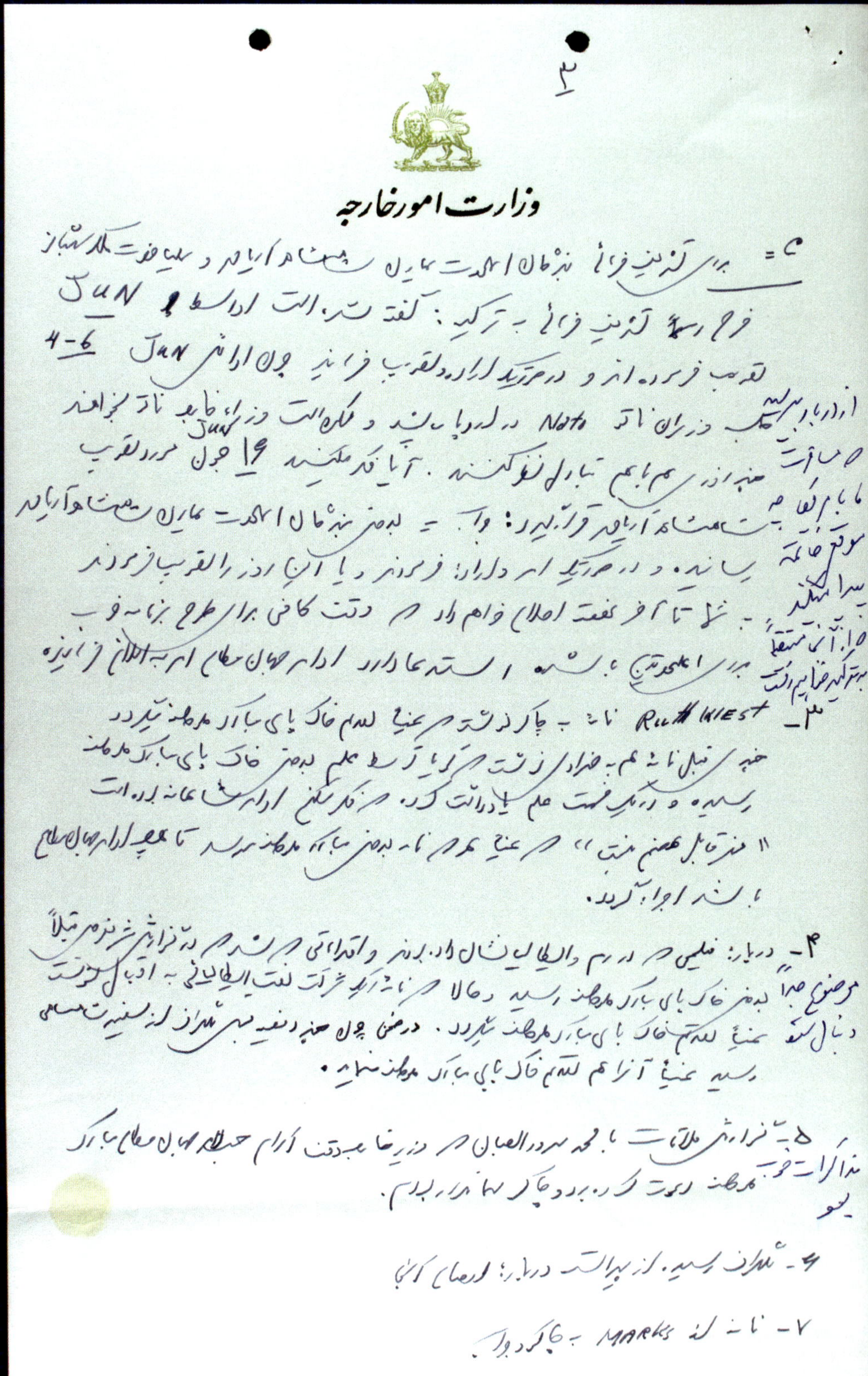

وزارت امور خارجه

20.1

Emblem

Ministry of Foreign Affairs

3

C = For the visit of the servants of His Imperial Majesty Shahanshah Aryamehr and Her Imperial Majesty Queen Farah's official visit to Turkey: It has been said early JUN [June] was approved and in case he should decide to approve because in early Jun 4-6 all NATO ministers will be in Europe and it is possible that the NATO foreign ministers may want to stay a few days more to exchange views. Does he think 16 June will meet the approval of Shahanshah Aryamehr?

Answer = It will be reported to the servants of His Imperial Majesty Shahanshah Aryamehr and in case he decides and orders or approves this day I will inform you by the end of the week so that there will be enough time for a good plan for their Majesties I beg that when your universally obeyed orders are issued to order it to be communicated to us.

Ask the Court when our trip to America will end so that we can go to Turkey directly from there]

—"Ruth KIEST" has written a letter to your servant that I am presenting to the dust of the auspicious Imperial foot Some time back she also wrote a letter to .... that it is said was brought to the attention of Your Majesty by Alam and Alam has made notes in the margin that I think are your Majesty's orders "................................" that again is brought to the attention of His August Majesty so that any universally obeyed orders will be executed.

4—About the film they had shown in Rome Italy that in the previous communication was brought to the attention of Your Majesty and now I present the dust of the auspicious Imperial foot the exact letter of the Italian oil company written to Iqbal. Additionally because some other news was received from his Majesty's Ambassador before the telegram I present the same to the dust of the auspicious Imperial foot.

5—Report of the meeting with Mohammad Sarvar Al-Aban foreign minister at the time of Aram per your your auspicious universally obeyed orders he was invited and I was his host

The matter should be pursued seriously]

6—Telegram received from Pirasteh about conditions there

7—Letter to your servant from "MARKS" and my response

The discussions were good]

۴

وزارت امور خارجه

۸- نامه و تلگراف درباره ۳۰ نفر دانشجوی الجزیره و ۵۸۰ نفر دانشجوی عراقی که امروز به خاک پای مبارک [illegible] برسانند نخست وزیر - وزیر کشور - وزیر جنگ - وزیر امور خارجه [illegible] خیلی زحمت کشیدند همه با جدیت و سرعت و علاقه زحمت کشیدند و آبروی کشور را حفظ کردند و از آن دوران پرمشقت حفظ خواهد شد. [illegible] بسیار همکاری کرد و [illegible] را مأمور دنبال کار نمود. سپهبد [illegible] چاکر را عصبانی کرد ولی [illegible] از روی حسن نیت و علاقه به خدمت به شاهنشاه عزیزتر از جان بوده است.

۹- مهمانی شب گذشته که چاکر در فرودگاه [illegible] و دیگر فرزندان عزیز را با چاکر تلفنا صحبت [illegible] بی نهایت از مراحم والطاف شاهنشاه عزیزتر از جان در سایه [illegible] سپاسگزاری میشود. چاکر زبانم لال است [illegible] از این همه مراحم والطاف [illegible] شاهانه تشکر کنم و خاک پا را بوسیدن [illegible] ... عزت [illegible] چاکر [illegible] خدای من

[illegible]

[illegible] شب ۱۰ بهمن ۱۳۴۸

[illegible]

20.2 4

8 – Letter and telegram about 30 Algerian students and 550 Iraqi students that has to be brought to the attention of Your Majesty; the Prime Minister—Minister of the Interior—Minister of War—Minister of Education who worked very hard all worked very hard with goodwill and speed and care saved the nation's honor and God willing will be maintained at this time too Nassiri cooperated very much and delegated Khonsari to follow up. Pirasteh made me angry but I think it was more out of his goodwill and affection to serve the Shahanshah, who is dearer than my life.

9 – Mahnaz [Zahedi] came last night and your servant was at the airport last night I kissed her and I have not seen her since but she spoke to your servant by phone and she was extremely thankful to the Shahanshah dearer than my life and to Her Majesty the Queen for their kindness and graciousness. Your servant is lost for words and does not know how to thank you for your majestic kindness graciousness and patronage and shame on me and I kiss you dear feet a thousand times

Any kindness to Mahnaz is natural because she is truly a very good girl]

Your servant and devotee, shadow of my God
Ardeshir
Tuesday night 10 Bahman
1345

Document 21
3 February 1967

This document is fascinating, not only for the details it reveals about Iran's foreign policy—from the shah's rapprochement with the Soviet Union, which began in earnest in 1965, to his twin sister Ashraf's renewed effort to play a more pivotal role in the United Nations—but also because it shows how the shah tried to manage the many competing actors and interests in Iran's foreign policy.

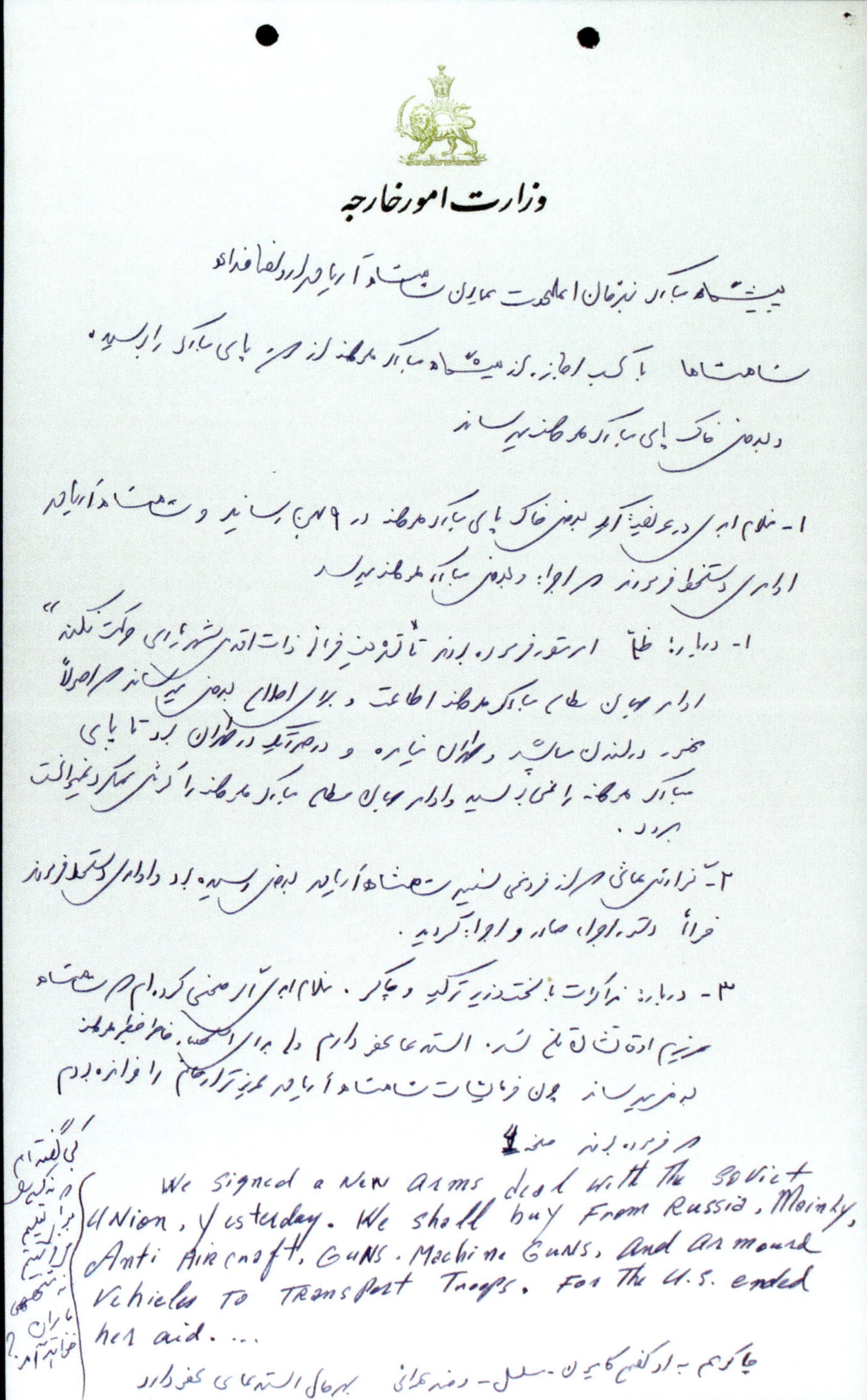

وزارت امور خارجه

پیشگاه مبارک بندگان اعلیحضرت همایون شاهنشاه آریامهر ارواحنا فداه

[illegible]

We signed a new arms deal with the Soviet Union, yesterday. We shall buy from Russia, mainly, Anti Aircraft, Guns, Machine Guns, and armoured vehicles to transport troops. For the U.S. ended her aid...

[illegible]

21.1 Emblem

Ministry of Foreign Affairs

The Auspicious Presence of His Imperial Majesty King of Kings (Shahanshah) Light of the Aryans (Aryamehr) May Our Souls be sacrificed for Him

O Shahanshah with permission of your auspicious Imperial Majesty, kissing your auspicious foot from afar and reporting to the dust of the auspicious imperial foot

1. As your humble servant brought to the attention of Your Majesty in the report of 9 Bahman and the Shahanshah Aryamehr issued some orders that were fulfilled and hereby report

1. About Zelli per your stated command "he should not depart before the arrival of your majesty" Your auspicious and binding imperial commands were obeyed and bring to your attention that essentially he is in London and did not come to Tehran and had he been in Tehran he could not have left before paying his respect and listening to your binding commands.

2. That reports that had been received from the Shahanshah Aryamehr's Ambassador Foroughi that had been brought to your attention and orders had been issued, immediately implementation orders were issued and were executed.

3. About the consultations between the Prime Minister of Turkey and your servant. If your humble servant has said something that has made the Shahanshah angry I beg his pardon but as a reminder to His Majesty's already burdened memory I submit that because I had read the Shahanshah Aryamehr dearer than my life's remarks in which he said Page 4

> We Signed a New arms deal with the Soviet Union, yesterday. We shall buy From Russia, Mainly, Anti Aircraft, Guns. Machine Guns, and armoured Vehicles to Transport Troops. For the U.S. ended her aid....

When have I said we will neither send anyone for training nor will any specialists come to Iran?]

Your servant told him trucks, machine guns, anti aircraft anyway I beg your pardon

۲

وزارت امور خارجه

۴- کرسپی رئیس دولت به بولستان رفته تا آخر هفته آینده مراجعت خواهد کرد از اداره
حمل سلاح ساز خبر ندارند و از اعلان خواهد شد برای شرح نیامد

۵- در مذاکرات با وزیر خارجه و جاکر باز هم از من سوء صحبت کرده ام پیروزی و اسلحه های
مصر را دیدم و اصلاً در همین کار مثلاً ابری تا کسب اجازه تکرار صحبتی نخواهم کرد

ولی بات شاهنشاه عزیزتر از جانم صحبت جاکر در صحبت گفته و معتقد هستم شاهنشاه
عزیزتر از جانم سایه خدا هستند و کسیکه را می پرستم و میخواهم و
آرزو میکنم فدایش شوم و جانم را فدایش کنم نمیتوانم تحمل کنم
ناصر بی ادب سوخته به عزیزتر از جانم به وزیر خارجه کشور دیگری بگوید
زبانم لال شاهنشاه عزیزتر از جانم را در دنیا خطاب کند و من خاک بر
سر نالایق و احمق خبر نداشتم و مثل لال ها نگاه کنم و یا بخندم!!؟
دیشب وزیر خارجه ترکیه این حرف را نیزد قلب من لطمه ای بیند و عبدالله را
در ترکی خود می شنیدم صفحه ۷ صحبت وزیر خارجه ترکیه

IN Reply Nassen Said Iman has Wnong Information About The Policies Followed by us. His Imperial Majesty WAS ATTRIBUTING To us Policies WHICH WE WERE NOT FOLOWING.

EVEN it has been Said That We Tried The Attempt ON His Life. This is ABSOLUTELY UNTRUE AND WE HAD NO SUCH INTENTION. SUCH RUMOURS do not help improvement in RELATION with IRAN.

21.2

Emblem

2

Ministry of Foreign Affairs

4- Kermit Roosevelt has gone to Saudi Arabia and will return by the end of next week and His Majesty's binding orders to attend an audience will be conveyed to him.

5- In the talks with the Prime Minister and your servant, again apologies if I spoke out of turn and I beg your pardon and in principle your eternal servant will never speak again without seeking permission

But Shahanshah dearer than my life, how could your servant who has always said and believes that the Shahanshah dearer than my life is the shadow of God and the one that I worship and want and wish to be sacrificed for him and will sacrifice my life for him could bear to hear that the father (good for nothing) Nasser call dearer than my life, may I be struck mute, a liar, to the Foreign Minister of another country and shame on worthless stupid me to say nothing and stare like a mute and with a smile!!?

When the foreign minister of Turkey was uttering these words my heart was beating so loudly that I could hear it in my ear Page 7 Conversation of the foreign minister of Turkey

> In Reply Nasser said Iran has Wrong Information About the Politics Followed by us. His Imperial Majesty WAS ATTRIBUTING to us Policies WHICH WE WERE NOT FOLLOWING.
>
> Even it has been said that that We Tried The Attempt on His Life. This is ABSOLUTELY UNTRue AND WE HAD NO SUCH INTENTION. Such Rumors do not help improvement in Relation with Iran [*sic*]

۳/

مقصود مطالب دیگر نیست بخصوص راجع به ارگانها

وزارت امور خارجه

این بود که چاکر در جواب ملتزم الرکاب ثابت کنم در دنیا دولت و کشور ما [illegible]

به هر حال از فکر سفیرها نیز مجبوری گفته ام البته [illegible] و [illegible] وقتی که [illegible] فرمان شده بود داشتم، با این سابقه کردم [illegible] اطاعت خواهد شد [illegible]

۲ــ چند روز قبل رئیس اداره حمایت سلاح [illegible] را درباره والاحضرت شاهدخت اشرف پهلوی [illegible] فرمودند. بعد حالا دکتر [illegible] در تهران است دنبال کار را گرفته [illegible] آلمان و فوراً به دکتر [illegible] اداره حمایت سلاح [illegible] آلمان و سپس سفیر چکسلواکی [illegible] شده به وزارت خارجه [illegible] و دکتر [illegible] با [illegible] صحبت کنند و اینجا هم شد

و [illegible] دکتر [illegible] نظر دارند که چون اصل چکسلواکی از طرف [illegible] برای اصل کافی است و آن مربوط به [illegible] فرانسه - انگلیس - آمریکا - و روسیه قول به عهده [illegible] حاضر سال آینده بعضی اصل از چکسلواکی پشتیبانی و قول داده چکسلواکی را کافی خواهد کرد و رأی خواهد داد [illegible] چکسلواکی اصل [illegible] میرود. و برای اینکه پیشنهاد کرده [illegible] تنها [illegible] این است که چاکر سفیر انگلیس - روسیه - آمریکا و فرانسه را به وزارت خارجه [illegible] با [illegible] این درخواست را بنمایم. بنابراین هرچه امر [illegible] سفیرها نیز اطلاعات شود؟ و اداره حمایت سلاح [illegible] را امر به آلمان فرمایید.

اقدام کنید

۳ــ روز گذشته قاسم رضایی [illegible] قبل از آنکه فردا به کانادا برود برای [illegible] به دیدن چاکر آمد و درباره [illegible] و نمایشگاه [illegible] از چاکر نظر [illegible] در [illegible] برای [illegible] - و تهیه - و مطالب [illegible] از [illegible] قابل توجه باشد و [illegible] باید [illegible] به [illegible]

21.3

Emblem

3

Ministry of Foreign Affairs

That is why in response your servant wanted to prove that it is he who is the liar and I said Nasser is a whore and....

I meant other matters particularly about the Americans

Anyway if you think I should not have said that I beseech your pardon and God willing, when you return and I receive the honor of kissing your foot whatever you command will be obeyed as always.

2. A few days ago per universally obeyed orders of his auspicious Majesty about Her Highness Princess Ashraf Pahlavi who had said that now that Vakil [Iranian diplomat in U.N.] is in Tehran [let him] pursue the matter was communicated and immediately the universally obeyed auspicious Imperial orders were communicated to Dr. Vakil and after that it was agreed that the Czechoslovak Ambassador be summoned to the Ministry of Foreign Affairs and Vakil and Hoveyda to talk to him and this too was done.

And afterward Vakil and Hoveyda opined that because this year Czechoslovakia is the candidate of the Socialist group and if the governments of France—England—America—and Russia promise that they would be ready to support Czechoslovakia next year instead of this year and promise that they will nominate Czechoslovakia and will vote for it, then Czechoslovakia will step aside this year and to carry this out they suggested that the only way is that your servant summon the ambassadors of England—Russia—America and France to the Ministry of Foreign Affairs and to request this from them. Consequently, whatever you command will be obeyed. And order the binding Imperial commands to be communicated.

3. Yesterday Deputy Prime Minister Ghasem Rezaie, before his departure for Canada tomorrow, came to your servant for lunch and asked your servant's opinion about tourist attraction and Montreal exhibition and I gave him in detail whatever came to my mind about publication—displays—and the faults, andthings that are attractive to tourists and in my opinion what must be done.

Take action

۴

وزارت امور خارجه

گفتم و در ضمن هم کارهائی وزارت خارجه تهران برای اینجا انجام داده و وظیفهٔ عمده‌اش این است
که با هم همکاری داشته و دولت به دولت هم به هم برای پیشرفت کارها.

۴- گزارش هفتگی ش ۳۰۲ در پیشگاه خاک پای مبارک ملوکانه می‌رسد. لطفاً بفرمایید ملاحظه فرمایند
در فهرست شماره ۲ و همچنین صفحه ۴ تشکیل جبهه با اصطلاح (آزادی خلیج عربی)
برده چون این گزارش عادی کارمند وزارت خارجه چاپ می‌شود چاکر گفتم در اینجا
نوشته شود "آزادی خلیج فارس" بنابراین اگر ملاحظه فرمایند در ترجمه انگلیسی آن توجه نشده
یا خواسته‌اند در عین حال نوشته باشیم.

۵- چند دقیقه قبل هم تلگرافی از کراچی رسید چون اعلیحضرت فردا صبح ساعتی را با [illegible] خانم
برای [illegible] را استدعا دارد فردا شب به عرض خاکپای مبارک ملوکانه خواهد رسید
تلگرافاً به عرض خاکپای مبارک ملوکانه رسانید.

از ترکیه دستخط مبارک را گرفته استدعای عفو کرده و از درگاه پای عنایت [illegible] خواهد
و نمی‌دانم. تصدقت گردم چاکر

سه‌شنبه ۱۴ بهمن
ساعت ۱۰/۳۰

21.4

4

Emblem

Ministry of Foreign Affairs

I said and additionally what can the Ministry of Foreign Affairs do for them and it is our duty to have cooperation with each other and to work hand in hand for progress of our affairs.

4. Weekly report number 3 that was presented to Your Majesty. As you can see in the index number 2 and also page 4 formation of the so-called Front (for the Liberation of Arabian Gulf) because these reports are printed on Ministry of Foreign Affairs paper, your servant said to write in there "Liberation of Persian gulf" therefore do not think that attention was not paid in preparation or we had wanted to have written falsehood.

5. A few minutes ago I received two telegrams from Karachi because this communication will be brought to you tomorrow morning by Salehi, who is traveling with Ms. Farideh to Switzerland and will be bringing the diplomatic mail, and it will be presented to Your Majesty tomorrow night so it was not presented telegraphically to Your Majesty.

I beg your forgiveness for taking up your auspicious time and from afar I kiss your dear foot and may I be dispensed as alms for you a thousand times

Your servant
Ardeshir
Friday night 14 Bahman
10 ½ o'clock

Document 22 Approximately March 1967

Much of this report revolves around the visit of Kermit Roosevelt to Iran (1899–1943, Theodore Rossevelt's second son, businessman, writer, and explorer, and by his own reckoning a key figure in the American effort to overthrow Mossadegh). The visit takes place while Zahedi was foreign minister (1966–71). Roosevelt was the CIA operative sent to Iran in 1953 to manage the American effort to topple the government of Dr. Mossadegh. After retiring from the CIA, Roosevelt entered the world of business, often working as middleman for American companies hoping to do business in Iran. Here he is apparently interested in seeing if he could get Zahedi interested in one of these deals. The detailed nature of the report to the shah is also interesting. Zahedi demurs. The exact date is not clear, but Lucius D. Battle was appointed assistant secretary of state on March 5, 1967.

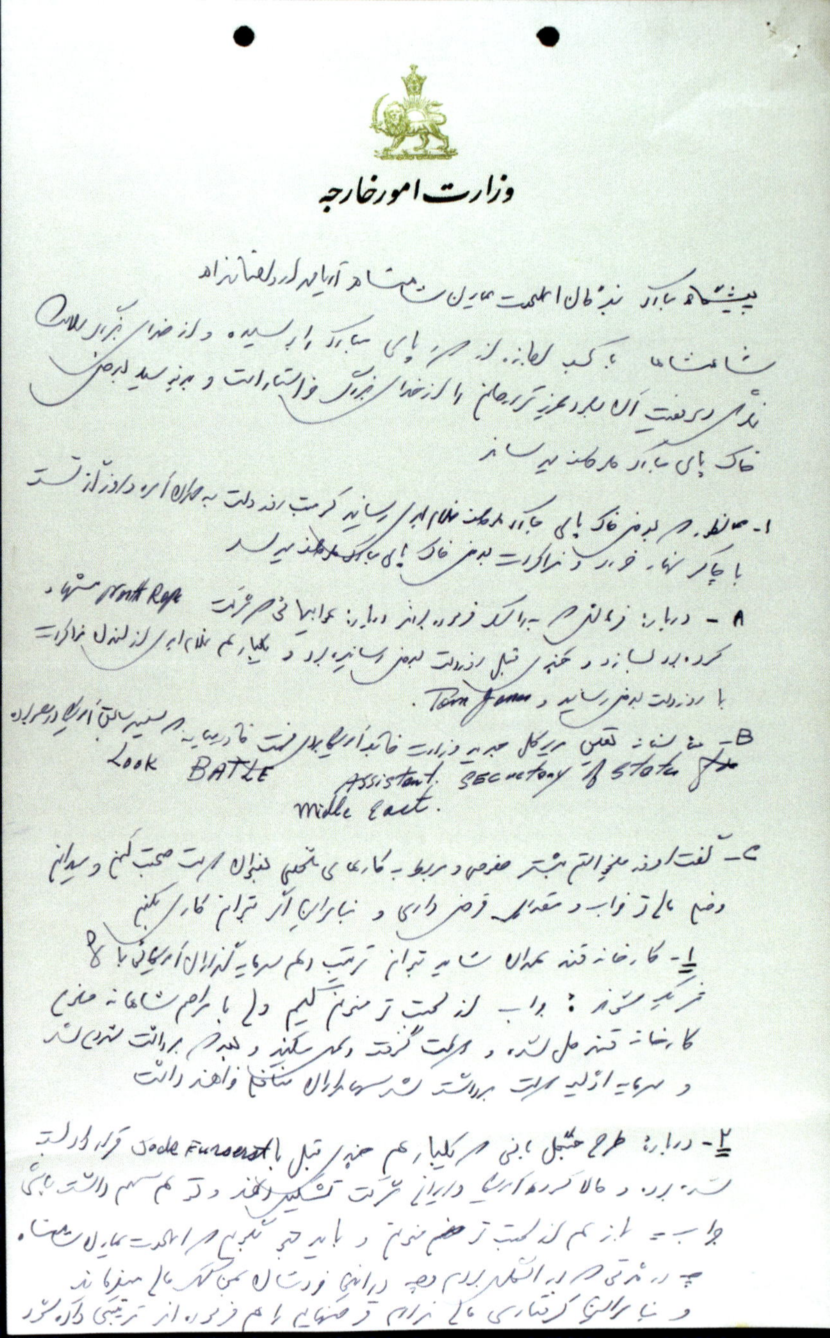

وزارت امور خارجه

پیشگاه مبارک بندگان اعلیحضرت همایون شاهنشاه آریامهر ارواحنا فداه

[illegible]

Look BATLE assistant secretary of state Middle East.

[illegible]

22.1 Emblem

Ministry of Foreign Affairs

The Auspicious Presence of the Servants of His Imperial Majesty the Shahanshah May Our Souls be sacrificed for Him

O Shahanshah With permission from afar kissing your auspicious foot and asking the great God for the good health of your being that is dearer than my life and hereby and report to the dust of the auspicious imperial foot

1. As reported by your eternal slave to the dust of the auspicious imperial foot Kermit Roosevelt has come to Tehran and had lunch with me yesterday and our discussions are hereby reported

A. About what you had told Rusk about the airplane that "North Rope" [Northrop] company has proposed to build that Roosevelt reported a while ago and one time too your eternal slave held discussions with Roosevelt from London that was reported and "Tom Jones"

B. Unfortunately the appointment of the Department of State for the Undersecretary of State for the Middle East is the former Ambassador to Egypt

"Look BATLE Assistant Secretary of State for the Middle East"

C. He said he wanted to talk privately and more as a friend about personal matters and I know your financial situation is bad and you have some debt and therefore if I can do something

> 1. Hamadan Sugar Factory I may be able to arrange for American investors to partner with you:
>
> Answer Thank you for your kindness but kingly blessings has resolved the issue of the Sugar
>
> Factory and the government has taken it over and is running it and later when payout starts and
>
> the government has recouped its initial investment the shareholders will receive their profits
>
> > 2. About the Forestry project that an agreement was reached with "Jode Furserst" [sic] some time ago and now the American and Iranian groups can form a company and you can also have a share in it

Answer: Again I thank you for your kindness and I must tell you that even the time I spent in England and now here His Imperial Majesty the Shahanshah has personally helped me financially and therefore I don't have financial problems and about my debts he said it will be arranged

Document 23
11 June 1967

In the aftermath of the Israeli victory in the 1967 war with Arab neighbors, the shah agreed to allow a few Soviet planes to use Iranian airspace to help rapidly rearm the Arab armies. Here the shah delivers a stern message of admonishment to the Soviets for their obvious breach of the bilateral agreement and the nature and number of flights that flew over Iran. This is the early phase in the shah's remarkable decade (1965–75), when he enjoyed an unusually independent and at times assertive foreign policy that put him on a collision course not only with the Soviets but also, in issues such as oil prices and the nuclear program, with firm allies like the United States.

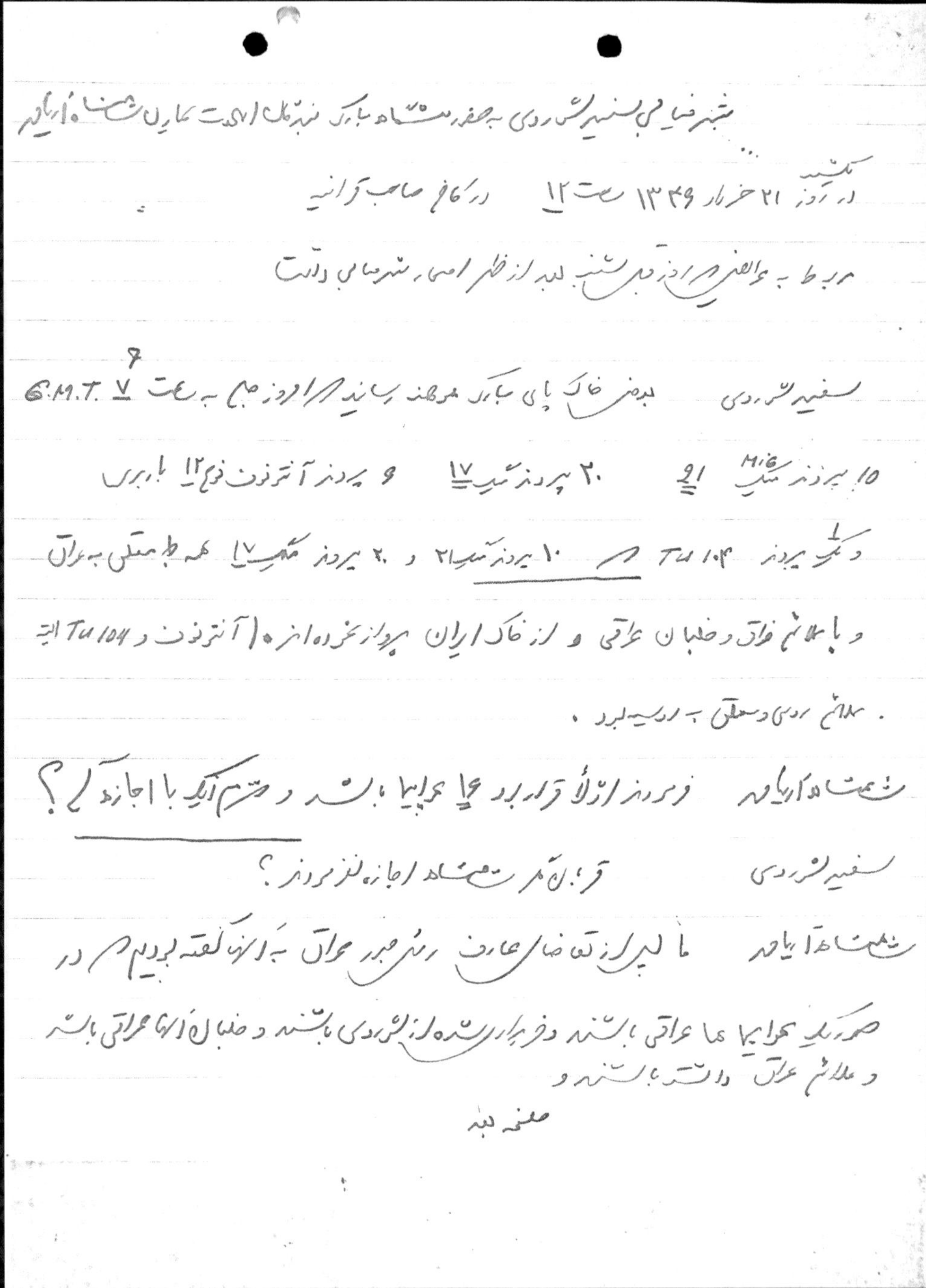

شرفیابی سفیر شوروی به حضور [illegible] اعلیحضرت همایون شاهنشاه آریامهر

یکشنبه
در روز ۲۱ خرداد ۱۳۴۶ ساعت ۱۲ در کاخ صاحبقرانیه

مربوط به [illegible]

سفیر شوروی بعرض خاک پای مبارک میرساند [illegible] از روز جمعه به ساعت ۷ G.M.T.

۱۵ پرواز میگ ۲۱ [illegible] ۲۰ پرواز [illegible] ۱۷ و ۶ پرواز آنتونوف [illegible] ۱۲ [illegible]

دیگر پرواز TU 104 [illegible] ۱۰ پرواز [illegible] ۲۱ و ۲۰ پرواز [illegible] ۱۷ همه جا منتقل به عراق

و با علائم عراق و خلبانان عراقی و از خاک ایران پرواز کرده اند ۱۰ آنتونوف و TU 104 البته

علائم روسی [illegible] به روسیه برد.

شاهنشاه آریامهر [illegible] قرار بود [illegible] هواپیما باشد [illegible] با اجازه کی؟

سفیر شوروی [illegible] اجازه [illegible]؟

شاهنشاه آریامهر ما [illegible] تقاضای عارف رئیس جمهور عراق به آنها گفته بودیم در

صورتیکه هواپیماها عراقی باشند و خریداری شده از شوروی باشند و خلبانان آنها عراقی باشند

و علائم عراق داشته باشند و

صفحه بعد

23.1 Page 1

The Soviet Ambassador's Audience in the Auspicious Presence of His Majesty Shahanshah Aryamehr

On Sunday 21 Khordad 1346 12 o'clock at the Saheb Gharanieh Palace

Soviet Ambassador Reporting to the Auspicious dust of the royal foot that this morning at 7 hours GMT 10 MIG 21s 20 MIG 17s 6 Antonov Type 12 cargo and one 1 TU 104 aircrafts, that 10 MIG 21s and 20 MIG 17s all belonged to Iraq and carried Iraqi insignia and with Iraqi pilots overflew Iranian soil. (Antonovs and TU 104 of course had Russian insignia and belonged to Russia).

Shahanshah Aryamehr Said first of all the arrangement was for 16 airplanes and secondly with whose permission?

Soviet Ambassador Sir, hadn't the Shahanshah issued the permission?

Shahanshah Aryamehr After the request of President Aref of Iraq, we told them that providing the airplanes are Iraqi and purchased from the Soviet Union and piloted by Iraqis and bearing Iraqi insignia and

۲- خلبانان آنها عراقی باشند

MARKING
۳- و قبلاً در مارکینگ عراق را داشته باشند و [illegible] MATRICOL
عراقی [illegible] داشته و قبلاً اطلاع داده باشند

۴- و در روز پرواز نمایند

۵- و قبلاً اطلاع داده باشند

۶- در هواپیماهای نیروی هوائی ارتش شاهی که آنها را اسکورت کنند

روسی اگر عراق کشوری مسلمان و همسایه ماست قبول کرده بودیم که

همانطوری که گفتیم اولاً تمام شرایط بالا را داشته باشند و ثانیاً خودشان [illegible]

و هر یک شرایط بالا را گفته بودیم و ثانیاً هواپیما بیشتر نبود

این جوابی بود که ما به سفارت دادیم. و حالا اینطوری که فکر میکنید

بنظر میرسد در سه ساعت است که این هواپیماها پرواز کرده باشند

** در این موقع [illegible]. با فرمانده نیروی هوائی ارتش شاهی تلفناً
صحبت فرمودند.

و بعد به سفیر شوروی فرمودند که ممکن است هواپیماهای ما [illegible]

2. Piloted by Iraqis

3. And with Iraqi markings MARKING and having Iraqi MATRICOL and with previous notification

4. And fly during the day

5. And with previous notification

6. So that the airplanes of the Imperial Iranian Air Force would escort them

Based on Iraq being a Moslem country and our neighbor, we had agreed, and as I said, first of all under all the above conditions and sixteen airplanes were agreed to and we had stated the above conditions explicitly and no more than sixteen airplanes

This was the response we had given Aref. And now as you are saying it seems that the airplanes were flown two three hours ago

** At this time the Shahanshah spoke to the Commander of the Imperial Iranian Air Force by telephone

And then told the Soviet Ambassador that our aircrafts may

خود را بزنند و کسی به شما اجازه داده ؟

[illegible] بسیار خیلی عصبانی و قیافه برافروخته گرفته بودند

سفیر شوروی خیلی دست پاچه و نگران شد و بعرض [illegible] رسانید.

در مورد همانطور که فرموده اید به عرض خودم گفتم پدرم دلش میخواهد

که شاید تقصیر از او نبوده ولی به عرض [illegible] درست گفته و این

اشتباه کرده اند و سپس بعرض رسانید نمیدانم من به عرض خودم چه بگویم؟

[illegible] زیرا من اتفاقی روز گذشته تلگراف فرستادم

به مسکو رفته و صحبت [illegible] به شما کرده پدرم [illegible] به [illegible].

خارج [illegible] و ما نمیخواهیم آزادانه [illegible] Khan tour [illegible] بین المللی باشیم و نمیخواهیم

در اینطور [illegible] دخالت [illegible]. ما [illegible] اجازه نخواهیم داد که اینطور شرطی را

با ما بکنند و کشور ما کشوری است مستقل و هیچ فردی اجازه ندارد کاری

بر خلاف مصالح کشور ما بنماید و به هیچ فردی اجازه نداده و نخواهیم داد

چنین کارهائی بر خلاف مصالح عالیه کشور ما بنماید

hit you and who gave you permission?

The Shahanshah was very angry and visibly inflamed

Soviet Ambassador became very nervous and worried and said to the Shahanshah that I had informed my government as you have stated and was trying to prove that he was not to blame and that he had informed his government and they made the mistake and then he said I do not know what to tell my own government?

Shahanshah Aryamehr said incidentally I sent a person to Moscow yesterday to tell Foreign Minister Gromyko exactly what I have told you and we do not want to be international adventurers AVANTEUR and do not want to get involved in such things. We will not allow anyone to play such tricks on us and our country is an independent country and no one has permission to do anything against our national interests and we have not and will not permit anyone to do such things against our higher national interests

ما اگر اجازه داده بودیم با آن شرایط می‌گفتند برای این بود که اینها کشوری

مسلمان و همسایه ما برادر و همجواران برادری دیگر موافقت کردیم اینطور عمل کنند

* و این ارزش را دارد که به عراقی‌ها هم گفتیم چنین اجازه‌ای نمی‌دهیم.

سفیر شوروی بعرض رسانید که آن عراقی‌ها گفته

شاهنشاه آریامهر عراقی‌ها شما را گول زدند و بسیار پشیمان هستند. فرمودند

همانطور که دیروز هم به شما گفتیم ما مخالف جنگ هستیم و رویه ما را در سازمان

ملل ملاحظه کردید و ضمناً فرمایشاتی که روز گذشته فرموده بودند تکرار فرمودند

و فرمودند مثلاً تأکید کردیم که اگر اسرائیل زیاده روی کند وضع خوب نخواهد شد

سفیر شوروی درباره صلح و تاشکند صحبت می‌کرد که چون شاهنشاه

صحبت‌شان اینجا می‌رسد و سفیر روس هم دولت ما چه شده بعد صحبت‌های او

خوب فهمیده نشده. و گفت ما که خبری نخواسته‌ایم و به ایران اجازه

Commercial TRANS PORT می‌دهیم همکار هر کس می‌خواهد ببرند داری کار یک

باشید

شاهنشاه آریامهر فرمودند مسئله این است ما چنین اجازه به هیچ آریا کشتی چنین

بردن ما با اینها هم هستیم که در اجازه ولی به عراق فقط PACT

If we had permitted them under those conditions as I said it was because they are a Moslem nation and our neighbor and we agreed for the sake of brotherhood and assistance to carry out this way

* And this is the last time that we provided permission to the Iraqis and you

Soviet Ambassador Sir the Iraqis told us

Shahanshah Aryamehr The Iraqis deceived you and then the Shahanshah said

As I told you yesterday we are opposed to war and considered your policy at the United Nation sensible, and he repeated all what he had said yesterday and said for example asserted that if Israel overplays its hand the situation will not be good

Soviet Ambassador was speaking about peace and Tashkent and because the Shahanshah seemed angry and white-faced he was nervous and could not be well understood and said we have not asked for anything and we will allow Iran to go wherever it wants and case was a COMMERCIAL TRANS PORT.

Shahanshah Aryamehr said we will never give such permission. If it were Pakistan because we are in a PACT with them we could permit but with Iraq only

از لحاظ بی‌ملاحظه بودن کمک کردیم کلی کار داشتیم.

سفیر شوروی   سعی میکرد ثابت بکند در این کار ما به عراق برای زمان [illegible]

سابقه داریم.

** در مسائل قراردادها   سعی شده   شاهنشاه فرمودند استعمارها

مشخص کردن با استقلال ایران است و ما به همین علت و همین کشوری را اجازه نخواهیم داد

** در جای دیگر فرمودند   این کار نه با همین که از قرارداد بین‌الملل رفت

تغییر نکند

** جای دیگر در مسائل قراردادها فرمودند ما خیال استقلال کردن بین‌الملل

داریم ولی این شخص ما را اجازه نمیدهیم.

** درباره مذاکرات   سفیر شوروی   عرض کرد   شاهنشاه اگر

جبهه نکرده باشند صحیح نمیشود

شاهنشاه ایشان   در جواب فرمودند چون ما [با اتحادها] تحمل کرده‌ایم و همانطور

هم به همراهی کار کرده‌ایم و با همه شرایطی که گفته بودیم باشد

because of being Moslem, we thought we would provide some help.

Soviet Ambassador was trying to say that this assistance to Iraq was only for its self-defense and nothing else.

*** In between the Shahanshah's remarks Shahanshah said that such acts make mockery of Iranian independence and we will not allow anyone or any country

** Elsewhere he said Your act does not reconcile with any international Law

*** Elsewhere he said we are not thinking of starting an international scandal but will not allow such mockery.

*** In between the discussion the Soviet Ambassador said what will happen if they have not crossed

Shahanshah Aryamehr in response said because we promised the Iraqis and as we have told them and if under the same conditions that we have said

قبول میکنیم و روی قول خود ایستاده ایم ولی هیچیک از آن شرایط را

کسب بوزنیم خلاف خواهد بود و کسی اعلام نکرده است.

*** همینها را تسلیم کردی   در متن مذاکرات بعضی را نشنیده‌ام

سری جزوانه مانده

توضیح، ارایه   زیر از جلسه مذاکرات ما باید تکلیف را با عراقی‌ها روشن

کنیم و معلوم شود چه بود و چه گفته اند. البته ما الان هم گفتیم چون

? اسیرانت نداریم الساعه [illegible] برای شما درست کنیم به روزنامه ندهید

مراتب را هم گفت ولی باید معلوم شود.

we will agree and we stand on our promise but if there is variance with the conditions we had laid, it would be an abrogation and we will not allow it.

*** Likewise the Soviet Ambassador during the consultations asked that this subject remain confidential.

Shahanshah Aryamehr How can this be we must clarify the situation with the Iraqis to see what happened and what was said. Of course as I said because

? we do not like to create an international scandal for you we will not tell the newspapers etc., but it must be clarified.

Document 24
Around 1967

During much of Zahedi's tenure as foreign minister, Armin Meyer (diplomat, 1914–2006) was the US ambassador to Iran. He was widely known to be sympathetic to the views of the shah. As the shah was in this period beginning to have a much more independent and assertive foreign policy, at times at odds with the United States, and as Iran was in those days no longer in need of US aid or grants, the relationship between the two countries had grown at times tense. This exchange was a harbinger of even tougher days to come. Meyer was ambassador between 1965 and 1969, and the shah visited Pakistan in 1967; thus this document is dated to around 1967.

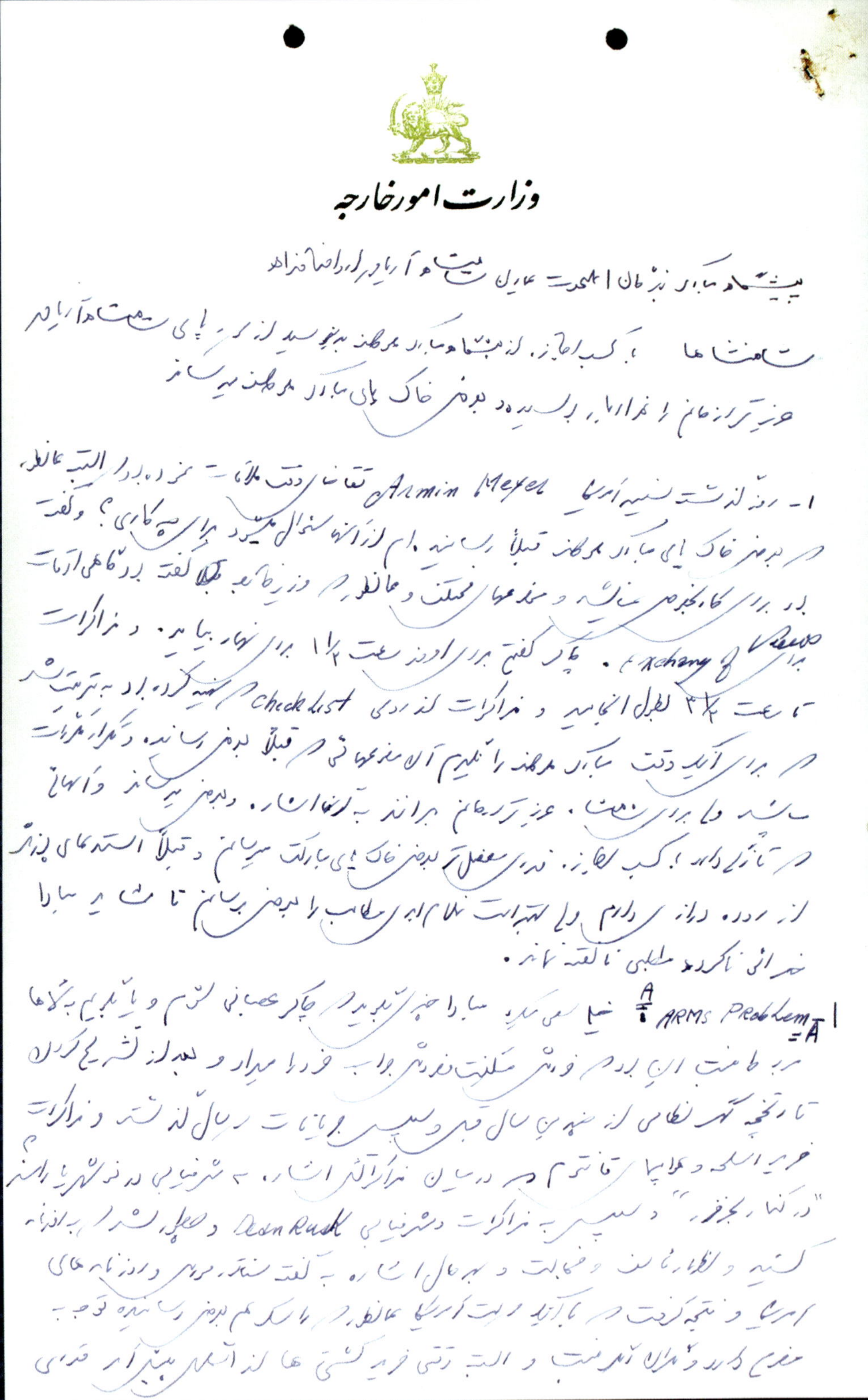

وزارت امور خارجه

پیشگاه مبارک بندگان اعلیحضرت همایون شاهنشاه آریامهر ارواحنا فداه

[illegible]

۱- [illegible] Armin Meyer [illegible]

[illegible] Exchange of views [illegible]

[illegible] Check List [illegible]

[illegible]

۲- ARMS Problem [illegible]

[illegible] Dean Rusk [illegible]

[illegible]

24.1

Emblem

Ministry of Foreign Affairs

The Auspicious Presence of His Imperial Majesty the Shahanshah Aryamehr (King of Kings Light of the Aryans) May Our Souls be sacrificed for Him

O Shahanshah

With permission of your Auspicious Majesty I hereby report

1. American Ambassador Armin Meyer requested time for a meeting yesterday and of course as I had previously reported to the dust of the auspicious imperial foot they were asked for what purpose? And he said it was for a particular business and various subjects and as the Secretary of State had said before once in a while for "Exchange of views". I told him to come today at 1:30 for lunch. And the discussions went on to 3:30 and the discussions followed the order of a "checklist" that he had prepared and so that His Majesty's time is not occupied by the subjects that had been reported before and repetition would be redundant but so that the Shahanshah dearer than my life knows, (they will be touched upon and reported and those that are fresh, seeking permissions, your devotee will go into detail for the dust of the auspicious royal foot and prior to that I beg your pardon for my long-windedness but it is better that your eternal slave report maybe lest God forbid a subject is left unsaid.

1. An "ARMS Problem" A He tried very hard not to say something that would make your servant angry or to make me say that it does not concern them and so he would say something and answer himself and after analyzing the history of military assistance from many years ago and then the incidents of the past two years and the talks about arms purchase and Phantom airplanes that he referred to in the middle of his discussions and his audience in Noshahr or Ramsar? "by the Caspian Sea" and then to discussions and audience of Dean Rusk and how it reached American newspapers and his lament and embarrassment and anyhow referred to Senator Morse's statement and American press and concluded that just as Rusk had presented although the American government pays attention to the subject and is not worried anymore and of course when the subject of purchase of the ships from England came up he became a little

۲

وزارت امور خارجه

حسود شدند و کلیه مذاکرات [illegible] بیشتر از

In Washington they became concern, but they finnaly understood the problem. Thanks God. ...

دل ناراحت شد گر روزنامه خبر از نفت ایران [illegible] صحبتی کرد والبته قدری دولت در واشنگتن با کنگره مشکل خواهد داشت و مثلاً Rusk و McNamara با کنگره ممکن است ناراحت کنند و سؤال مطرح کنند ولی حل خواهد شد.

جواب چاکر: خیلی مختصر و متکلم [illegible] ما را [illegible] والبته [illegible] شده دولت [illegible] اخبار [illegible] والبته باید اضافه کنم [illegible] باز [illegible] انجام شد و [illegible] باید [illegible] به کاری که [illegible] خبر را [illegible] دولت [illegible] منتشر [illegible] و [illegible] شده و [illegible] امر را تنبیه کرده اید.

B- Review [illegible]: با [illegible] شد و [illegible] این مذاکرات را باز به چاکر شرح داد و بالاخره اظهار امیدواری کرد که این مذاکرات در [illegible] حل خواهد شد [illegible] شماره ۵ [illegible] واشنگتن امیدوار است این حل شود که [illegible] شماره ۵ [illegible] و لازم [illegible] باشند در [illegible] مذاکرات [illegible] صحبت کرد.

[illegible] در مورد A صحبت کرد [illegible] دولت [illegible] پنجاه میلیون برای [illegible] سال گذشته و سال آینده پنجاه میلیون [illegible] خواهد بود [illegible] پنجاه میلیون کمتر [illegible] برای [illegible] استفاده [illegible] شد.

2= [illegible] پاکستان

H.I.M.'s TRIP TO PAKISTAN

jealous and then when the subject of purchase of arms from the Soviets came up "In Washington they became concerned, but they finally understood the problem, thank God...."

but one must not be offended if a newspaper reports something or a Senator says something but of course the government in Washington will have some problems with the Senate and for example Congress may upset "McNemara" and "Rusk" and question them, but it will be solved.

Your servant's response: Very briefly I am glad you have understood and understand us and of course you yourself pointed out that the Imperial government has authority over its own affairs and of course I must add that we were purchasers and will do what benefits our country and although you yourself pointed out I must say you did a bad thing to release the news before the Imperial Government did and anyhow you yourself became aware of your mistake and are saying that the official has been punished.

B. A. E. Review Have discussed with Samiie and likewise he explained to your servant the history of this issue and finally he said he hoped that the issue will be solved in April and May and until the visit of the Shahanshah Aryamehr to Washington he is hopeful that it will get resolved so that at that time the Shahanshah Aryamehr would not see a need to address this issue and can talk about other issues.

Your eternal slave must report that when he was talking about the issue in "A" *[sic]* he referred to two hundred million in credit and that about fifty million for airplanes last year and next year another fifty million will be in the airplane column and he is hopeful that the cost will be less than fifty million so that other uses can also be made of this money he pointed out.

2= The visit of the slaves of His Imperial Majesty Shahanshah Aryamehr to Pakistan

"H.I.M.'s TRip To PAKistan"

وزارت امور خارجه

بازهم به مذاکرات گذشته و تاریخچه ایران برگردم و شکرانم برای آمدن چاکر سال
کرد و آیا فکر میکنید تیرانی قبل از گذشتن فردا شرفیاب بشوم؟ و نظر اعلیحضرت به
پاکستان چیست

فکر میکنم وقت داشته باشم

جواب چاکر: البته اعلان کردم تا به حال اعلیحضرت همایون ساعت ده ارباید در خزانه
گذشتن فردا و لیکن از گذشتن فردا بلافاصله به پاکستان گذشتن فردا خواهد شد

سفیر امریکا: سب ضبط میرسد در اینجا ترجمه نبرده و سپس از وقت شصت. ارباید
خطا گرفته است.

چاکر: منظور تلگراف را به عهده است بعض خاک‌های مبارک ملوکانه خواهم رساند
و در صورتی که دقتی شده تا اینکه عاطفه که گفتم برنامه شصت. ۱ ارباید لیکن
شنلی دگرفته است شاید درصورتیکه برنامه شصت. ۱ ارباید تغییر کرد ترتیب و
اجازه شرفیابی داده شود

سفیر امریکا: بسیار فکر خوبی است ولی چون این تلگراف قبل از ایران رسیده و من همین تلگراف
را به همه نشان داده‌ام همین مطالب را به سفارت هم برگشتم روی کاغذ خوب زده‌ست
فردا برای همه سفیرستم هم بعض خاک‌های مبارک ملوکانه برسانند و فکر میکنم
با برنامه شنلی شصتاد ارباید لیکن از مطالعه تلگراف لازم بدانند که شرفیاب بشوم
Battle
تجدید هم لیکن از گذشتن فردا شصت. از پاکستان اینکه شرفیابی را
کردیم و بسیار سپاسگذار و مفتخر هستیم که تا اینکه شصتاد ارباید الحمدالله گرفته هستند
اجازه صحبت فرموده شرفیاب بشویم و خیلی خیلی خوشحال و مفتخریم و B هم سرافراز است

* تلگراف را تا تکمیل صحبت دوم برای چاکر بفرستند که با عملی عرایض بعض خاک‌های مبارک
ملوکانه برساند.

- B : Reading Material : B + A :

چون وقتی کاسیکین به ترکیه رفته بوده اینجا مقامات ترکها صحبت کرده بوده

again he referred to past discussions and history of the matter and showed your servant the telegram he had received and do you think I can get an audience before his visit? And your opinion about Pakistan?

I don't think we will have time

Your servant's answer: Of course you know that His Imperial Majesty Shahanshah Aryamehr are in Khuzestan and after the visit will be leaving for Pakistan immediately

American Ambassador: Yes it seems that Washington was not attentive and knows Shahanshah Aryamehr's schedule is very tight

Your servant: In my opinion give me the telegram and I will bring it to the attention of His Majesty and in case there happens to be time, although as I said the schedule of the Shahanshah Aryamehr is very heavy maybe if there happened to be a change in Shahanshah Aryamehr's schedule arrangements can be made for an audience

American Ambassador: It's a very good idea but because the telegram was received just before I came and I showed you the actual telegram I will write the exact subjects on good paper and will send it to you immediately so that you can bring it to the attention of His Majesty but I think that with the heavy schedule of the Shahanshah Aryamehr after perusing the telegram an audience will not be deemed necessary particularly because after the visit of Shahanshah to Pakistan we will have the honor of an audience with "Battle" we are very grateful and honored that even though the Shahanshah Aryamehr is extremely busy he permitted and honored us with the audience and we are very very pleased and honored and "B" is also proud

* He will send your servant the telegram in an hour and it will be forwarded with this letter to Your Majesty.

B. "Reading Material": B + A :

Because when Kosygin went to Turkey and talked to Turkish leaders

وزارت امور خارجه

گفته بودم با ملاقاتهایی که ایران و ترکیه شکل فلانند با ما باشند یک نامه خصوصی به سفیر خودمان

در فلان نوشته بودم در آن گزارش برای من فرستاده‌اند و فکر کردم برای مطالعه شما

جالب توجه باشد. همین نامه را به چاکر داد و فرستید لطفاً به خاکپای مبارک ملوکانه عرض شود

در ضمن گزارشی دنباله گزارش چین کرده است که در هفته گذشته برای شما نوشته بودم

و فکر می‌کنم جالب توجه باشد.

جواب چاکر: به گزارش قبلاً مطالعه کردم بسیار جالب بود و تشکر می‌کنم این گزارش را

برای من آوردید: همین گزارش لطفاً به خاکپای مبارک عرض خواهد گردید.

4 - C.I.A Hullabaloo: البته این روزها در روزنامه و تلویزیون راجع به C.I.A سروصدا [illegible]

متأسفانه تصور می‌کنم درست است CIA به بعضی‌ها کمک کرده ولی این اصلاً جنبه این را

نداشته که دانشجویان و غیره برای ما جاسوسی کنند و کمک به گروه‌های مختلف

بوده و البته باید قبول کنیم باعث خجالت و ناراحتی همه ما امریکائی‌ها شد.

And el Leader everyone in States were shocked about The publicity in The papers.

چاکر از سئوال مطرح کردم راجع به اینکه چه باید ترتیب اتخاذ شود چیزی نگفت و گفت فقط

متأسفانه شما میدانید و البته خبرهائی که من دارم تمام باید و همه درست چون این روزها

اغلب روزنامه‌ها همه این بحث درباره [illegible] کرده و می‌کنند.

5 - Releas of Sgt. Whipkey: شرحی شرح داد و چاکر گزارش دادم

و همان را به تازگی در سفارت به سفیر برده کرد.

چاکر گفتم اعلیحضرت این مسئله خیلی در حال حاضر بی‌اهمیت است و در عین حال

اهمیت دارد اگر شماها بخواهید اصرار می‌کنند و روی آن سروصدا بلند شود

شما در نامه خود گفته‌اید تا زمانی که سفارت به سفیر برد برای شما Victory

بود آیا واقعاً انتظار داشتید و سروصدائی روی آن راه افتاد

خوب بود؟ در جواب گفت باید تصدیق کنم که ما اشتباه کردیم [illegible]

he had said that we would like to see Iran and Turkey be like Finland with us I had written a private letter to our Ambassador in Finland that he sent me a report that I thought would be interesting for your perusal. I hereby present the exact text that was sent to your servant and the second report is the continuation of Jean Kerr Nesbitt report that I had sent you last week and think it would be of interest.

Your servant's response Yes I studied the previous report it was very interesting and I thank you for bringing this report for me: The exact report is hereby presented.

4. "C.I.A. Hullabaloo:" [sic] Of course these days you must have heard of what the newspapers and others say about the "C.I.A." I wanted to say that it is true that the "CIA" helps some people but this never meant that students and others spy for us and rather it was help for various groups and of course I must agree that it has embarrassed and upset all of us Americans.

"And it looks every one in States were shocked about the publicity in the papers."

However much your servant asked him what other news do you have he got red and said nothing and only said I wanted you to know and of course the news that I have you have too and all others have too because these days most newspapers have and continue to discuss this issue every day.

5. "Release of Sgt. Whipkey:" He explained for some time and I listened and then he referred to the law that Mansour took to the Majlis. [Mansour law refers to a Status of Force Agreement ratified when Mansour was the Prime Minister in 1964.]

Your servant said In my view this issue is unimportant at this time but at the same time is important if you all want to insist needlessly and create noise about it. In your talk you said the law that Mansour took to the Majlis was a "Victory" for you do you really think so and the ruckus that it created was good? Replying he said I must agree that we thought that

وزارت امور خارجه

در انگلستان [illegible] Victory را برد و حالا همه متوجه شده‌اند [illegible] حق با شما است

و نه تنها Victory را نبرد بلکه نتیجه معکوس داشت. [illegible] چاکر به سفیر

[illegible] کشتن یک دختر ۱۷ ساله در ۱۹۸۱ کردم و [illegible] گفت صد در صد حق

با شما است و اصلاً اشتباه [illegible] بوده و [illegible] حاضر شدیم

[illegible] تمام خواهد شد گفتم [illegible]

و [illegible] تمام خواهد شد

و بالاخره گفت [illegible] امروز [illegible] دستور [illegible]

[illegible] را برای [illegible]. گفتم [illegible] آمریکائی بوده از

[illegible]

[illegible]

[illegible] یک آمریکائی [illegible] قاتل [illegible]

[illegible]

[illegible]

کرد.

6- [illegible] منزل [illegible] سفارت

آمریکا [illegible] وزارت خارجه و

سفارت [illegible] گفت [illegible] در جواب گفتم من تشکر کردم

[illegible] تشکر کنید درست است [illegible] در هیچ کشوری [illegible]

[illegible] سفارتخانه [illegible] کشور [illegible]

[illegible] و گفت [illegible] من اشتباه کردم

و اصلاً [illegible] تشکر کنم و متشکرم [illegible]. چاکر [illegible] گفتم [illegible]

[illegible]

at the time it was a "Victory" and now we all came to realize that you were right and not only it was not a "Victory" but rather it had the opposite outcome. And then your servant I (mentioned) the case of Dr. Harris and murder of an eleven-year-old girl in 1951 and then he said you are right one hundred percent and basically it was the fault of my administration and do you think if we get ready that the Sergeant comes back for interrogation the case will end I said that of course I am not a judge and jurist but we can tell you that baseless insistence will work against you and he finally said I give up and when I return today I will order that your view is agreed to and they send the aforementioned for interrogation. I said thank you because there were two Americans and if legal procedures are not allowed to follow the same senators that you mentioned will make noise the same people or other groups will create a ruckus about why the Embassy did not allow the law to pass judgment over the killing of an American! Again he concurred and after that he profusely thanked the Shahanshah for his kindness for pardoning (the culprit) in another murder that occurred the previous year.

6. Relates to the issue of the Armenian's house and the Russians that an Armenian who worked at the American Embassy and Intelligence agents and the police without confrontation through the Ministry of Foreign Affairs and his Embassy arrested the aforementioned and took him away in response I said I thought you wanted to offer your thanks it is true that no country will allow another country to use officials of another embassy to create a center for spying but in any event this matter was in your favor and worked in your favor he got very red and said yes I made a mistake and in principle I would like to offer thanks and I am thankful. Your servant laughed and said anyway if our northern neighbors complained about as they put it why we have arrested their functionaries

وزارت امور خارجه

با تبدیل اینها منزل هم متعلق به ما که کارمندان سفارت اجاره گرفته‌ایم به اینها مبلغی که از اطلاع
نرسید کمیسیون کنند. خواهید دید هم‌اکنون را با کمک سفارت آمریکا هم کرده‌ایم و کسب کنیم
ولی بعد از شرحی خبری بدهید به شما تبدیل هم دولت شاهنشاهی به هیچ فرد خارجی نه اجازه
وکالت و نه اجازه کاپیتولاسیون خواهد داد. گفت بله بله می‌دانم و اوامر بگذارید
و باز هم متشکرم.

ح = بعد Amb. Battle's Visit : باز تکرار کرد هم بسیار متفق و سپاسگزارند هم
شاهنشاه. از اینکه اجازه فرمودند شرفیاب بشوند و گفت چون بعضی‌ها فکر می‌کنند
او نگهدار مصر و ناصر است این خیلی خوب شد هم ناصر هم از این شرحها را پیدا می‌کند
و از نزدیک به عظمت بزرگی شاهنشاه. بیشتر از هیچی پی خواهد برد و شهر [illegible]
به اینکه شاه [illegible] خواهد داد از نزدیک شاهنشاه. ایران را هم همه به عظمت
و بزرگی و لیاقت شاهنشاه نه تنها در ایران بلکه در دنیا همه تحسین و تمجید می‌کنند
فقط [illegible] و بین یک مرد بزرگ جهانی و یک مرد متظاهر - در [illegible] دماگوگ
را می‌بیند و فرق می‌گذارد.

۲ - روز گذشته نماینده اسرائیل به وزارت خارجه اطلاع داد هم وزیر خارجه اسرائیل [illegible] وارد
فرودگاه مهرآباد خواهد شد و یک ساعت توقف خواهد نمود و خواهش کرده بود که یکی از اعضای [illegible]
ولو یک کارمند پایین رتبه در فرودگاه باشد. چاکر قبول کردم در ضمن با تفسیری که
صحبت هم یک نفر مرد هم از طرف ما به فرودگاه فرستاده‌ایم و به [illegible] دستور دادم
[illegible] و اگر [illegible] گزارش [illegible] و [illegible] گزارش
[illegible] و صحبت وزیر خارجه اسرائیل وارد [illegible] خاک ایران [illegible]
شد.

۳ - [illegible] اجازه از شاهنشاه [illegible] تهران [illegible] رسیده [illegible] و [illegible]

6

or as they would say we have taken a house that belonged to one of their Embassy's functionaries we would tell them if you don't know then investigate and you will see that we have done the same with a functionary of the American Embassy and then I said all jokes aside I must tell you the news that the Imperial government will not permit any foreign person either to interfere or to spy under any circumstances. He said yes yes I know and forget it and again I thank you.

7. "Amb. Battle's Visit:" He repeated again that he was very proud and thankful to the Shahanshah Aryamehr for granting an audience and said because some think he favors Egypt and Nasser it is very good that the aforementioned will have the honor of an audience to observe from close and he will discover the great personality of the Shahanshah even more than before and his audience will provide him the chance to get to know the Shahanshah of Iran in all his grandeur, greatness, and leadership not only in Iran but that all the world has come to admire and praise and will give him a chance see and differentiate between a great worldly man and a show-off liar and demagogue.

2—Yesterday the Israeli representative informed the Ministry of Foreign Affairs that the Israeli Foreign Minister will land at Tehran Airport tonight and for a one-hour stopover and had requested that a member of Protocol even a lower echelon official to be at the airport. I accepted additionally I told Nassiri by phone that one agent should be sent from the secret division and I ordered the head of the fifth department of the Ministry of Foreign Affairs to also go but to keep it confidential and if any discussions should occur, to report it and that is exactly how it was carried out and the original report of .... and the conversations of the Foreign Minister of Israel with him is presented to Your Majesty.

3—With permission of the auspicious Imperial presence the telegrams received up to this hour and some other material

Document 25
13 November 1968

These are the minutes of a meeting between the shah of Iran and the Saudi monarch, King Faisal (1906–75, reigned 1964–75). Faisal discourses about the difficulties of establishing ties with the "godless Soviet Union," and the shah's careful advice about how to establish such relations is a fascinating facet of this document. In that period, the shah had cautiously moved to normalize Iran's fraught relationships with the Soviet Union.

- ۲ -

وزارت امور خارجه

بکلی سری

شاهنشاه آریامهر: روزنامه های کویت با حمله میکنند. از سفارت ما خوشحال هستند.

اعلیحضرت ملک فیصل: در کویت بعضی از روزنامه های کویت دست چپی و افراطی هستند.

شاهنشاه آریامهر: با ناصر ارتباط دارند.

اعلیحضرت ملک فیصل: مخصوصاً دو روزنامه: السیاسه والطلیعه

شاهنشاه آریامهر: در بیروت هم روزی یکی دو تا روزنامه منتشر است. بعضیها پول خرج میکنند.

اعلیحضرت ملک فیصل: پول خرج میکنند ولی نه بمیزان سابق.

شاهنشاه آریامهر: راجع به ما دشنام بگردن میکنند. انتظارات دارند.

ملک فیصل: با مطبوعات انگلیسی که مقصد اغراضی دارند.

شاهنشاه آریامهر: شما که حمله به سفارت ما هم داده اند. ما یکی از اولین دولی بودیم که کویت را برسمیت شناختیم.

بکلی سری

25.1 [Minutes of a November 13, 1968 meeting between the Shah of Iran and King Faisal of Saudi Arabia. Ambassador Zahedi was in attendance. Minutes prepared by Iran's Foreign Ministry.]

2

Ministry of Foreign Affairs
Totally Confidential

Shahanshah Aryamehr	Kuwaiti newspapers attack us. They are not happy with our visit.
His Majesty King Faisal	Unfortunately some Kuwaiti newspapers are leftists and extremists
Shahanshah Aryamehr	They have connections with Cairo
His Majesty King Faisal	Particularly two newspapers: *Al Siasah* and *Al Tali'ah*
Shahanshah Aryamehr	Also in Beirut one or two newspapers have behaved similarly. The Egyptians spend money.
His Majesty King Faisal	They spend money but not as much as the past.
Shahanshah Aryamehr	They vilify you and me. They have expectations.
King Faisal	They say explicitly that they intend to extort.
Shahanshah Aryamehr	They have chanted slogans against our visit. We were one of the first governments to recognize Kuwait.

وزارت امور خارجه

اعلیحضرت ملک فیصل: در این قسمت از دنیا معمولاً طبقه جوانان دست دارند جوانان صحیح و منطقی فکر نمیکنند و افکار و عقاید عجیبی در سر دارند.

شاهنشاه آریامهر: بدون شک. در این مرحله از زندگی پرخروش تغییرات افراد احتیاج به راهنمائی و دلالت دارند.

ملک فیصل: —

شاهنشاه آریامهر: ما به کویت همیشه کمک و مساعدت را نموده ایم.

ملک فیصل: به کویت باهم حمله نکنند در حالیکه در ابتدا ما با آنها کمک نظامی کردیم

شاهنشاه آریامهر: ما از کویت چیزی جز خیر و صلاح آنان نمیخواهیم و مایلیم که استقلال خود را حفظ نمایند و مستقل و سعادتمند باشند. اگر خدای‌نکرده کویت در دست دیگران افتد اثرات بدی خواهد داشت.

اعلیحضرت ملک فیصل: در درجه اول با خود آنهاست که در فکر خودشان باشند. تمام ناراحتی کویت از جانب خارجی‌ها ناشی میشود. آنها هستند که راه اصلاح کویت را گرفته‌اند. متأسفانه تمام آنها عرب هستند. همانطور که ما با شاهنشاه [illegible] اتحاد - اتحاد اسلامی [illegible] خلیج میدهیم.

25.2 3

Ministry of Foreign Affairs
Totally Confidential

His Majesty King Faisal	In these demonstrations, usually the youth are involved.
Shahanshah Aryamehr	The youth do not think right and rationally and have strange thoughts and beliefs in their heads.
King Faisal	Without doubt at this stage in life they undergo changes and are in need of guidance and reasoning.
Shahanshah Aryamehr	We have offered Kuwait all sorts of aid and assistance.
King Faisal	We too are attacked in Kuwait although at the beginning we provided them military assistance.
Shahanshah Aryamehr	We do not want anything from Kuwait but their welfare and best interest and also for them to preserve their independence and not fall victim to antagonists. If Kuwait's wealth falls in the hands of others it will have important consequences.
His Majesty King Faisal	In the first place it is up to them to think for themselves. All Kuwait's troubles are promoted by foreigners. They instigate native Kuwaitis. Unfortunately all of them are Arabs. They have labeled our consultations with the Shahanshah Unity—Islamic Unity and Gulf Unity.

وزارت امور خارجه

این نوع کشتار چه اشکالی دارد.

شاهنشاه آریامهر: این اساس ساخته و پرداخته فکر آنها است. روابط ما طوری است که همکاری با آنان ندارم.

اعلیحضرت ملک فیصل: باید ایشان مطالب زیر را با تمام اسلامی. اگر منطقه‌ای از بین [illegible] می‌گردد.

(شاهنشاه آریامهر: از کشتی و [illegible] استفاده. چون آنها میل ندارند [illegible] اتکای [illegible] گردند.)

اعلیحضرت ملک فیصل: به امید خدا اتحاد اسلام تحقق خواهد یافت.

(شاهنشاه آریامهر: [illegible] است. روسها [illegible] با یک نفر [illegible] قرار گرفته‌اند در این احوال بهتر [illegible] نفوذ خود را توسعه دهند ولی اگر دور هم جمع شویم قوی خواهیم شد و سد راه آن‌ها خواهیم بود.)

اعلیحضرت ملک فیصل: متأسفانه در مخالفت با اتحاد اسلامی عوامل عرب و شرقی [illegible] دست دارند و هر کدام بطریقی با این امر مخالفت می‌کنند. دول عرب راه‌های دارند ولی تا آنها [illegible] نیست همین [illegible] را [illegible] مدیریت [illegible] [illegible] روشن است در آنها [illegible] و تکلیم [illegible] ملل اسلامی [illegible] نکنند.

Ministry of Foreign Affairs
Totally Confidential

Shahanshah Aryamehr	What is the problem with this type of connection?
His Majesty King Faisal	This is the basis of the construct of their thinking. Our relations are such that we have no need for it.
[Shahanshah Aryamehr	We know where matters related to Islamic Unity—Regional Unity originate from. They come from Moscow and Cairo. Because they do not like such a unity to take shape.]
His Majesty King Faisal	God willing Islamic Unity will become a reality.
[Shahanshah Aryamehr	God willing. The Russians would like to establish relations with us on a singular basis, and as a result, to be able to expand their influence but if we come together we will become strong and will be an obstacle in their path.]
His Majesty King Faisal	Unfortunately in opposition to Islamic Unity Western and Eastern elements are both involved and each opposes it in some way. Western governments have agents but they are not to be blamed. We Muslims must blame and reproach ourselves, for the policy of westerners is clear and they are opposed to closeness and strengthening of the principles of friendship among Muslim nations.

- ۵ -

بکلی سری

وزارت امور خارجه

شاهنشاه آریامهر: باید دید از آنکه این سیاست مستقل چه از سیاست بد هیچ وجه تکمیل نکنیم.

اعلیحضرت ملک فیصل: بالست چیست نمردم در کویت تقاضا دمنات خبر از دشمنان داریم و حالت خرگوش داریم. ثبات سیاسی برای آنها نیستیم.

شاهنشاه آریامهر: درین باره هم عیناً همین است.

اعلیحضرت ملک فیصل: کشتیها و زرهی و حرکت حرفی دولت ما را بیجانی آورند و نمیخواهند مثلاً این ایران و سعودی توقع اندازند. چیزی نشد مشکلی نیست که چه دیگری عمل کنند. شما ایراد و بران با آنها نشد واقع شود.

شاهنشاه آریامهر: در وزارت خارجی هم مطالعه میکنند.

اعلیحضرت ملک فیصل: با هم همینطور رفتار میکنند. قسم میخورم که نیت این سیاست کمونیستی داریم.

شاهنشاه آریامهر: درین باره هم همین است.

اعلیحضرت ملک فیصل: طبق گزارشی که داریم از قرار معلوم عوامل بعثی در کویت خیال کودتا دارند ولی معتقدم اشخاص مسلمان را با آنها گفتیم مبادا ما را شریک جرم حساب آورند.

25.4 5

Ministry of Foreign Affairs
Totally Confidential

Shahanshah Aryamehr	By adopting an independent policy, we must see what we lose and what we gain.
His Majesty King Faisal	Our objectives and intentions toward the people and the government of Kuwait are benevolent and [we] are desirous of happiness and the establishment of political stability for them.
Shahanshah Aryamehr	Our policy is exactly the same.
His Majesty King Faisal	Kuwaitis do not value or respect our friendship and kindness and want to create discord between Iran and Saudi. They tell you one thing but do another. Coming face-to-face with them may be beneficial.
Shahanshah Aryamehr	They are confrontational in private negotiations too.
His Majesty King Faisal	They behave the same way with us. I swear we have no malevolent intentions toward Kuwait.
Shahanshah Aryamehr	Our policy is the same.
His Majesty King Faisal	According to reports that we have, apparently Baathist agents in Kuwait intend a coup d'état, but we are afraid to tell them this matter lest we be blamed as coconspirators.

- ۶ -

[illegible]

وزارت امور خارجه

شنبه ۱۰ آذرماه — ما هم درباره این فعالیت که چند بار با انگلیسها تذکر داده‌ایم [illegible] است اشتباه، [illegible]

در تعقیب ۱۹۵۸ عراق تکرار کرد چه حاضر نشستند این مطالب را بطور جدی [illegible]

دستوری می‌فرمایند.

اعلیحضرت همایونی — قبل از کودتای ۱۹۵۸ عراق به نوری سعید گفته شد ما اسم [illegible] کودتا کننده ولی او این حرف را نپذیرفت و گفت ما اسم [illegible] است.

شنبه ۱۷ آذرماه — روزنامه‌ها انگلیسها برای ما روشن نیست.

اعلیحضرت همایونی — ما هم در موارد [illegible] از فهم سیاست انگلیس عاجز هستیم شاید علت [illegible] و هم [illegible] نیست و دفاع آنها را [illegible] با [illegible] در احوال باشد. روزنامه [illegible] تعقیب [illegible] [illegible] است. سال گذشته موقعی که در روزنامه‌ها [illegible] [illegible] [illegible] است [illegible] [illegible] [illegible] [illegible] به آنها گفتم باید [illegible] حفظ امنیت را [illegible] [illegible] این اختیارات را [illegible] [illegible] ندارد [illegible] نباشد.

یکشنبه ۱۵ آذرماه — ما هم با انگلیسها گفتم که دانشگاه [illegible] [illegible] [illegible] [illegible] همیشه [illegible] [illegible] [illegible] [illegible] [illegible] که [illegible] با آنها [illegible] [illegible] [illegible] دارد و [illegible] آنها جواب در [illegible] که [illegible] [illegible] چه خواهند شد؟

Ministry of Foreign Affairs
Totally Confidential

Shahanshah Aryamehr	We too have warned the English a number of times about such activities. It is probable that the 1958 mistake in Iraq will be repeated because they are not willing to discuss and study these matters seriously and are dismissive of them.
His Majesty King Faisal	Before the 1958 Iraqi coup d'état, Nouri Saeed was told Ghassem wanted to mount a coup d'état but he did not accept this word and said Ghassem is like my son.
Shahanshah Aryamehr	The policy of the English is not clear for us.
His Majesty King Faisal	In some cases we too are incapable of understanding the policy of the English. Maybe the reason is ignorance and unfamiliarity with the situations and conditions. The policy they are pursuing may also threaten their interests as well. Their policy toward southern Arabia presages this same matter. Last year when I was in London I told them either take responsibility for security or cede the authority to responsible officials
Shahanshah Aryamehr	We too told the English that the London School of Economics cannot always predict the outcome of events. Lives of individuals whom you are dependent upon depends on a bullet and in their absence what will happen to your pipe dreams?

خیلی سری

وزارت امور خارجه

اعلیحضرت ملک حسین   صحیح است

شاهنشاه آریامهر   شاید انگلیسها قصاص گناهان گذشته را میدهند

اعلیحضرت ملک حسین   مگر بیش از این اهمیتی را داشتند و حالا به ترتیب درجه سوم و یا چهارم شده اند. اگر در آن گاه فعال ولا از تجربیات خود قبلها بیش از وشغل ماهیگیری را در پیش گیرند اقلا با گرفتن ماهی شکم خود را پر کنند دیگران این راه و روش خود را تعیین نمایند بخصوص از زمان این انقلاب کبیر و یا کشف آنچه ها ... ماهیگیری با آنها روابط خوب داشته باشند.

شاهنشاه آریامهر   ما هم با انگلیسها دوست هستیم ولی هرگز از آنها انتظار کمک و اتحاد صحیح کرد.

حضرات سفیر کبیر ...   انگلیسها حالا به زیارت حج اهمیت میدهند.

شاهنشاه آریامهر   بله حتی انتظار نتایج این زیارت را دارند و این مطلب از روش روزنامه‌های آنها مشهود است گرچه تظاهر انگلیسها متعرضیم که کاری با این جریانات ندارند.

اعلیحضرت ملک حسین   بله زیرا خودشان را با مسئله ثبات در منطقه محشور می‌کنند.

شاهنشاه آریامهر   یا باید مشترکاً حفظ الصلح و امنیت را برای منطقه بدهند و یا مردانه بیایند و از دخالت کاری بمانند.

Ministry of Foreign Affairs
Totally Confidential

His Majesty King Faisal	That is correct.
Shahanshah Aryamehr	Maybe the British are being punished for their past sins.
His Majesty King Faisal	They had the largest empire and now they have become a third- or fourth-rate power. If they really want to stick to their island and take up the fishing profession, they should at least tell us so that we know our task, and based on that determine our policy. By mentioning these matters I do not mean to belittle or discount the English. I want to have good relations with them.
Shahanshah Aryamehr	We too are friends with the English but it is possible to fault them and criticize them correctly.
Saudi Ambassador Marwan	The English attach a lot of importance to current consultations.
Shahanshah Aryamehr	Yes, they are quite anxious about the outcome of these talks and this matter is evident from the attitude of their newspapers, although outwardly the English say that they are not interested in these proceedings.
His Majesty King Faisal	Yes, they don't want to be associated with the issue of stability of the region.
Shahanshah Aryamehr	They must either give the responsibility for order and stability to the people of the region or come and bravely request their cooperation.

بکلی سری

وزارت امور خارجه

اعلیحضرت همایونی: این مسائل را باید جدی گرفت.

ژنرال ضیاءالحق: بلی نگرانند و تأکید میکنند که چینی‌ها و غربیان نمی‌توانند ببینند و [illegible] پیشرفت کنند.

اعلیحضرت همایونی: آنچه [illegible] ولی به نحو دیگری عمل میکنند و در نتیجه [illegible] کار خلاف انتظار است.

ژنرال ضیاءالحق: این یک دلیل ضعف است و [illegible] و جبلی آنها است. کمونیست‌ها [illegible] منظورشان [illegible] اوضاع را آشفته و درهم سازند که کسی [illegible] بدست نیاورد.

اعلیحضرت همایونی: و تا مردم [illegible] آنها حس [illegible] نکنند.

ژنرال ضیاءالحق: [illegible] صحیح را در روزنامه‌ها - با [illegible] - [illegible] - [illegible] بخش آورده‌اند.

اعلیحضرت همایونی: در مورد [illegible] هم تغییر با آنها است.

ژنرال ضیاءالحق: پس باید همه گرفت که [illegible] و جبلی است.

اعلیحضرت همایونی: در پاکستان [illegible] هم صحیح [illegible]. سرداران هم صحیح [illegible] دارند [illegible] شمال [illegible] و اجازه [illegible] و با هم ارتباط داشته باشند. اوضاع [illegible] که حکومت [illegible] شوروی [illegible].

Ministry of Foreign Affairs
Totally Confidential

His Majesty King Faisal	They must accept this responsibility.
Shahanshah Aryamehr	But they don't say and keep insisting that they cannot do this or that, but we know it is not so.
His Majesty King Faisal	They say one thing but act differently, and in some instances the result is opposite to expectation.
Shahanshah Aryamehr	This is either due to weakness or their conniving nature. After leaving an area, they are accustomed to creating such a mess and disarray that no one will have a clue.
His Majesty King Faisal	Or so that the people will regret or be envious of their departure.
Shahanshah Aryamehr	They created these conditions in Rhodesia—Biafra—Nigeria—Malaysia and Aden.
His Majesty King Faisal	About Palestine also they are to blame.
Shahanshah Aryamehr	So it can be concluded that it is their conniving nature.
His Majesty King Faisal	The same conditions exist in Pakistan and India. Sudan also has similar conditions. Northern Sudanese are not permitted to travel to the southern region or to have communication with each other. Conditions in Nigeria are so bad that their Federal Government is becoming inclined toward the Soviets.

وزارت امور خارجه

بکلی سری

شنبه ۱۰ آذرماه — کمیته مرکزی شوروی این روزها در جلسه است.

[illegible] — فقط شرکت در مراسم رسمی هستند و [illegible] شمال [illegible] مشغولند ...

[illegible] — در حضور اعلیحضرت [illegible] اظهار کردم که انگلیسی‌ها با [illegible] سر خود مشغولیت لازم دارد

پرسیدند که چرا چنین شکلی گفت برای اینکه فکر کنم چه لذتی دارد وقتی این کار را بکنم.

عرض کردم اعلیحضرت که راست برفتار ناشیانه جرج براون با ناصر بدانیم.

[illegible] — چون نمیدانیم چه حمله‌ای دیگری داشته باشد و بنابراین آنرا بحساب سیاست انگلیس نگذارد.

جرج براون که در مصر [illegible] نکند و سیاستش را آشکار دارد.

[illegible] آذرماه — وزیر خارجه ما اخیراً با جرج براون مصاحبه لفظی داشت.

[illegible] — اخیراً آدمی [illegible] و خدمات چشمگیر خاصی [illegible] دارد.

شنبه ۲۰ آذرماه — خیلی اوقات گفته است وقتی جرج براون و وزیر خارجه ما [illegible] وزارت خارجه انگلیس [illegible] با هم

صحبت میبرده بعضی از اعمال و حرکات او نشانه آدم مستقل نیست

[illegible] — [illegible] تاجر لبنانی واسطه [illegible] جرج براون و ناصر گردید.

[illegible] آذرماه — [illegible] چند هفته [illegible] طول [illegible].

Ministry of Foreign Affairs
Totally Confidential

Shahanshah Aryamehr	A Soviet economic commission is in Nigeria these days.
His Majesty King Faisal	The people in eastern Nigeria are Christians and the people in the north and center are Muslim....
Shahanshah Aryamehr	I recall a proverb that says a person kept hitting his head with a hammer. They asked him why he was doing so. He said so that I can imagine the pleasure when I stop doing it. I would like to know His Majesty the King's view about the friendly behavior of George Brown toward Nasser.
His Majesty King Faisal	I guess it was private and personal in nature and must not be credited to the English government. George Brown lived in Egypt for a while and has some friends there.
Shahanshah Aryamehr	Our Foreign Minister recently had a verbal quarrel with George Brown.
His Majesty King Faisal	Essentially he is not a bad person but has [his] own unique ethical traits.
Shahanshah Aryamehr	He is drunk most of the time. When our Foreign Minister and George Brown were appointed to their positions, they were very good friends. Some of his actions and behavior are indications of an irresponsible person.
Mr. Ardeshir Zahedi Foreign Minister	Emil Boustani the Lebanese businessman was the intermediary responsible for the friendship between George Brown and Nasser.
Shahanshah Aryamehr	He was thinking of implementing some financial projects.

- ۱۰ - .....

وزارت امور خارجه

اعلیحضرت همایونی — با تشابه رسمی زیادی کشور دوستمان بود تا تقدم و نزدیکی هست آن در موقعیت خود را تحکیم نمایند.

تیمسار آریانا — در صورتیکه با … بانگلیسها داریم و بیشتر با آنها احتیاج داریم و بالعکس روابط حسنه دوستانه با آنها داشته باشیم و چرا نمیخواهند خود را با اوضاع و احوال فعلی تطبیق دهند؟

اعلیحضرت همایونی — این نظر در مورد ما هم صادق است. ما هم میخواهیم با آنها روابط دوستانه داشته باشیم و توقع داریم حداقل نظریات ما را تا حدودی رعایت نمایند.

تیمسار آریانا — قبلاً هم عرض کردم که سیاست ما دشوار است با این تفاوت که شما خوشبختانه با شوروی که روابط سیاسی ندارید و ما بحکم تعهدات منطقه‌ای باید با آنها رابطه داشته باشیم.

اعلیحضرت همایونی — (در مورد رابطه با شوروی) مسئله‌ای که برای ما وجود دارد این است که قرآن صراحتاً قانون اساسی برای ما دارد و حکم قرآن است که با اشخاص لامذهب محشور نباشیم.

تیمسار آریانا — مقصود همین است.

25.9 10

Ministry of Foreign Affairs
Totally Confidential

His Majesty King Faisal	He mingled with and was intimate with many high officials in order to gain rank and stature and to solidify his success.
Shahanshah Aryamehr	Anyhow, we do not have a bad view of the English and are in need of trade with them and are inclined to having normal friendly relations with them. But why don't they want to reconcile themselves to current conditions and circumstances?
His Majesty King Faisal	This view is true in our case as well. We too desire to have friendly relations with them and expect that they will at least consider our views to certain extent.
[Shahanshah Aryamehr	I can say that our policy and yours are one with the difference that fortunately you do not have relations with the Soviets but due to geographic necessity, we must have relations with them.]
His Majesty King Faisal	About relations with the Soviets, the problem that exists for us is that the Koran has the role of a constitution for us, and it is Koranic law that we do not associate with people of no faith.
Shahanshah Aryamehr	You mean irreligious.

وزارت امور خارجه

اعلیحضرت ملک فیصل — آنها کوشش نمودند که با ما رابطه سیاسی برقرار کنند. ما موافقت نداریم شرط اینکه عقیده خود را عوض نمایند.

(شاهنشاه آریامهر — چون شما با آنها ارتباطی ندارید لابد تعهداتی هم در قبال آنها ندارید.)

اعلیحضرت ملک فیصل — قبلاً ما با روسها رابطه داشتیم و در حجاز سفارتخانه داشتند و بعد از الغاء و اکنون حجاز دیگر شوروی روحانی ... بوده که این است آنکه را با ... گفت و همین حالت در زمان پدرم عبدالعزیز بمسکو رفتم ولی امروز وضع کلاً تغییر کرده است.

(شاهنشاه آریامهر — باید در جهان آزاد بهتر است با اینکه احتیاج بهم و در ارتباط تجاری با شوروی هست معهذا با آنها روابط سیاسی برقرار نمود.)

اعلیحضرت ملک فیصل — اینها در این دوره از فرصت برای ما هم خالی از اشکال نیست. دیروز شیخ عبدالله سالم الصباح بشدت با تعارف بعمل داشت.

شاهنشاه آریامهر — من تصور نمیکردم او از طرفداران ناصر بود

اعلیحضرت ملک فیصل — اطلاع دارید ... در ملاقات رئیس جمهوری لبنان از ضعف ایشان اظهار نمود در جواب گفته بودم ما موافقت نمودیم که ... هم از آنها حمایت میکنیم. با وجود این کیفیات

Ministry of Foreign Affairs
Totally Confidential

His Majesty King Faisal	They tried to establish political relations with us. We don't mind on the condition that they change their beliefs.
[Shahanshah Aryamehr	Because you don't have relations with them, you do not need to be considerate of them.]
His Majesty King Faisal	Previously we had relations with the Russians and they had representation in Hejaz and after …………….. and after annexation and unification of Hejaz and Najd the Soviets were the first government to congratulate this unity and it was for this reason that during my father's time I went to Moscow but today the situation has changed completely.
[Shahanshah Aryamehr	It must be seen why Kuwait, which had no pressing need or commercial relations with the Soviets, nonetheless established diplomatic relations with them.]
His Majesty King Faisal	Origination of such policy on the part of Kuwait has not been without wonder for us either. The late Sheikh Abdullah Salem al Sabah had a favorable view of the Soviets.
Shahanshah Aryamehr	I assumed he was a supporter of Egypt.
His Majesty King Faisal	That is the way it was.… In an official visit to Kuwait some members of Parliament expressed to me that some youth demonstrated against me and were supported by the Prime Minister. Regardless of these happenings,

وزارت امور خارجه

ما طالب هستیم کویت ضعیف و دستخوش نفاق و پراکنده‌ای باشد. بنابراین ما از کمک با آنها مضایقه نداریم. ما طرفدار ضرب المثل عرب هستیم که باید انقلاب و نظام را به هم کمک کرد با این تفاوت که کمک انقلاب خود نفسه تعیین در حق اوست.

[illegible] آذرماه — کویت پول گزافی و زمینه از مصرف دارد که نمی‌داند چگونه و در چه راه خرج نماید. بهترین راه این است از کویت اخاذی کنند. [illegible] از جمله کسانی است که از کویت پول می‌گیرد.

[illegible] — با عراقی‌ها در اطراف آنها که فعالیت خاصی ندارد و انگیزه خرج کرده‌ها نباید و [illegible] شده که دیگران را منحرف سازد و کویت را از آنها تبعیت نمایند.

[illegible] آذرماه — هر درجه پول به اخاذی نفس عمل مشخصی است ... اشکال عمده دیگر در کویت این است که فاقد دستگاه رهبری است که تعداد انسجام و هم بستگی ما را تأمین و تضمین نماید.

[illegible] — جمعیت کویت در حدود ۴۰۰٬۰۰۰ نفر است که فقط ۱۲۰٬۰۰۰ نفر آن بومی هستند و بقیه بیگانه هستند و ساکنین کشور با این جمعیت قلیل ۸۰٬۰۰۰ کارمند دولت دارد. حال آنکه احتیاجی با این تشکیلات عریض و طویل ندارد و یک وزارت بلدیه می‌تواند کویت را اداره نماید.

25.11 12

Ministry of Foreign Affairs
Totally Confidential

We do not want Kuwait to be weak and prone to discord and factionalism. Nevertheless, we will not spare them any assistance. As the Arabic saying goes, one must assist both the cruel and the oppressed; the difference is that assisting the cruel is inherently punishment in its own right.

Shahanshah Aryamehr — Kuwait has an enormous amount of money, more than its expenses, which it does not know how or on what to spend, and it is for this reason that there are some who extort Kuwait. For example, Nasser is one of these people who receives money from Kuwait.

His Majesty King Faisal — No one is particularly opposed to their lavish spending and wastefulness but this type of spending should not become a means of leading others astray and making others blindly comply with their wishes.

Shahanshah Aryamehr — Paying money to an extorter is a heinous act … the main problem with Kuwait is that it lacks a leadership apparatus capable of providing and guaranteeing its unity and solidarity.

His Majesty King Faisal — The population of Kuwait is about 400,000, of which only 12,000 are native and the rest foreign. But this country with this small population has 80,000 civil servants. In reality it has no need for such a large and expansive administration and a city council can administer Kuwait.

وزارت امور خارجه

بکلی سری

جناب آقای ریاحی: کاملاً صحیح است. بخاطر دارم موقعی که تنزل نرخ نفت در جریان بود کمپانیها بما اطلاع دادند و گفتند ۳۰ میلیون دلار از عایدی نفت ما کسر خواهد شد. ما آنها جواب دادیم این امر از دخل ما در برنامه کشور ما است و نقص با هم دارد. بدان حد مقاومت کردیم تا بالاخره کمپانیها تسلیم شدند و بعد آ شنیدیم که همان مبلغ را از دیگر کمپانیها جبران کردند و آنها عصبانی هستند. ما جواب دادیم اجباری نداریم این تفاوت را بپردازیم و حال آنکه این تفاوت بالغ بر ۹۰ میلیون بالغ شد.

اعلیحضرت ملک سعود: در آمد ما از نفت تقریباً هم سطح در آمد ما است و در واردات آنها نیز نزدیک بهمان واردات ما است و حال آنکه جمعیت آنها فقط در حدود ۴۰۰/۰۰۰ نفر است.

جناب آقای ریاحی: ما اصلاً در خصوص خرید اسلحه عراق از انگلستان گذشت. ایران و عربستان سعودی نقشه واحدی علیه کسی ندارند و ... قصد ندارند ... اگر ... پول بگیرند.

اعلیحضرت ملک سعود: بهمین جهت است که ما میخواهیم با دوست خود دوست باقی بمانیم تا ... برای آنها ... دائم ...

جناب آقای ریاحی: با عراق هم میخواهیم دوست و متحد باشیم.

اعلیحضرت ملک سعود: ولی ما هم بهتر است ... آنها باید در درجه اول خودشان در فکر مصالح خود باشند.

بکلی سری

Ministry of Foreign Affairs
Totally Confidential

	Absolutely correct. I recall when the subject of devaluation of the Pound was prevalent, the companies came to us and said that 30 million dollars would be deducted from our oil revenue. We replied that it was their own internal matter and did not concern us. We resisted so much that the companies finally gave in. Later we heard that they had broached the same subject with the Kuwaitis who because of their wealth replied you have no obligation to pay us the difference, although this difference amounted to 90 million Pounds.
His Majesty King Faisal	Their national income is about the same as ours and their imports are also close to the level of our imports, while their population is only 400,000 people.
Shahanshah Aryamehr	One can fly over Kuwait in minutes. Iran and Saudi Arabia have no plan or design against anyone, but the Egyptians are determined to receive money from Kuwait under any guise.
His Majesty King Faisal	That is the reason we want to remain friends with Kuwait so that we can be useful to them.
Shahanshah Aryamehr	We too want to be friends with and useful to Iraq.
His Majesty King Faisal	That is how we think as well but in the first place they themselves must think of their own interests.

بکلی سری

وزارت امور خارجه

شاهنشاه آریامهر — در ایران ثبات و استقرار وجود دارد. در پشت حکومت کمونیستی و قسمتی آن وجود دارد.

اعلیحضرت ملک فیصل — ما هم معتقدیم که کمونیستها مسئول این وضع در عراق هستند

شاهنشاه آریامهر — بین تکریتی و عماش اختلاف نظر وجود دارد. عماش بعثی و دست چپی تلقی میشود.

اعلیحضرت ملک فیصل — فعلاً بصورت ظاهر عماش از بعثی افراطی تر شده است.

شاهنشاه آریامهر — البکر هم رویه ثابت و مشخصی ندارد. گاهی از عماش جانب داری میکند و گاهی تکریتی را نسبت بخود نزدیک میسازد.

اعلیحضرت ملک فیصل — البکر شخص مریض و تقریباً نیمه مریض است و نمیتواند موجبات اداره و ابتکار ترازان را بین حزب بعث در عراق فراهم سازد.

شاهنشاه آریامهر — گر این بار تحولی در عراق رخ دهد شاید وضع خوبی خواهد بود. عراق قصاص خیانت مجموعی را که نسبت به فیصل و خانواده اش مرتکب شده پس میدهد.

اعلیحضرت ملک فیصل — خداوند قادر و بهتر داور است. آنها بزرگ و کوچک ما را از دم تیغ بیدریغ گذراندند و بیچاره ها را آتش زدند و جسدشان را از بین بردند.

شاهنشاه آریامهر — مسئله برای ما این است که با عراق ۸۰۰ کیلومتر مرز مشترک داریم. امکان تجزیه

Ministry of Foreign Affairs
Totally Confidential

Shahanshah Aryamehr	There is no stability in Iraq. There is no government or administration in the real sense.
His Majesty King Faisal	Some think the Baathists are responsible for the situation in Iraq.
Shahanshah Aryamehr	There is a difference of views between Takriti and Ammash.Ammash is not considered a leftist Baathist.
His Majesty King Faisal	Ammash has been portrayed as an extremist Baathist superficially.
Shahanshah Aryamehr	Al Bakr does not have a stable and identifiable policy. Sometimes he supports Ammash and other times he reassures Takriti of his support.
His Majesty King Faisal	Al Bakr does not seem to be a prudent and strong person and will not be able to bring about balance between the two poles of Baath in Iraq.
Shahanshah Aryamehr	If this time there is another upheaval in Iraq, it will be bloody. Iraq will be punished and will pay for the brutal crimes committed against Faisal and his family.
His Majesty King Faisal	Without a doubt that is true. They massacred big and small cruelly and unsparingly and destroyed them like insects.
Shahanshah Aryamehr	Our problem is that we share 800 kilometers of border with Iraq. We have holy sites

وزارت امور خارجه

در آنجا داریم و هم چنین عده زیادی از آنها در عراق زندگی می‌کنند. از اعراب عراق مثلاً نگران هستیم چرا حزب بعث دست چپی که روی کار آمده و در امور [illegible] از دریای احمر تا دهانه شط العرب مجدداً [illegible] است.

[illegible] تصدیق می‌کنیم که زمینه خطر وجود دارد و به همین جهت باید با جناح بعث دست راستی مدارا کرد چرا [illegible] دست چپی در دست سیاست‌های خطرناک آنها [illegible] قرار گیرند. باید عوامل معتدل حزب بعث را در دست داشت. ما گاهی اوقات وقایع و تعدیات مرزی را از ناحیه عراقی‌ها نادیده می‌گیریم و از انتشار اخبار مربوط به این وقایع جلوگیری می‌کنیم.

[illegible] همیشه برای مدارا و همکاری با عراقی‌ها آمادگی داشته‌ام و به همین جهت با [illegible] عارف [illegible] [illegible] ولی عارف هم روی [illegible] و سقوط کرد و حالا هم [illegible] همراه با ایران بسازند. [illegible] مخالفتی نداریم ولی نمی‌دانم حکومت فعلی تا چه وقت دوام دارد.

[illegible] عوامل میانه‌رو و معتدل [illegible] باید مورد حمایت قرار گیرند.

Ministry of Foreign Affairs
Totally Confidential

	there, and also many Iranians live in Iraq. For these reasons we are very worried lest the leftist Baathists come to power and quickly establish a red empire in the neighborhood from the Red Sea to the mouth of Shat al Arab.
His Majesty King Faisal	I concur that it seems that danger exists and that is why the rightist faction of Baath must be tolerated lest the leftist extremists become tools in the hands of dangerous policies. Moderate elements of Baath must be brought under our influence. We sometimes overlook border incidents and incursions caused by the Iraqis and prevent the dissemination of news about such incidents.
Shahanshah Aryamehr	We have always been ready for moderation and cooperation with the Iraqis and for this reason we have held discussions with Mohammad Aref and Taher Yahya, but Aref did not last long and fell and now Takriti does not want to come to Iran. Of course I have no objection but do not know how long the current government will last.
His Majesty King Faisal	Moderate, centrist elements such as Takriti must be provided support.

Document 26
25 January 1969

Once again, Zahedi reporting in minute detail the conversations he had with the Soviet ambassador. In this period (1965–75) Iran had extensive ties with the Soviet Union, but as this document clearly shows, there was beneath the veneer of amity an enduring sense of mistrust, particularly from the Iranian side.

وزارت امور خارجه

پیشگاه مبارک بندگان اعلیحضرت همایون شاهنشاه آریامهر ارواحنا فداه

با عرض [illegible] با [illegible] و کسب اجازه به عرض خاک پای

ساحت [illegible]

مبارک ملوکانه می‌رساند

۱– غلام این هفته پس از تلگرافی که به پیشگاه مبارک ملوکانه عرض و محتوای جریان ملاقات

سفیر شوروی را به عرض خاک پای مبارک ملوکانه رسانیدم در روز تلگراف رسیده که St Moritz

رسیدم که به عرض مبارک ملوکانه رسید و اوامر مطاع [illegible] صادر [illegible]

آزاد هستند و [illegible] به [illegible] خودشان [illegible] مطبوعات [illegible])

[illegible] [illegible] ملاقات [illegible] چون [illegible] باشد

[illegible] تشریح کنم و با کسب اجازه به عرض می‌رساند

سفیر شوروی [illegible] صحبت [illegible] سفیر شوروی ۲۴ [illegible] گفت

[illegible] صحبت کنم [illegible] به پایان [illegible]

و او دو کار [illegible] گفت مجله [illegible] اخبار [illegible] گذشته چاپ می‌شد

و [illegible] برای چاپ فرستاده‌ایم چاپ نکرده، گفته سازمان امنیت

دستور داده چاپ نشود.

[illegible] اظهار [illegible] اطلاعی کرده و گفتم [illegible] و مطبوعات در ایران

آزاد هستند و نه وزارت اطلاعات و نه سازمان و نه وزارت خارجه [illegible]

نه تنها دخالتی نمی‌توانیم بکنیم بلکه [illegible] نخواهیم [illegible]

26.1 Emblem

Ministry of Foreign Affairs

His August Majesty

O Shahanshah With a thousand times kissing your foot and seeking permission presents . . .

1. Your servant presented your auspicious Majesty a telegram on Thursday the day before yesterday and briefly presented to His Majesty the proceedings of the meeting with the Soviet Ambassador that yesterday a telegram was received from "st Moris" that was presented for the attention of your auspicious Majesty and your orders were thus relayed (the newspapers are free and in principle it would be better if you did not enter in the business of journalism)

Dearer than my life I think in my telegraphic report I was not able to clearly describe the case because I wanted it to be brief and seeking permission I submit

The Soviet Ambassador after finishing his talk about the arrival of the Soviet Prime Minister said there was a matter I would like to discuss with you privately and in confidence this was why Pooyani went out and he and your servant stayed he said a magazine named Akhbar that used to print in the past but this time we sent for printing and they did not print saying the security organization has ordered it not to be printed.

Your servant expressed total ignorance and said I don't think so and the press is free in Iran and the Ministry of Information or the Organization or the Ministry of Foreign Affairs first of all not only cannot interfere but if we want to even do so as a favor or for friendship

وزارت امور خارجه

از این تقاضا نمی‌کنیم باعث خواهد شد هم مطبوعات ما حمله کرده و بگویند

کارمند رسمی سفارت در [illegible] دخالت و این خلاف قانون است . . .

تبلیغات این به عهدهٔ سفارت [illegible] مربوط است نه با مطبوعات و فقط برای

چاپ فرستاده بودیم و آنها چاپ نکرده و گفته‌اند از مقالات مرتب [illegible] را از

گفتم من اصلاً وارد نیستم و تعجب می‌کنم و سعی خواهم کرد تحقیق کنم و خواهشمندم که

مرتب این مقاله‌ها در جراید نگذارید و کاملاً [illegible] برگردید و باز شروع کرد

مثل جزوه‌ها را زدن

اشاره گفتم همه این البته صحبتی هم نمی‌کنند چه باشد و سعی می‌کنم

تحقیق کنم چون همه این قبیل کنم نامربوط است بعد از به مطبوعات یا

شرکت چاپ چنین دسته‌ای برگه‌ها را بعداً هم در [illegible] لندن داستانی

ما را در هم کنایه زده بودند [illegible] و سعی می‌کنند و خودشان سفینه بوده و اعلان

را در کشور ما کارهایی عجیبی نشان داده‌اند ما در کشورشان به کشور دیگر

حمله کنند چون این کار به زحمت باشد و آنها قوانین کشور ما و منجمله ایران است

شاید منظور جناب سفیر چیزی است در این باره. و آنها به قضاوت خودشان واگذار

کنند و غیره . . . هم فهمیدم در میان این درباب هم گفت متأسفم که ملاقات

و اگر مطلبی باشد بزنید هم به او گفتم کار را [illegible] سفیر کشور [illegible]

مثل [illegible] احتیاج به این جزوه‌ها ندارد و اگر کارمندی که اشتباه کرده خودش

متوجه و تنبیه شده و . . . . .

این جواب صحیح است

و اما اصل برای ایران هم جای اصلاح داشتن ولی اصلاً برای خودش [illegible] بود

26.2 2

and request them it will cause the press to attack us and say that a tenured government employee of the fourth division interfered and this is against the law. . . . then he said this is related to the Soviet Embassy magazine and not to the press and we had sent it only for printing and they did not print it and have said government authorities ordered them I said I don't have the knowledge and am surprised and will try to investigate and I request that you explain it to me better and give me more complete information and again he started to repeat what he had said.

I told him I don't know what the issue is that they are talking about and will try to investigate because I cannot accept that a government employee can give such an order to the press or a publishing company but just as it is in Moscow—London Washington Paris and elsewhere in the world all operate according to the Treaty of Vienna you yourself are an Ambassador and know that countries do not allow embassies in their country to attack other governments because this causes hardship and that is the Law of nations as well as of Iran Perhaps the Honorable Ambassador had something in mind about this and I will leave it to you yourself to judge etc. . . . . before and in the middle of this response he said you can check it and if there is an issue delete it I told him that is not my job and the Ambassador of a friendly country like yours does not need such talk and if your employee has made a mistake he will realize it and . . . .

This is the correct answer

But as to the real story your servant had the information but did not let on at all]

وزارت امور خارجه

جناب آقای نخست وزیر:

۱- سفارت شوروی چند هفته قبل این مقاله را به چاپخانه گراور مصور میبرند که چاپ کنند و آنها معذرت خواسته اند و چاپ نمیکنند تا اینکه سفارت شوروی تکلیف کند بسیار خوب ما حاضر هستیم در چاپ کنند به چاپخانه تیپهایی میبرد که انجام جواب رد میدهند

۲- همینطور سفارت شوروی مقالاتی با پول و رشوه دیگر برای اغلب روزنامه نویسها توسط کارمندان سفارت میبرد مدت ۵ سال است اینها مقالات را چاپ کنند بعضی ها اصلاً صدایش را در نیاوردند و همه چاپ کردند و بعضی ها اصلاً نمیخواهند که تکلیف نکنند.

** شاید ها اگر نظر ساواک مقدور باشد چند ماه قبل هم که روزنامه‌ها برای عرض گزارشی درباره‌ی شهربانی بردم همه که گزارشها مربوط به این امر بعضی که سفارتخانه ها مقالاتی به روزنامه ها میدهند و به آنها پول هم میدهند و بعضی روزنامه ها رسیدند نشانه

A - این عمل آنها را خاتمه بدهند و خارجی [illegible] بکنید

B - اصلاً خلاف تقریب نامه دولت در این سالها منتشر شده است

ت منن. اراده فرموده بلکه به دو غلطی است و موضوع را در هیئت دولت مطرح کنند و چاره کار را در جریان سازمان ساواک ملاحظه اطلاعات و در هیئت دولت

مطرح و در آنجا هم همه تأیید کردند در وزارت اطلاعات باید به روزنامه ها گوشزد کنند در خلاف عمل نکرده و حتی تحت دستورالعمل اگر انتشار را تکرار کنند جلوی اعلانات آنها را خواهیم گرفت و دیگر به آنها اعلان نخواهیم داد

** همینطور تکرار شد وزارت خارجه در مرتب تقریب نامه را به سفارتخانه ها

26.3 3

and did not give away any information:

1. A few weeks ago the Soviet Embassy takes their magazine to the printing house of Tehran Mosavvar for printing and they apologize and do not print it the representative of the Soviet Embassy says okay we have another place that will print it and takes it to Kayhan printing house and they too refuse

2. The same way the Soviet Embassy sends articles along with money and a bottle of vodka to most journalists through their representatives so that they print the articles for the occasion of the 50th anniversary some don't utter a word and say nothing about it and some report it and ask for guidance.

** O Shahanshah If your auspicious Majesty recalls a few months ago one of the days when I was in audience to present reports and pay respect one of the reports was related to this that some embassies provide articles to newspapers and they also give them money

> A. This action was brought to your attention that unfortunately it nurtures them as whores and makes them worship foreigners
>
> B. It is altogether against a government resolution passed a long time ago

Shahanshah Aryamehr said yes it is a wrong action and report the matter to the Ministerial Council and your servant obeyed your auspicious Majesty's commands and brought it before the Ministerial Council and there too all confirmed that the Ministry of Information must remind newspapers not to do any illegal activity and the Prime Minister said if they did such a thing we will prevent them from receiving advertising and will not give them advertising

** In the same manner it was resolved that the Ministry of Foreign Affairs will communicate the resolutions to the embassies

وزارت امور خارجه

ابلاغ کتبه و انیکا بعرض خواهد اجرا شد و به عرض رسید که وزارت تقریب نامه
۱۳۴۹/۷/۹ و ۱۳۴۸/۷/۴ را تقدیم خاکپای مبارک ملوکانه بنماید

۲- امروز سرپرست سفارت شوروی که عقب مکتوب گفتم با بی‌نیاز و با اداره مربوط ملاقات
و در تمام قرار بر ... آنها اراده کردند ۲ تا ۸ آذر ماه ایران ... برای
بلا مانع وزارت ... وسایل خواهد شد از نامه ... را
ضمیمه گزارش ... تقدیم خاکپای مبارک ملوکانه می‌دارد

۳- چنانکه ... تشکیل مطالعه در اطراف ... و ... کار ... عالی
گزارش ... را ... به عرض ... رسید. در ... عادی
مطالعه ... و ... تقریب ... اجرا گردد.

۴- نگرانی و دستور زراعتی به عرض تقدیم خاکپای مبارک ملوکانه می‌گردد

که ... مبارک را هزار بار چاکر

شنبه ۵ بهمن

ساعت ۲۳/۳۰

26.4 4

and this too was executed immediately and herewith is the text of the copy of the resolutions 7/9/1339 and 4/7/1338 presented to Your Majesty.

2 – Today the Soviet Embassy will visit twice I told Pooyani the head of the related section and on the face of it they were to receive our answer about the 2 to 8 April visit of the Prime Minister of the Soviet Union that there is no problem and the Imperial government will be happy but the aforementioned brought up the second subject about which Pooyani's exact report is presented here to Your Majesty.

3 – This afternoon a commission met to study the subject and its implications that the exact report of the commission and their views is presented to your imperial Majesty which I beg you to study and in case of approval it will be implemented.

4 – Telegrams and a few other reports are presented to Your Majesty.

From afar I kiss your auspicious foot a thousand times
your servant

Saturday 5 Bahman
Ardeshir
Time 23/30

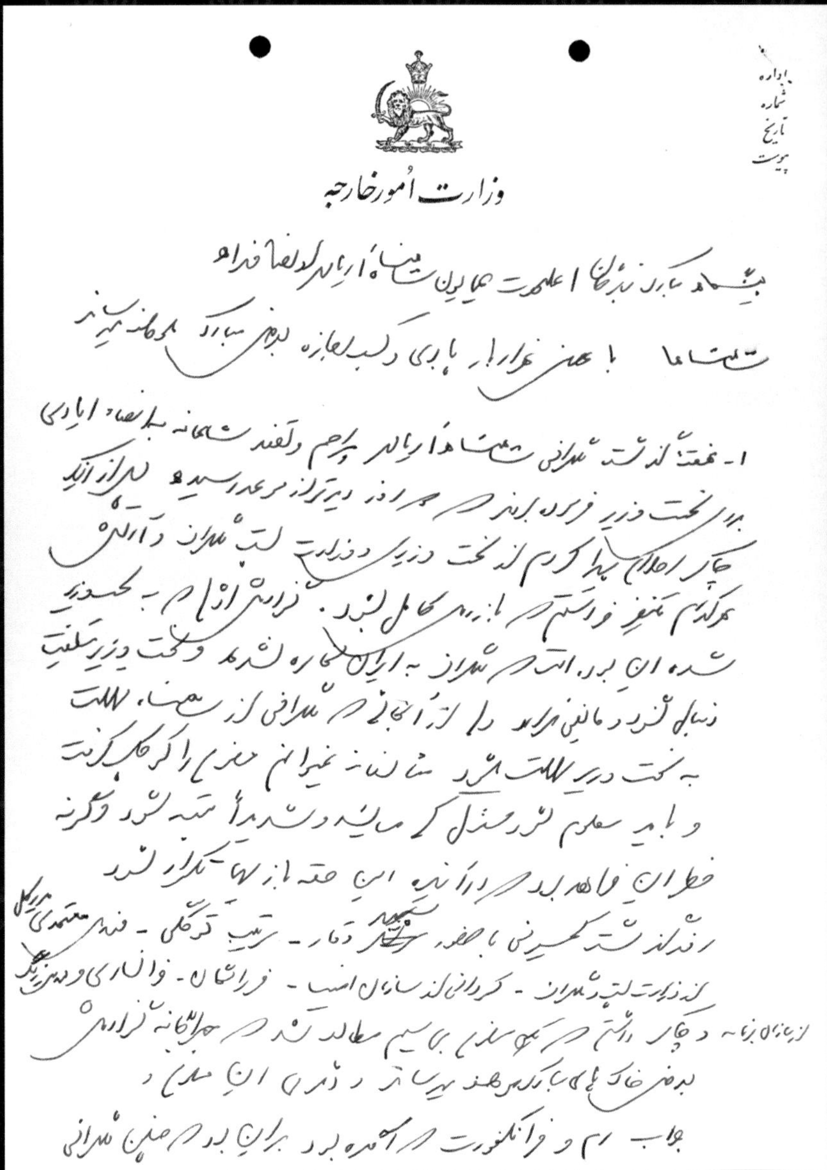

Document 27
10 February 1969

This letter from Ardeshir Zahedi, then foreign minister, to the shah, who was at the time vacationing in Switzerland, is revealing in several ways. While traveling, the shah's private physician, General Ayadi (1907–79), often acted as a de facto chief of staff, conveying critical messages to and from the shah. Secondly, the document reveals the kind of ongoing tensions between Zahedi and the prime minister, Amir Abbas Hoveyda (1919–79, prime minister 1965–77). Third, the document shows that the shah was

27.1 Emblem

Ministry of Foreign Affairs

Imperial Majesty the Shahanshah Aryamehr May Our Souls be sacrificed for Him

O Shahanshah Humbly seeking permission to present to his auspicious Majesty

1. Last week Shahanshah Aryameh's telegram signed by Ayadi for the Prime Minister said that it was received two days later than scheduled after your servant found out I asked for one person each from the Prime Minister's office the Ministry of Post and telegraph and the Army to conduct a complete inspection. The first report made to the Prime Minister said that the telegram had not been wired to Iran and the Prime Minister said do not pursue and it does not matter but from the point of view that a telegram is sent from the Shahanshah of the country to the Prime Minister of the county unfortunately one cannot make light of the matter and the culprit must be found and punished severely otherwise the danger is that in the future these shenanigans will be repeated.

Yesterday a commission was convened with participation of General Veghar—Brigadier General Tavakkoli—Engineer Motamedi Director General from the Ministry of Post and Telegraph—Kardani for Intelligence Organization—Farzanegan—Khonsari and Engineer Zerang from the Plan Organization and your servant one issue studied was the wireless the report of which will be presented separately to Your Majesty and the other was this issue and the response from Rome and Frankfurt that had been received that stated that such a telegram

اداره
شماره
تاریخ
پیوست

۲

وزارت امور خارجه

تهران را چون اکنون از مرکز منحرف ساختیم و به دستگاه‌های وزارت خارجه و وزارت [illegible] شیراز
[illegible] و کاملا رسیدگی شده و برای آنکه صدور [illegible] خاطرم راحت باشد دستور
ثابت دادم [illegible] از وزارت خارجه و [illegible] [illegible]
وزارت [illegible] شیراز را [illegible] کردم و [illegible] با [illegible] به [illegible] بروند
و از آنجا هم به [illegible] و کاملا روشن شود که چه [illegible] شیراز
فرستاده شده و با مقصد [illegible]

با [illegible] های [illegible] [illegible] [illegible] [illegible] [illegible] [illegible]
[illegible] [illegible] [illegible] [illegible] به [illegible] [illegible]

۱ - [illegible] [illegible] به کی صادر شده

۲ - چه [illegible] [illegible] [illegible] [illegible] [illegible] را خورده اند

۳ - [illegible] از [illegible] [illegible] به [illegible] [illegible] [illegible] [illegible]
به [illegible] و یا [illegible] [illegible] [illegible] [illegible] [illegible] کرده [illegible]
برده اند

۴ - چون این احتمال [illegible] [illegible] [illegible] [illegible] [illegible] [illegible] از [illegible]
[illegible] [illegible] [illegible] [illegible] باشد و [illegible] را [illegible] و یا
[illegible] [illegible] [illegible] باشد و [illegible] [illegible] شده [illegible]
[illegible] با هم ساخته باشند

با استعجال
به تهران [illegible]
[illegible] [illegible]
[illegible] [illegible]
[illegible] [illegible]
[illegible] [illegible]
دارد

27.2 2

did not exist but because I wanted live evidence and the instruments of the Ministry of Foreign Affairs and Ministry of Post and Telegram were thoroughly checked but so that my mind would be at ease one hundred percent that this was not a snow job I appointed Shilati from Ministry of Foreign Affairs and Engineer Akhavani head of the communication section of Ministry of Post and Telegraph for the two to fly to Frankfurt tomorrow morning and from there to St. Moritz to get to clarify what exactly happened what time the telegram was wired and who was to blame

With apologies and begging your pardon I request that if you desire and if your servant's request is accepted to inform your servant

1. Who were you Imperial commands issued to

2. When were your Imperial commands issued

3. In case from the time the Shahanshah issued the order to a person and that person relayed the command to a second or third person who were these people that received the imperial command

4. There is also the possibility that the two or three people responsible for communications either before wiring or while writing the telegram may have forgotten and left the telegram in their pocket or on their mind and when they realized instead of telling the truth, colluded out of fear

Either directly to Bahrami or through Ayadi in any case Bahrami says he has the confirmation of the receipt of the telegram from Tehran

۳

اداره
شماره
تاریخ
پیوست

وزارت اُمور خارجه

سیستم‌ها را از هم استدعا کنم که ما هم در این تشکیلات را [illegible] سازیم و آنهم
مستقلاً برای روشن شدن مطلبی می‌باشد در ادارات شاهنشاهی باید اسامی
و خطاکاران را به کیفر مجازات سخت رساند چون گناه گناهی است بسیار
بزرگ.

۲- سفیر آمریکا در مهمانی [illegible] جنرال [illegible] گفت شاهنشاه آریامهر
دقیقاً چه موقع به ایران تشریف فرما خواهند شد چون سلطان [illegible] می‌خواهد
و نمی‌دانست کی برسد. چاکر عرض کردم شاید [illegible] به [illegible] بروند
شاید خواسته باشند [illegible] شاهنشاه آریامهر را بدانند. ولی چون مطلقاً
خبر چاکر نبود و برای آرام [illegible] کند ممکن شاید در حدود دهم و یا یازدهم ماه
ولی قطعی نمی‌دانم و شاید هم زودتر تشریف فرما گردند. آیا اگر
علاقه دارید [illegible] حدود چه روزی [illegible] تحقیق کنم. گفت تا چند روز
دیگر خواهد گفت که قطعی دانستن تاریخ [illegible] لازم است و آیا در صورت
سفر قطعی شاهنشاه ممکن است زودتر تشریف فرما گردند یا نه

۳- [illegible] رسیده [illegible] تقاضای [illegible] آمده که از روز [illegible] بعد از ظهر رسیده
فوراً [illegible] شد [illegible] سفیر [illegible] رسیده فوراً [illegible]
شد و چند دقیقه قبل [illegible] عیناً [illegible] شد
حضرت [illegible] خاک پای مبارک [illegible]

قاعدتاً [illegible] از آن [illegible] برگردیم [illegible] امر البته اگر [illegible] می‌توانم زودتر هم بیایم

27.3 3

O Shahanshah again I beg your pardon for posing these questions and that is only to clarify the issue that is the commands of the Shahanshah Aryamehr and the culprit must be punished very severely because the sin is a very big sin

2. At Hesarak's [Zahedi's residence in Tehran] Abgoosht party [a favorite Persian food] the American Ambassador was asking when exactly is Shahanshah Aryamehr returning to Iran because he was not sure and could not say what he wanted your servant thought maybe Nixon who is going to Europe maybe wanted to know Shahanshah Aryamehr's schedule. But because he was not sure I replied I think maybe around the tenth or eleventh of March but I do not know for sure and he may return earlier. If you would like to know exactly one hundred percent I can find out for you. He said he will say in a few days whether it is essential to know the exact date or not and if there is an important issue whether the Shahanshah could return earlier or not.

Probably I will not return later than 5th of March of course if it is a very important matter I can return earlier

3. Telegrams received from Iraq and the confidential report that was received this afternoon that was telegraphed immediately also tonight Pirasteh's detailed report was received that was telegraphed immediately and a few minutes ago Khalatbari's telegram was received that too was telegrammed verbatim Minutes of discussions are hereby presented to Your Majesty

۴

وزارت امور خارجه

۵- تظاهرات مختلف در چاپار فکر کردم ممکن است در روز کوچ شاهانه و گرنه بعد
هر نوع رسید لیکن خاک های مبارک [illegible] شود.

۶- تلگرافی از [illegible] رسیده در حین لیکن خاک های مبارک [illegible] شود در
در صورتیکه استدعای چاکر حدود قبل [illegible] ارائه [illegible] گردد
گردد از آنجائی که ممکن است سرعت عمل لازم باشد و در صورتیکه نامه‌ای
بعد مبارک باید برسد مانعی نداشته باشد

۱- جواب نامه تهیه شود و فوراً برای [illegible] ارسال گردد

۲- غلام اجازه برای هواپیما [illegible] اجازه [illegible] داشته باشم که مجدداً
خبر رسید که [illegible] تهران هواپیمای فوری بخواهم

۳- هرگونه خبری مربوط به این [illegible] و [illegible] وقت کم کردن
خطر داشته باشد چاکر اجازه داشته باشم از روی مصلحت
و با مشورت [illegible] وزیر و سایرین اقدام لازم بعمل آید

اختیارات کامل دارید

درباره [illegible] و غیره با [illegible] صحبت کردم و [illegible]
[illegible] لازم خواهد داشت فوراً [illegible] با هواپیما برای آوردن
ایشان [illegible] بفرستند
البته اینها در صورتی است که [illegible] عمل شود

27.4 4

5. Various reports that your servant deemed may be of interest to His Majesty are hereby presented to Your Majesty.

6. A report was received from Zelli that is hereby presented to Your Majesty.

7. In case your servant's plea is accepted by Shahanshah Aryamehr dearer than my life since there may be times when speedy action is necessary and in cases when letters that need to be brought to the honored attention and there is no objection

1. Response to the letter to be prepared and sent immediately for signature

2. Your servant to have prior permission for military aircraft so that as soon as information is received I can request an aircraft from the Air force Staff

3. Any type of information that was related to this issue and it was possible that when lost would be dangerous your servant to have permission in the interest of and consultation with the Prime Minister and others to take immediate action

I spoke to Nassiri about protection etc. and because he was leaving today for Saudi Arabia he appointed a representative who will immediately provide the group that will be immediately needed to fly and bring back this son of a bitch.

You have full authority

Of course all this in case God willing the issue becomes local

۵

اداره
شماره
تاریخ
پیوست

وزارت امور خارجه

غلام ابداً تا امروز وقتی عرضی ابراز نکردم و امیدوارم در اثنا از سلامت کامل
برخوردار باشند و در اینجا خجل هستم که وقتی در انجام [illegible] شاهنشاه عذر تأخیر کردم
برای اینکه همت گذارند خواهشمند هستند مرتب مراسم [illegible] را داشته باشند [illegible]
و همراه با [illegible] [illegible] چاکر
[illegible]

دوشنبه ۲۱ بهمن
ساعت ۲۰

27.5 Your servant does not have anything new or worthwhile to report and hope that God willing he will be healthy and successful and I am constantly ashamed that even when the Shahanshah who is dearer than my life has gone for rest I am constantly intruding and I beg forgiveness

Your servant
Ardeshir
Monday 21 Bahman
Time 20

THE ROYAL PALACE,
Amman, Jordan,
July 28, 1969.

our Imperial Majesty My Good Brother,

I extend to Your Imperial Majesty my sincere and brotherly greetings, oupled with my repeated gratitude for the kindness with which You receive e whenever I have the pleasure of visiting Teheran.

I recall with satisfaction our talks during my last visit and I regret o inform Your Imperial Majesty that the situation in our area has not mproved since. On the contrary, we find ourselves slowly moving away from ny hopes of a just, lasting, and peaceful settlement. We fear that we might e confronted with a resumption of hosilities even sooner than we had expected.

This, naturally, increases our burden, and makes it necessary for us to repare ourselves for the worst. We can only do that if we have the support f our dear brothers in the Muslim World. Thus I find myself turning to Your mperial Majesty for help, since I have always regarded you as my dearest and loset brother.

The Royal Jordanian Air Force is in need of at least two or three C-130 ransport aircraft. We are also in need of any number of antiaircraft guns. sincerely hope that Your Imperial Majesty will consider our request favourably nd deem it proper to loan us some of this badly needed equipment.

I am grateful for Your Imperial Majesty's indulgence, and I pray to the lmighty to preserve You so You may continue Your noble efforts for the glory f Your brotherly nation and the Muslim World as a whole.

Your Sincere brother
Hussein

is Imperial Majesty
ohammad Reza Pahlavi,
hahinshah Aria Mehr,
E H E R A N.

28.1 **Document 28**
28 July 1969

The shah had a particularly close relationship with King Hussein of Jordan (Hussein bin Talal, 1935–99, reigned 1952–99). In the 1960s and 70s, the Jordanian monarch was often a welcome guest in Tehran, enjoying the hospitality of the shah and receiving on many occasions gifts and grants from the Iranian government. As Iran's income from oil increased, this hospitality and the accompanying grants and gifts increased and often helped the beleaguered Jordanian monarchy, which faced at the time an increasingly militant Palestinian population in the kingdom. Jordan was not among the places that offered the shah even temporary refuge after the revolution when the latter was in a desperate place for exile.

Document 29
10 February 1970

Here is another example of Ardeshir Zahedi's detailed reporting to the shah. By this time, tensions between Iran and Iraq were reaching new heights. Zahedi seems to be advocating a show of force and the shah suggesting that Iran had to at least appear to be calm and deliberate. Zahedi also seeks justice for a colleague who seems to have been denied fair treatment. Also of note is Zahedi's effort to influence the shah in the appointment of senators. According to the constitution of Iran, the sixty-person senate was composed of two types of senators: those directly elected by the people (half of the entire body) and the remaining thirty to be appointed by the shah. Zahedi had a long-running feud with Iran's Freemasons, thought commonly in Iran to be agents of the British conspiracy and exemplifying the omnipotent "British hand" in Iranian politics. Here Zahedi is trying to convince the shah to appoint a new senator in place of the deceased Taqizadeh, known to be a leading member of the Freemasons, and one of the leaders of the constitutional revolution (1905–07).

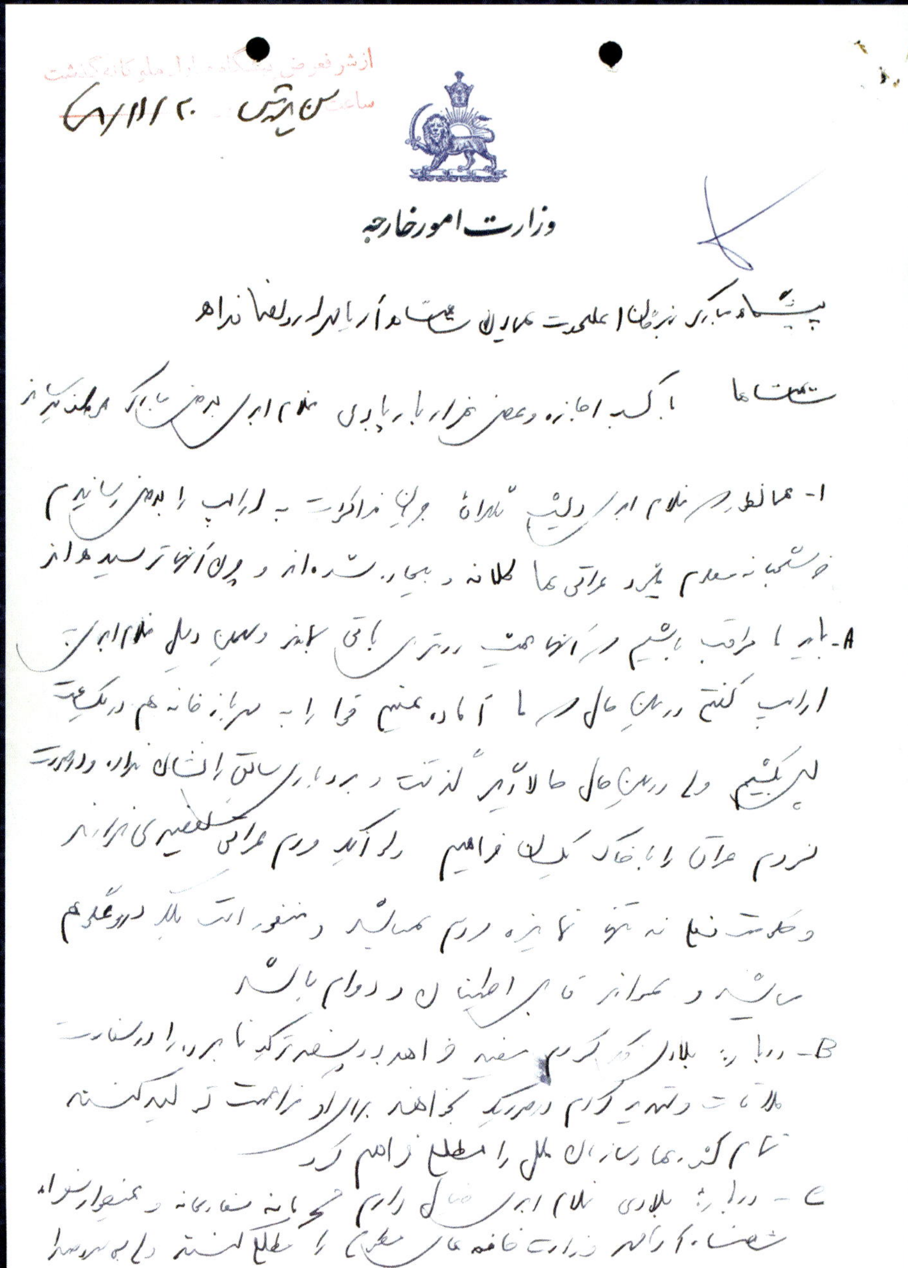
وزارت امور خارجه

29.1 Presented to His Imperial Majesty
Time St. Moritz 20/11/38

Emblem

Ministry of Foreign Affairs

His Auspicious Majesty the Shahanshah Aryamehr May Our Souls be sacrificed for Him

O Shahanshah Seeking permission and humbly presents to his auspicious Majesty

1. As your servant reported telegraphically last night regarding discussions with Eramp fortunately it is understood that the Iraqis are enervated and enfeebled and because they have become frightened

A. We must be careful that they always remain two meters away and it is for this reason that your servant told Eramp While we are ready to withdraw our forces to barracks within one hour but at the same time this time we will not have the tolerance and patience of the past and if necessary we will raze Iraq to the ground despite the fact that the people of Iraq have no blame and the current government not only is not representative of the people and is hated but rather is a liar who cannot be trusted and cannot last

B. About Beladi I thought it would be useful for the Turkish Ambassador to meet the aforementioned at the embassy and threatened him that if he wanted to create problems for him I will inform all the countries of the United Nations

C. About Beladi your servant has in mind to confidentially inform all the embassies and Shahanshah Aryameh's ambassadors as well as the related Ministries but without a lot of noise

وزارت امور خارجه

D- نظام ایران که ما می‌گوییم حالا بیشتر از هر وقت [illegible] قطعاً [illegible] قوا و قدرت ما لازم است [illegible] و همین [illegible] در هر [illegible] به یک [illegible] و وحشت [illegible] خودکار [illegible] [illegible] بر عراق شده

(حاشیه: [illegible])

E- چون در حالت ترس و وحشت [illegible] دیگر است [illegible] دست کنیم شده [illegible] در [illegible] حال [illegible] مراقب شده [illegible] باشیم [illegible] کلاه [illegible] یک بار وحشت [illegible] ما [illegible] خواسته [illegible] شده [illegible] و [illegible] [illegible] آتش [illegible] ۳ آتش [illegible] آتش [illegible] خاک [illegible] کنند

F- نظام ایران وضع [illegible] و [illegible] ما [illegible] و آنچه [illegible] [illegible] عراق [illegible] بادی [illegible] [illegible] نه [illegible] بلکه [illegible] برای [illegible] ما [illegible] است

۲- همه [illegible] نظام ایران [illegible] خرج می‌کنیم وقت صرف می‌کنیم و از همه [illegible] حسن نیت داریم و بالاتر از همه اراده [illegible] شاهانه [illegible] به [illegible] مردم برسانیم و از [illegible] پرهیز کنیم و [illegible] [illegible] نیاز داریم ولی [illegible]

29.2 2

D. Your servant thinks that now more than any other time we must demonstrate our forces and power and this demonstration on the border may have been the reason for the fear and terror of these wild barbaric Iraqi bloodsuckers

On the contrary we must demonstrate calmness

E. Because they live in fear and terror they may have split into two groups and at the same time we must monitor them very closely so that because of frustration or fear or to create terror among us they do not take some action and if they want to do it they are rebuffed solidly and as you have said wherever a fire is started the fire and the area of fire should be razed to the ground

F. Your servant sees the conditions as good and very very much in our favor and what we had wanted to achieve as punishment for the Iraqi government and regime we may have achieved more and the result was not only defeat but success and the Iraqis have no reputation left

2. Dearer than my life in the view of your servant we spend money we spend time and most important of all we have goodwill and above all it has been and is the royal determination to help the people and to stay away from dragging our feet and not to keep for tomorrow what can be done today but unfortunately maybe we have not yet succeeded in this department

۳

وزارت امور خارجه

موفق شده‌ایم

تمام این مدت هشت ماه را با در خبر نرده‌ام رسیده‌اید نه در چند روز قبل هم

کار را همکاری به وزارت خارجه می‌رفتم و معمولاً از منزل تا سر جاده را پیاده

می‌روم. درس فرانسه را به جای کار از راحت و با یک لغات بزرگ

لغت مترادف فرانسه را آنان ببرند. با ... سال قرار ...

آنان نزد خودشان آرام باشند هم مترادف به هر کار نزد دقت

برای دفاع ... بازگذاشتن و به طرف او ببرند و منصرفشان کردم

... این بیچاره به گریه ... برای ... متأسفانه چرا انکار

... مترادف نکنند چون بیش از ۶ ماه است که از وزارت

خارجه به تخت ... و تخت ... به وزارت کار و خلاصه

این ... ۷ بچه مثل ... به انتظار ...

... شده و بالاخره هم کسی به کارشان نرسیده

متأسفانه این روزها که آمده ... باشد ... بیش از صد سال

... در تهران زندگی کرده و در نجف به دنیا آمده ...

احساسات ایرانی داشته ... و شکسته ... و بالاخره

29.3 3

one hundred percent

I don't know whether or not it was brought to the attention of Shahanshah Aryamehr dearer than my life that a few days ago your servant was going to the Foreign Ministry from Hesarak [Zahedi's residence] and usually I walk from my house to the main road. A man threw himself in front of your servant and with two large bottles said [he] wanted to set fire to himself. I must say that if instead of wanting to set fire to himself even if he wanted to hit me on the head with a stone there would be no time for defense anyway I prevented it and jumped toward him and dissuaded him and after that the poor man started to cry and lament do you know why he wanted to do that because it is more than six months that he is being passed around from the Ministry of Foreign Affairs to the Prime Minister's office and from the Prime Minister's office to the Ministry of Labor and in short this unfortunate man with seven children was thrown around like a football and finally no one resolved his problem and do you know where this man came from he is an Iranian whose family lived in Iraq for over a hundred years and was born in Najaf and because he had Iranian sentiments he was tortured and finally

۳۰

وزارت امور خارجه

به کشور شما صلح آمده است و سرگردان و بیچاره دیگر نیست فقط دفعه
روی زیستن علاقه و وحیدان نامردی بابان زور را نشان اداره انتظار عمل میکنند
اگر هم اینها موردی به ایران رجعت کنند خواهد گفت این رفتاری که بود
ریا با شده.

اگر عراقی‌ها بخواهند تردد دوستی در کشور ما راه اندازند از ایران آزاد
بیچاره و گله همه خبر که نیست خوب میتوانند استفاده کنند که سید از
گرسنگی بیچارگی و ستمکاری در دجله در عذاب است که هم فکر دیگر ندارد

چاکر منتظرم شکایت و گله از هیچ نزدی نسبت فقط میخواهم لذتی ببرم
تنها موردی که مشکل است که دست عمرت و خود بی‌آزاری را کلانه در کجا نیز
نامه [illegible] [illegible] این هم این است که اگر در فرمایند به دولت آمد [illegible]
با مقامات مربوط این [illegible] شده باشد این مسائل را چه از لحاظ انسانی و چه
وضع ما از لحاظ رهبرانی قدری جدی‌تر گرفته و [illegible] بخصوص ایالات
روشن کنید در دولت دیگر ایران هستند برسند. [illegible] صبح با
تحت [illegible] صحبت کردم الحمد لله [illegible] کرده و الله [illegible] خود [illegible]
مطالب را [illegible] به عرض برسانم

29.4 4

came to the imperial country and hapless and poor and hungry only and only because of heartless officials who do not care and treat such people like this and if these people go back to Iraq someday they will say this is the way we were treated.

If the Iraqis wanted to create fear and terror in our country they could use these poor and hopeless people those who from hunger wretchedness and responsibility for wife and children who are in agony maybe cannot think or breathe your servant does not mean to complain about any particular person but wanted to bring to your attention how can it be possible that a royalist who is also harmless is frustrated and offended as such your eternal slave entreats you to order and prescribe without referring to any complaints about anyone that these types of cases be taken more seriously from a human and moral point of view to help people particularly this group who are helpless and disoriented. Thursday morning I spoke to the Prime Minister at length of course he said he will also order it but I saw it as my duty to bring it the attention of my God's shadow.

You are assigned to take up the issue with relevant officials and clarify the situation

۵

وزارت امور خارجه

۳- عزیز ترزا جان [illegible] شاید [illegible] [illegible] از نظر ما [illegible] باشد

که سه سال قبل اداره [illegible] [illegible] هویدا [illegible] فرمودند و او اخیراً هم باز

ادارات [illegible] به جهت دیر اجرا. نظر ما [illegible] [illegible] در سال گذشته

در امور [illegible] [illegible] و [illegible] اگرچه [illegible] پول میخواهد حسب الامر هم

گفت در مقابل شاه هم من جواب میدهم ولی پول نمیدهم چون وظیفه خودمان

[illegible] [illegible] [illegible] کار کردم با [illegible] [illegible] [illegible] دارد با احساسات

[illegible] [illegible] [illegible] [illegible] حالا [illegible] [illegible] مرحوم شده از دیگری

تقی زاده [illegible] [illegible] [illegible] [illegible] باشد [illegible] [illegible] شاید صلاح بدانند

تقی زاده [illegible] [illegible] [illegible] [illegible] [illegible] تقی زاده با هویدا [illegible] هویدا فعلاً

[illegible] [illegible] [illegible] [illegible] تقی زاده [illegible] اگر [illegible] بهر حال

[illegible] [illegible] [illegible] [illegible] و [illegible] هویدا [illegible] [illegible] و [illegible] باشد

در حقیقت [illegible] [illegible] [illegible] [illegible] [illegible] [illegible] [illegible] خجالت

کشیدم.

[illegible] [illegible] [illegible] [illegible] [illegible] [illegible] خدا [illegible] [illegible] [illegible]

[illegible] [illegible] [illegible] [illegible] [illegible] [illegible] [illegible] [illegible]

شنبه ۱۸ [illegible]

29.5 5

3. Dearer than my life maybe I am meddling again anyhow if you recall from three years ago you issued some orders about Heda and also recently again your royal commands to the Prime Minister were executed Your auspicious memory recalls that in the past year you ordered and your servant told him how much money he wanted so that I can pay it per your orders He said for my king I will give my life but will not accept money because I see it as my duty

Anyhow dearer than my life I thought with your charitable view of the aforementioned and the sentiments that I know he possesses now that two senators have passed away and one is Taqizadeh who is from Azerbaijan I would like to remind you that maybe you would deem it advisable to make him a Senator because the difference between Taqizadeh and Heda in your servant's view is that Heda was and is a devotee of the Shah and Taqizadeh was a devotee of what the English ordered. Anyhow this is what came to your servant's mind and Heda himself is totally unaware and is in Azerbaijan and it is a shame that as of late I used to hide from him because I was ashamed.

Taghizadeh was not a senator anymore

I will not bother the one who is dearer than my life and shadow of my God and kiss the foot of dearer than my life a thousand times and God willing you will enjoy yourself

Your servant
Ardeshir
Saturday 18 Bahman

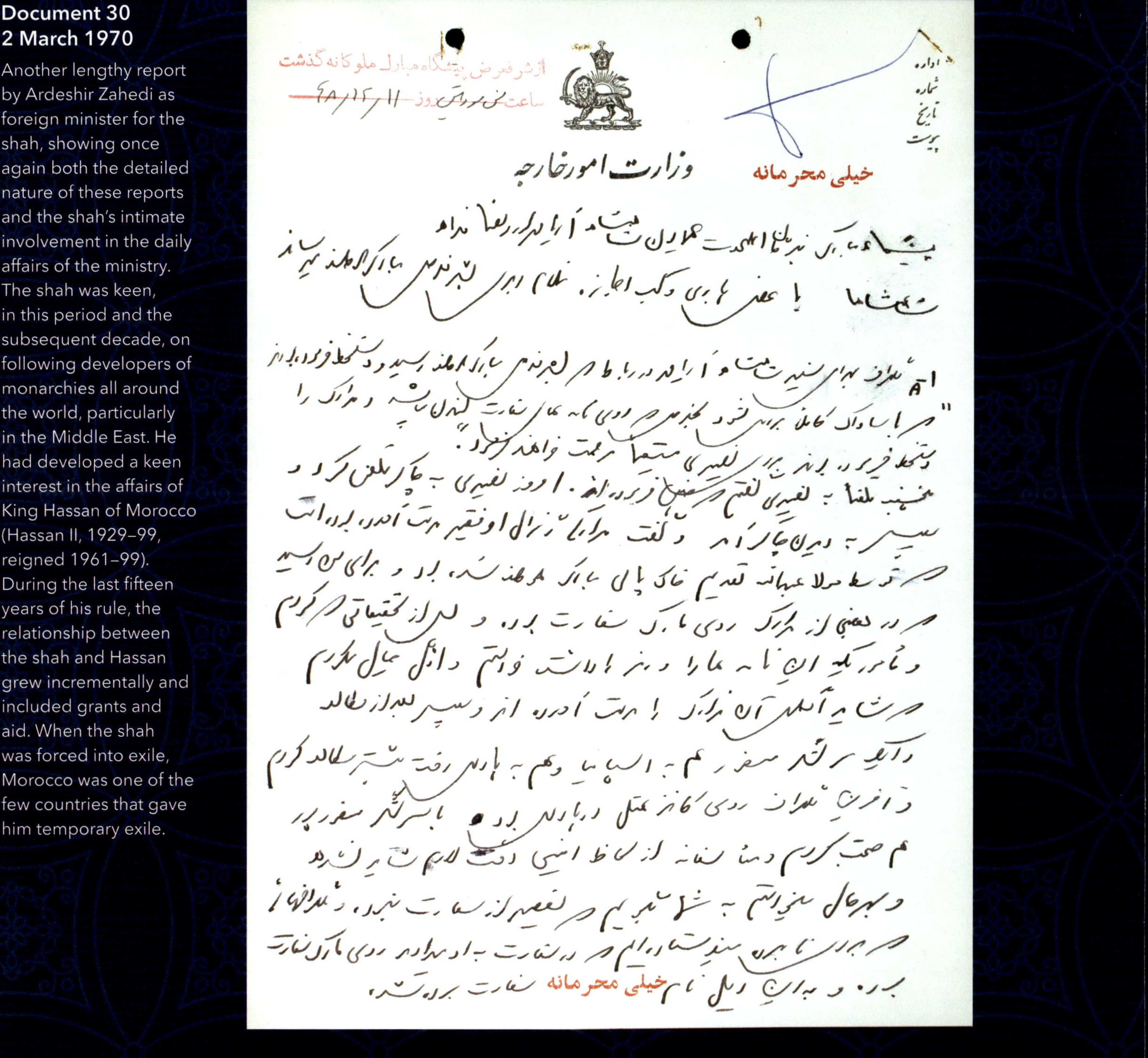

Document 30
2 March 1970

Another lengthy report by Ardeshir Zahedi as foreign minister for the shah, showing once again both the detailed nature of these reports and the shah's intimate involvement in the daily affairs of the ministry. The shah was keen, in this period and the subsequent decade, on following developers of monarchies all around the world, particularly in the Middle East. He had developed a keen interest in the affairs of King Hassan of Morocco (Hassan II, 1929–99, reigned 1961–99). During the last fifteen years of his rule, the relationship between the shah and Hassan grew incrementally and included grants and aid. When the shah was forced into exile, Morocco was one of the few countries that gave him temporary exile.

از شرف عرض پیشگاه مبارک ملوکانه گذشت

ساعت ... روز ۴۸/۱۲/۱۱

اداره
شماره
تاریخ
پیوست

وزارت امور خارجه

خیلی محرمانه

خیلی محرمانه

30.1 Viewed by His Majesty

Time St. Moritz Day 11/12/48 Very Confidential

Emblem
Ministry of Foreign Affairs

His Imperial Majesty the Shahanshah Aryamehr May Our Souls be sacrificed for Him

O Shahanshah Seeking permission your servant presents to your auspicious Majesty

1-A The telegram from Bahrami His Majesty's Ambassador in Rabat was brought to His Majesty's auspicious attention and you had jotted down "that should be investigated by SAVAK particularly because they are on letters of the embassy in London and you had jotted the documents will be sent to Nassiri directly"

I called Nassiri Thursday and told him it was so ordered. Today Nassiri telephoned your servant and then came to see me and said that he had received the documents General Oufkir has obtained that were presented to His Majesty by Molay Abdullah and some of the documents had the Embassy emblem and after the investigation that I performed and questioned the agent who had examined the documents at first I thought that the English might have had their hands on the documents but after studying it and that Lieutenant General Mansour traveled to Spain and Paris and I studied it more and the last telegram was on paper from a Paris hotel I also spoke to Lieutenant General Mansourpour and unfortunately from a security standpoint maybe enough attention was not paid and anyhow I want to tell you that the fault was not with the embassy and the telegrams that we used to send to the aforementioned that was given to him at the embassy was on embassy paper and that is why the name of the embassy is mentioned

اداره
شماره
تاریخ
پیوست

وزارت امور خارجه

خیلی محرمانه

و بنظر می‌رسد در پاریس [illegible] به دست آنها افتاده و عکس برداری کرده‌اند
تا گزارش کامل را مستقیماً به عرض نخواهم رسانید و چون نام سفارت لندن بوده
خواستم به عرض مبارک برسانم که می‌توانید کسی برسانید که سفارت در این مورد
تقصیری ندارد.

B - درباره کارهای امنیتی با هم صحبت کردیم و تأکید شد که صلاح باشد
وزارتخانه فقط مأمورینی در سفارتخانه‌ها داشته باشند که پوشش دیپلماتیک
داشته باشند چون سفارتخانه متعرض و لقب [illegible]
خواهد برد اصلاً کاری نشاید چون وقتی توسط سفارت ایران متعرض
شوند به هر حال هیچ کسی مطلع خواهد شد و کمک در کارهای
دانشجویان در ایران ما کمک می‌کنیم آنها باید مأمورین ساواک را بفرستند
وگرنه [illegible] بدون نتیجه خواهد ماند. قرار شد تصمیمی در این
باره فکر کنند و نتیجه آن را اطلاع بدهند.

۲ - هاری کرن روز یکشنبه به ایران خواهد آمد و بعد روز دوشنبه از راه
از طریق بیروت به عربستان سعودی برای دیدار اعلیحضرت ملک فیصل می‌رود
A - شکایت در [illegible] را به تهران فرستاده و سفیر
با نخست وزیر [illegible] ملاقات خواهد کرد

خیلی محرمانه

B - از وضع عربستان سعودی اظهار نگرانی می‌کرد

and it seems that these documents got into their hands in Paris and were photographed and the entire report will be presented and because it was the London embassy I wanted to tell you that you can apprise (his Majesty) that the embassy had no blame in this matter.

B. We spoke about security measures maybe it is advisable that from now on only agents that need diplomatic cover should be introduced as members of the embassy and the surname of all others should not be known to anybody because when they are introduced through the embassy a few people will know anyhow and particularly on issues concerning students and Iranians I think they should not recognize SAVAK agents otherwise their efforts will be in vain. It was agreed that Nassiri would think about this and tell us the result later.

2. Harry Kern had come to Iran Thursday and left the next day for Saudi Arabia via Beirut for a meeting with His Majesty King Faisal

A. He said that Nixon had replied to the Shahanshah's letter telegraphically and that the Ambassador will meet the Prime Minister this week

B. He expressed concern about the situation in Saudi Arabia

اداره
شماره ۳
تاریخ
پیوست

وزارت امور خارجه

خیلی محرمانه

۲- درباره اسرائیل و ایران از قول سفارتی شما صحبتی کردم چون از مطالب
جواب نگرفتن با اطلاع [illegible] که کردم شاید سفارتی شما به او گفته‌ام
با چاکر در میان گذارده و به این دلیل [illegible] و جواب چاکر
به او را لازم دیدم که فرصتی [illegible] اطلاع برسانم

* [illegible] آنها به او گفته از ارتش نیروی هوائی قرار دادی با Israel Aircraft Ind.
بزرگترین کمپانی اسرائیل بسته شد و همه او را می‌شناسند. قرار دادی
برای تعمیر هواپیما بسته. هواپیماهائی از نوع C130. و F.5. F.4.
و هواپیماهای شرکت هواپیمائی ایران و هلیکاپتر انگلیس را خواهد کرد و
قرار است ۲۰۰ اسرائیلی به ایران بیایند و مبلغ این پروژه ۲½ میلیون دلار
و به ۳۰ میلیون دلار خواهد رسید و قرار دادی بسته شد در همین شرکت [illegible] بعد
[illegible] را خواهد داشت و [illegible] آمریکائی [illegible] همکاری ایران
و [illegible] است و [illegible] متخصصین اسرائیل از حالا میخواهند در مورد
F.4 مطالعه کنند.

به [illegible] گفتم: اولاً از چنین خبری بی‌خبر هستم ولی مسخره است
که ما ایران [illegible] داریم [illegible] هم خدا را میخواهد و هم خرما
[illegible] آمریکائی [illegible] هم خدا را میخواهید و هم خرما

خیلی محرمانه

30.3 3

C. He discussed what the people at the embassy said about Israel and Iran and because he knew the contents of Nixon's response I thought maybe the people at the embassy had told him so that he shares it with me and for this reason I will relate his exact words and your servant's response as I saw it necessary to have the honor to present it to your auspicious imperial Majesty

* He said they had told him that the Army Air Force had an agreement with [Israel Aircsraft Ind.,] which is the largest Israeli company and everyone knows it has made an agreement for repair of aircraft for aircraft types "F.4 F.5, C130." and will be repairing aircraft of Iran Airlines Company and helicopters and 200 Israelis are to come to Iran and the start of this project will cost 2½ million dollars and will reach 30 million dollars and is an agreement that no other company will have the capability of performing and the Americans are worried about the relations between Iran and Saudi Arabia and particularly because from now Israeli specialists want to *study about "F.4"*

I told Kern: first of all regarding this news I am unaware of such news but it is farcical here that we Iranians have a saying that "they want God and the dates" (want to have the cake and eat it too) and you Americans in reality want to have your cake and eat it too.

۴

اداره
شماره
تاریخ
پیوست

وزارت امور خارجه

خیلی محرمانه

از شما شخصاً میخواهم امروز و فردا میکنید از شما خواهش میخواهم همراه معذور
هر از گاهی شاه را نادیده برای تضمین و بهره اشغال تراشی میکنید و چرا چه
اسرائیل و یک کشور دیگری ما نمیتوانیم دخالت نکنیم شما خودتان با اسرائیل
صحبت و همکاری میکنید وقتی وقتی رئیس جمهور فرانسه مهمان کشور شما است
شهردار شما در یک میهمانی شام او را بدرقه کمک میکنند هر
با اسرائیل هم رزمی نمیکنند و همین فرانسوی ها هستند در ۱۹۴۷
به مصر حمله کردند و شما هم جلوی آنها را گرفتید و حالا هنوز صحبت
میکنید من دائماً هم در صحبت هستم

گفت مغرضی در میکنید تبدیل دارم ولی شما میگوئید عربستان سعودی
از نجات رسیده و تجارت ایران متوقف میکند آمریکا هم از پول
حمایت میکند خود شما گفتید ما از آمریکائی ها هم معروف شده ایم به
طرفداران اسرائیل دیگر رزمی نخواهیم با ملک فیصل میکنیم نه تنها او را
تکذیب نکرده ایم بلکه به او صدمه زده ایم و همکاری بیشتر
عربستان سعودی قراردادهای مهم با F.5 میدهد و برای تضمین و غیره
آن به ایران احتیاج داشت ولی حالا از اینها دستکاری
به اسرائیل ها شده و افسران اسرائیل آنها را اداره کنند

خیلی محرمانه

30.4 4

We ask you for specialists and you hedge we ask you for airplanes and you give us a thousand lame excuses for repairs and screws you create blocks and why should we not go to Israel or any other country ourselves to arrange it you yourselves are friends and allies with Israel and even when the President of France is your country's guest the Mayor or Congressional Representatives boycott him because they think he is not closer with the Israelis and it is the same French who attacked Egypt in 1947 [1957] and you stopped them and now you make such statements and I really cannot make sense of it

He said: I agree with the points you are making but you want to rescue Saudi Arabia and what Iran can do America cannot because as you yourself said we Americans have come to be known as supporters of Israel and any cooperation that we would want with King Faisal not only have we not helped him but we have hurt him As you know Saudi Arabia is to get "F-5" aircraft and for their repairs etc. needed Iran but now if this setup is attached to Israel and Israeli officers operating it

اداره
شماره
تاریخ
پیوست

اولاً شرکت غیر نفتی را است
ثانیاً با سیستم اسرائیل نیست
۵

حق امریکائیها میخواستند این کار را بکنند
و اینها دلسوزی فقط برای حقوق ما است
بعلاوه ما با حکم حکومت کنید آیا سفیر میتواند قرارداد علیه نفوذ کرد؟

وزارت امور خارجه

خیلی محرمانه

حتی چرا ملک فیصل خواهد توانست با ایران همکاری نظامی کند؟ گفتم عالقدر
[illegible] گفتم که از این منطقه بی اطلاع و فکر نمیکنم عاقل هم باشم و
شما هم آنرا دانسته اید گفتم به حال ملک فیصل [illegible] اعلیحضرت
شاهنشاه را چه درباره [illegible] چه درباره [illegible] و لیبی
گذشته اید و چرا این مسائل را مجاناً در اختیار ایران گذاشته اید
ما میتوانیم به آنها هم کمک کنیم

۳- Lord Geo Brown در ملاقات [illegible] ناهار بود و شنید ایشان در [illegible]
و بسیار ساده دانش وزارت خارجه شد [illegible] زن او [illegible] شرفیابی بدهاند
همین شب [illegible] بود و [illegible] دنیای [illegible] و [illegible] و خلا و [illegible]
بودند بعد از شام و [illegible] یک ساعت و نیم بعد از شام با ایشان
درباره نفت - خلیج فارس - عراق - و عراق صحبت کردم
از هندوستان و پاکستان [illegible] و [illegible] را خراب و [illegible] پاکستان را
در حال حاضر [illegible] متوسط و شکایت [illegible] در پاکستان آدمهای
خوب را در [illegible] اداره [illegible] و بعد از [illegible] سؤالات
مشغول برای جواب.
درباره عراق [illegible] شخصاً معتقد هستم این [illegible] غیر ممکن است [illegible]

خیلی محرمانه

و عراق با این [illegible] خواهد رفت و [illegible] به هر حال [illegible]

30.5 5

how will King Faisal be able to cooperate militarily with Iran? I said as I told you I have no knowledge of this and do not think there is such a thing and if you all really sympathize with King Faisal why did you not listen to the Shahanshah: whether it is about Saudi Arabia or about Sudan and Libya. You did not listen and why did you not put this equipment at the disposal of Iran for free so that we are able to help them

First of all the company is non-military (civil) Secondly it is not in Israel's name

The Americans themselves wanted to do this and this sympathy is only for themselves Nonetheless speak to Khatam can a concluded agreement be canceled?

3 – "Lord Goe Booth" who supposedly was "Sir" and was the English Ambassador to India and later became the Permanent Under-Secretary of Ministry of Foreign Affairs had the honor of an audience in London He was your servant's guest Thursday night and also Dennis Robert and O'Brien and Zelli and Dr. Eghbal were there and before dinner and an hour and a half after dinner we talked about oil — Persian Gulf — the Islands — and Iraq.

He comes from India and Pakistan and sees the situation in India as bad and the current situation in Pakistan medium from a political point of view and was saying that today in Pakistan some good people have been brought into government but the future and what will happen after the elections are hard questions to answer.

About Iraq he said I personally believe the current situation is impossible to continue and with this government either Iraq will be destroyed or in any case the government will fall

اداره
شماره
تاریخ
پیوست

۹

خیلی محرمانه وزارت امور خارجه

ولی شاید نظر دولت دیگری بعضی از همکاران قدیم من در وزارت خارجه
با نظر من فرق کند و عقیده آنها سازش با دولت حاضر باشد
راجع به نفت حق را به ایران میدهیم ولی دیگری با ... از لحاظ امنیت خلیج فارس
و کاندید منطقه و شهرهای ایران گرفتیم و معتقد هستیم باید وزارت خارجه
به شرکت های نفتی فشار وارد آورد ولی نمیدانم همه با من هم عقیده هستند
یا نه. ولی من دلیل خود را بازگشته کردم و معتقد هستم هر حال عده طرفدار
کار ایران هستند و راه وسطی پیدا خواهد شد

از ایران به لیبی میروند و میخواهند از وضع حاضر دولت لیبی طرفداری
کنند ولی اکنون اشتباه بزرگی ... دارند و اعضای ... ایران ...
با اتحاد نفت و معامله دارند میخواهند از کودتا آنها بگیرند. و اعمال ...
احتمالا و قدیمی انگلیس را دارند. ولی اکنون شکست خواهند خورد

... کابینه ...

۴-۱ در کابینه فرانسه خیلی به آمریکایی ها حمله میکرد و میگفت ولی اکنون صحبت
... با انگلیس خوب بود ولی حمل آنها خلاف ... بود. و اگر بخواهند
این اعمال را ... کنند عده ای از ما در وزارت معتقد هستیم که ...
تا به ... باید فوراً ... را ... اقدام ترک ...

خیلی محرمانه

but unfortunately the views of the Government and particularly some of my old colleagues at the State Department are opposed to my views and they believe in colluding with the current government

About oil he said I side with Iran and specifically with you for the security of the Persian Gulf and the future of the region and the progress of Iran I agree with and believe in the State Department should pressure the oil companies but I don't know if everyone agrees with me and that is why I retired and believe that anyhow there are some who support the Iranian view and will find a middle road.

He was going to Libya from Iran and wanted to support the current government and conditions there even though he blamed .... and your servant's feeling was because with Libya they have oil and dealings they want to kiss their ass. And they have the same stupid old English beliefs. Although they will be defeated.

4. At the farewell lunch for the Tunisian Ambassador the French Ambassador was attacking the Americans very much and was saying that although the President's discussions with Nixon were good but their actions were against common courtesy. And if they want to continue these actions some of us in France believe that the President should not stay in New York and as a protest should leave New York at once

۷

اداره
شماره
تاریخ
پیوست

خیلی محرمانه

وزارت امور خارجه

۵- بار مشکلات عراقی‌ها - اول گفته بودند که ما آماده بودیم چندی قبل با ایران قرارداد جداگانه به بندیم ولی ایران حاضر نشد و مسئله را به تمرکز قوا در چهار چوب دادن ایران حاضر بود. دولت و در سازمان ملل متحد هم گفته‌ایم ولی آنها حرف را تصحیح نمودند که اگر قرارداد شرکت حاضر بودند لیکن چهار ماه پروتکل را به شط هم تکرار کرده‌اند و اگر قرارداد حرکت بود که پروتکل مساعد باشد و قرارداد ۱۹۳۷ برای ایران مضره و خود آنها به ۴ و ۵ اجرای تحدید سرحد و ۲ هم که عراق همراه از وارث امپراطوری انگلیس گشتند. سفیر فرانسه اضافه کرد قبل بار شکایت که نماینده آنها به عراقی رجوع داده گفت شما که گفته بودید حاضر به ایران هم که حالا میگوید حاضر است لیکن گرفتاری کجا است و عراقی‌ها گفته‌اند ما حاضریم بشرط اینکه قرارداد ۱۹۳۷ باشد و شط العرب مال عراق است و تو از این استفاده کرد و شکایت انقدر دیروز گفته‌اند که دولت ایران هم همراه او چه میکنند و سپس نزاع گرفت به صحبت عمانی و تکذیب او از آنها گذشتم که دولت ایران سفیر بلژیک - انگلیس - و آنها از این هم بودند که عراقی‌ها را استفاده میکردند و شکایت در تاریخ دیپلماسی بی سابقه است!

خیلی محرمانه

30.7 *7*

5. Brar was saying that the Iraqis had told him we were ready some time ago to sign a separate agreement with Iran but Iran was not ready and the same way about concentration of forces

that I answered Iran has been and is ready and we have said so at United Nations but they change our words If they were ready for an interim agreement then how did they repeat the name of the protocol to you also and if it was an interim agreement then there is no protocol and the 1937 agreement is dead for Iran and they themselves did not abide by 4 and 5 and 2 also that Iraq cannot become the inheritor of the British Empire. The French Ambassador quoting Brar today was saying that their representative reverted to the Iraqi and said you had said that you are ready and Iran now says it is also ready so where is the problem and the Iraqis have said we are ready on the condition that it is the 1937 agreement and Shatt Al Arab belongs to Iraq and he was making fun of them and was saying that they have lied so much that that they themselves do not know what they are saying and then I forced the discussion to what Omani had said and U Thant's denial and at this time the Ambassadors of Belgium—England—and Argentina were present and all were making fun of the Iraqis and were saying this is unprecedented in diplomatic history!

۸

اداره
شماره
تاریخ
پیوست

خیلی محرمانه

وزارت امور خارجه

۶- [illegible] دستخطی که فرموده بودید [illegible] شعرا از اعلیحضرت ملک حسین
«با شاه و ملکه ملاقات کنید» [illegible] بعد از ظهر طبق دعوت که دیشب [illegible]
شده و مفصل صحبت شد که مخصوصاً نتایج آن را که [illegible] مبارک [illegible]
میرسد چون امشب [illegible] خصوصی [illegible] شد با عجله و مختصر [illegible]
که به عرض برسد گزارش جداگانه [illegible] خواهد کرد

خاک پای [illegible] شد و [illegible] مرتب و [illegible]
[illegible]

غلام
[illegible]

شنبه ۱۲ اسفند
ساعت ۲۳/۳۰

خیلی محرمانه

30.8 8

6. Per your universal order and note that you had said about the telegram of His Majesty King Hussein "discuss with Staff" today afternoon per request of General Jam conference held and detailed discussions held the results of which I will present in brief Because there was a special courier tonight it was attempted to prepare a summary in haste to get it to the airplane in time A separate report A separate report Majesty will command

Nothing further worth reporting situation is orderly and all await kissing the foot of Shahanshah Aryamehr dearer than my life I kiss your blessed foot

Your servant
Ardeshir

Saturday 12 Esfand
Time 23/30

Document 31
19 February 1974

In 1974, the shah granted an interview to Mike Wallace (1918–2012), of *60 Minutes* (in this document his name is misspelled as Dalas). Angry with the tone of the interview, the shah tries to use the offices of the US ambassador in Tehran as well as the Iranian ambassador in Washington to stop the broadcast of the interview. The effort eventually failed, and the controversial interview was aired (24 February 1974). A few other interviews with European and American media became the subject of similar controversies.

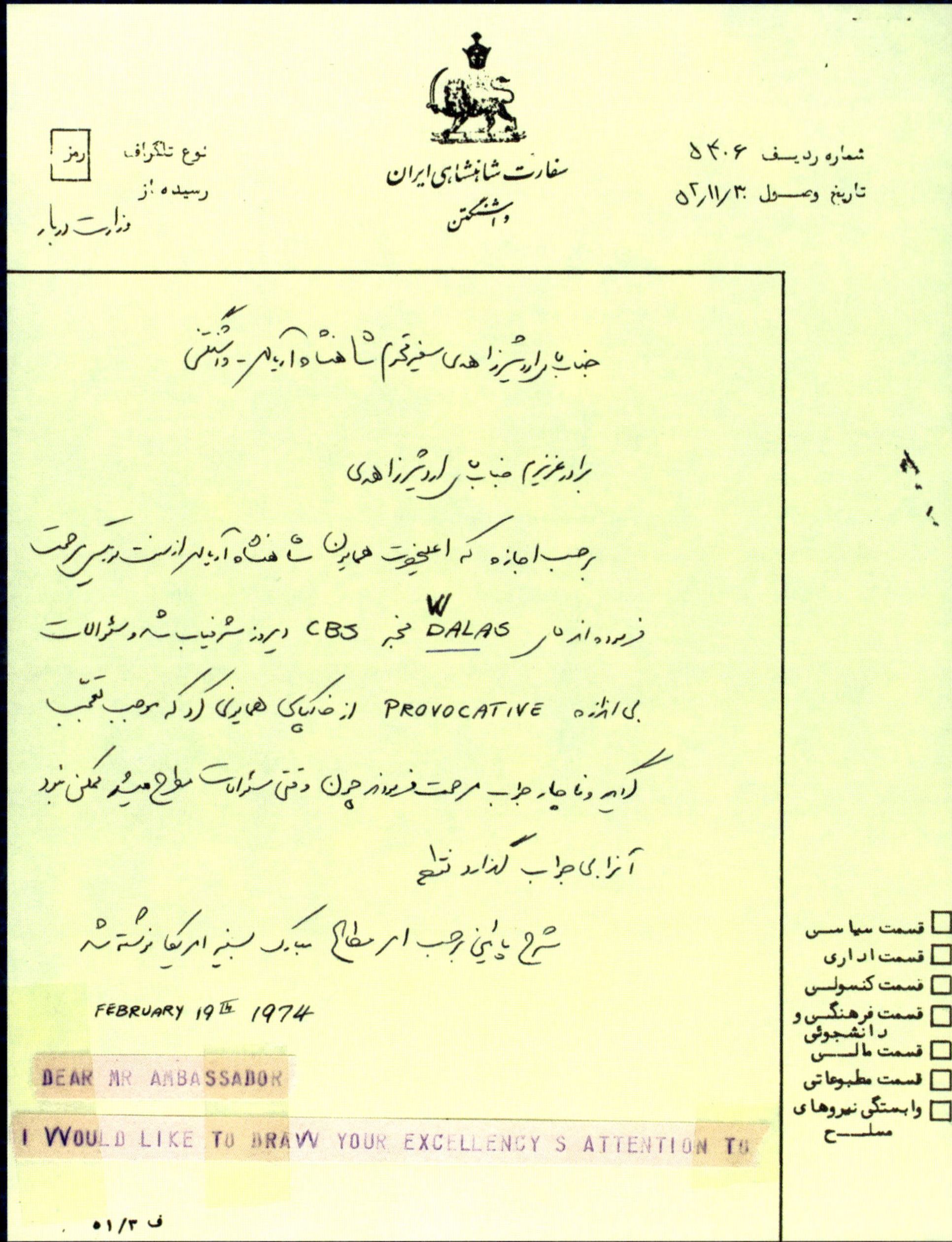

نوع تلگراف رمز
رسیده از وزارت دربار

سفارت شاهنشاهی ایران
واشنگتن

شماره ردیف ۵۴۰۶
تاریخ وصول ۵۲/۱۱/۳۰

جناب اردشیر زاهدی سفیر کبیر شاهنشاه آریامهر - واشنگتن

برادر عزیزم جناب اردشیر زاهدی

برحسب اجازه که اعلیحضرت همایون شاهنشاه آریامهر از [illegible] صحبت

فرموده اند با DALAS (W) مخبر CBS دیروز ضبط شد و سؤالات

بی اندازه PROVOCATIVE از ذات همایونی کرد که موجب تعجب

گردید و ناچار جواب مرحمت فرمودند چون وقتی سؤالات مطرح میشد ممکن نبود

آنرا بی جواب گذارد قطع

شرح پائین جواب [illegible] سفیر امریکا نوشته شد

FEBRUARY 19TH 1974

DEAR MR AMBASSADOR

I WOULD LIKE TO DRAW YOUR EXCELLENCY S ATTENTION TO

قسمت سیاسی
قسمت اداری
قسمت کنسولی
قسمت فرهنگی و دانشجوئی
قسمت مالی
قسمت مطبوعاتی
وابستگی نیروهای مسلح

ف ۵۱/۳

31.1

Emblem

Type of Telegram [Encripted]
Received From Ministry of Court

Imperial Iranian Embassy
Washington

Number 5406
Date Received 30/11/52

Excellency Mr. Ardeshir Zahedi Honorable Ambassador of His Imperial Majesty King of Kings Light of the Aryans — Washington

My Dear Brother Mr. Ardeshir Zahedi

With permission granted from Saint Moritz by His Imperial Majesty King of Kings Light of the Mr. W DALAS [Wallace] reporter for CBS was received in audience and posed some extremely provocative questions to his Imperial Majesty that caught him by surprise and he was compelled to answer because when the questions were posed he could not leave them unanswered stop

The following note was written to the American Ambassador by orders of his Majesty

February 19th 1974

dear mr. ambassador

i would like to draw your excellency's attention to

- Political Section ☐
- Administrative Section ☐
- Cultural and Student Section ☐
- Financial Section ☐
- Press Section ☐
- Armed Forces Attachés ☐

نوع تلگراف: رمز
رسیده از

سفارت شاهنشاهی ایران
واشنگتن

شماره ردیف
تاریخ وصول

٢

THE FACT THAT IN THE INTERVIEW GRANTED BY HIS IMPERIAL MAJESTY TO THE CORRESPONDENT OF THE CBS MANY OF THE QUESTIONS SUBMITTED BY HIM WERE OF AN IMPERTINENT UNFRIENDLY AND PROVOCATIVE NATURE. ~~NOGTEH SARESATR~~

IN VIEW OF THIS AS FAR AS VVE ARE CONCERNED VVE WOULD PREFER THAT THIS INTERVIEW NOT BE TELEVISED OR GIVEN ANY PUBLICITY ~~NOGTEH SARESATR~~ I SHOULD BE GRATEFUL IF YOU WOULD KINDLY TAKE UP THIS MATTER WITH THE COMPETENT AUTHORITIES.

WITH HIGH ESTEEM AND KINDEST PERSONAL REGARDS.

YOUR SINCERELY

ASSADOLLAH ALAM MINISTER OF THE IMPERIAL COURT

ف ۳/۰۱

31.2 the fact that in the interview granted by his imperial majesty to the correspondent of the cbs many of the questions submitted by him were of an impertinent unfriendly and provocative nature.

in view of this as far as we are concerned we would prefer that this interview not be televised or given any publicity i should be grateful if you would kindly take up this matter with the competent authorities.

with high esteem and kindest personal regards.

yours sincerely

assadollah alam minister of the imperial court

UNITED STATES SENATE
WASHINGTON, D. C.

EDWARD W. BROOKE
MASSACHUSETTS

از شرف عرض پیشگاه مبارک شاهنشاه آریامهر گذشت
تاریخ ۱۰ ر ۵ ر ۵۳

July 9, 1974

Dear Ardeshir:

It was a bang-up fourth enriched by your kind and generous gift of my favorite caviar.

I am still waiting for you to accept my invitation to be my guest on Martha's Vineyard and hope that time will permit you to do so before the end of the season. Also, keep in mind our retreat to St. Martin in late fall or early winter.

In the meantime, keep well and remember that "I love you"!

Sincerely yours,

Edward W. Brooke

His Excellency Ardeshir Zahedi
Ambassador of Iran
3005 Massachusetts Avenue, N.W.
Washington, D.C. 20008

EWB:brw

32.1 **Document 32**
9 July 1974

One of Ardeshir Zahedi's strongest points as an ambassador was his truly extensive network of friends, acquaintances, and cooperating colleagues in the ranks of America's elite as well as the diplomatic elite of the world. Senator Brooke (Edward William Brooke, 1919–2015, Republican senator) was among Zahedi's closest friends.

Document 33
6 May 1976

Assadollah Alam (1919–78, prime minister 1962–64) was a close confidant of the shah. At the time he wrote these two letters, he was a powerful court minister. Despite the amicable tone of these letters, his relationship with Zahedi was often testy, if not tempestuous. Another interesting subtext of the note is the obvious tension between Iran and Saudi Arabia at the time—two oil giants vying at the time for a leadership role at OPEC. Some scholars have argued that eventually Saudi Arabia, with goading from the United States, refused to allow an increase in the price of oil, and that fact contributed to the fall of the shah.

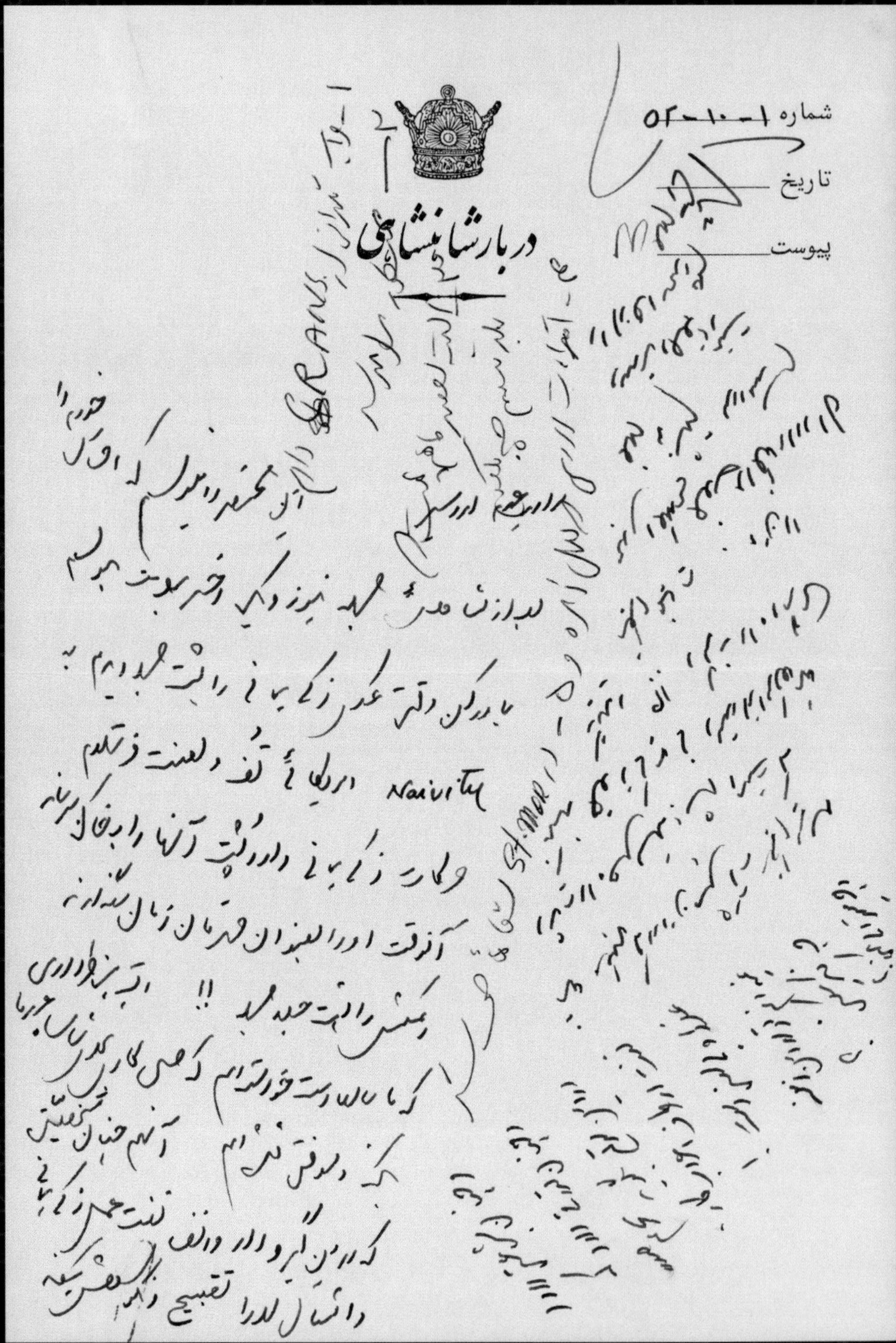

دربار شاهنشاهی

شماره ۵۲-۱۰-۱

تاریخ

پیوست

33.1

Emblem

Imperial Court

Number 2-10-52
Date ………………………..
Reference ………………..

My dear brother Ardeshir

I am writing briefly to tell you about my feelings after viewing the last issue of *Newsweek*

Believe me when I saw the picture of Zaki Yamani on the cover I cursed and spat on American's naïveté.

Zaki Yamani's actions are pinning America's back to the floor yet they select him as the champion of the epoch and put his picture on the cover!! Of course you remember that we have tried for many years to do a similar thing for our dear King of Kings and have not succeeded. And that such a personality who in these unsettled times has criticized and condemned the actions of Zaki Yamani and his likes.

And has such ______ and such power as to say at this time that the boycott of oil exports by the Arabs is wrong and meaningless! I don't know what you think about this issue?

The only thing about this incident that comes to my mind and may be a solution to the problem is that could it not be that Zaki Yamani himself takes orders from America?! Otherwise I can't see it another way.

I wrote this for your information and to intimate my own thoughts. I kiss you

And I ask God for the good health of your precious self

Assadollah Alam

1. Telegraphic response from Crans
2. He understands my intent
3. Of course it is also our fault because we don't know what to do
4. Administrative action has been taken
5. Will be used in "St. Moritz

This letter from Princess Ashraf, the shah's twin sister, to Ardeshir Zahedi is yet another example of their complicated, evolving relationship.

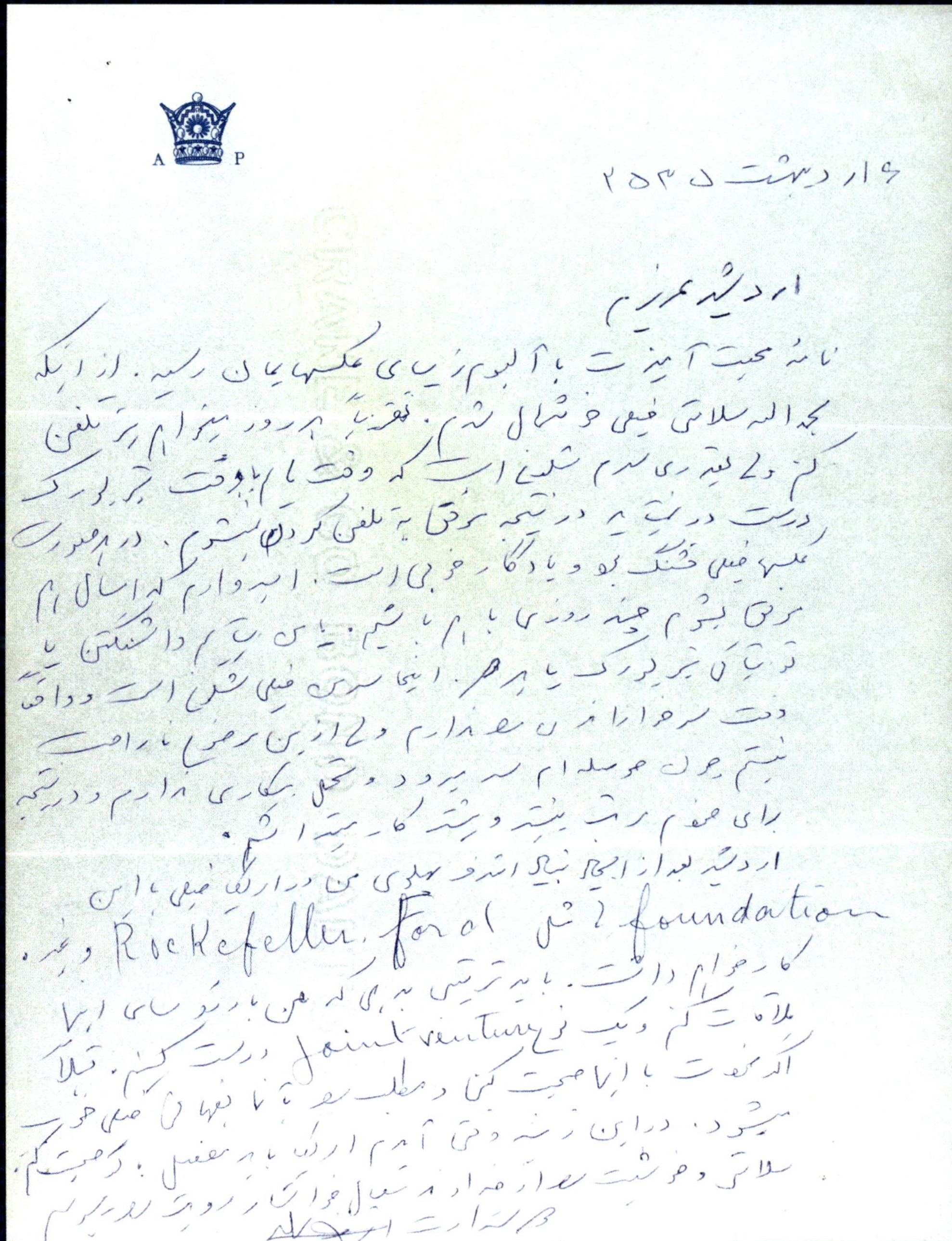

A P

۱۶ اردیبهشت ۲۵۳۵

اردشیر عزیزم

نامه محبت آمیزت با آلبوم زیبای عکسهایتان رسید. از اینکه بحمدالله سلامتی خیلی خوشحال شدم. [illegible]

[illegible] Rockefeller, Ford و foundation [illegible]

[illegible] joint venture [illegible]

33.2 My Dear Ardeshir

Received your affectionate letter with the beautiful album of our pictures. I am happy you are well thank God. Almost every day I want to call you but I am so very busy and our time with the time in New York does not match as a result I don't succeed in calling. Anyway, the photos were very beautiful and a good keepsake. I hope this year too I will succeed in spending a few days together. Either I will come to Washington or you come to New York we will see. I am very busy here and really don't even have time to scratch my head, but I am not bothered by it because I get bored if I have nothing to do. I cannot stand being idle, so I create more and more work for myself.

Ardeshir after creation of Ashraf Pahlavi Foundation, I will have a lot to do in America with foundations such as the Rockefeller Foundation and others. You must organize meetings with their heads so that we can form a sort of a joint venture with them. If you can talk with them first and apprise them of it, it will be very good. When I come to America we will talk in detail about this issue.

I ask God for your health and happiness and kiss your face from afar.

Ashraf

Document 34
20 December 1976

As an ambassador, Ardeshir Zahedi was known, amongst other things, for the lavish, caviar-laden parties he threw at the embassy. The political elite and well-known figures in the world of entertainment, media, and business often mingled at these famous parties. Zahedi was also known for giving his friends and Washington leaders generous gifts of caviar. This document shows that the shah also had a role in offering some of these gifts.

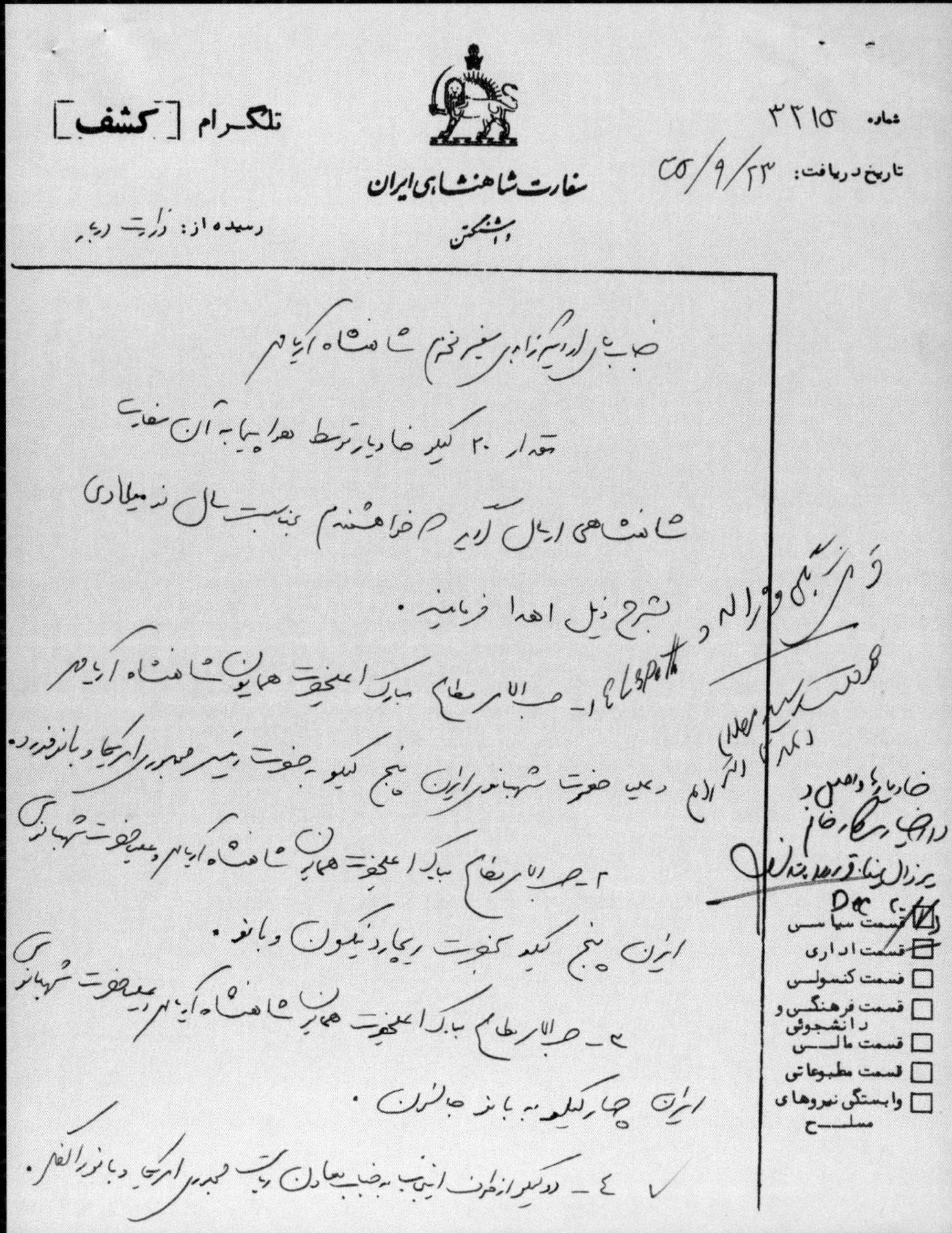
تلگرام [کشف]

شماره ۳۳۱۵

تاریخ دریافت: ۵۵/۹/۲۳

سفارت شاهنشاهی ایران
واشنگتن

رسیده از: وزارت دربار

جناب آقای اردشیر زاهدی سفیر کبیر شاهنشاه آریامهر

تعداد ۲۰ کیلو خاویار توسط هواپیما به آن سفارت

شاهنشاهی ارسال گردید، خواهشمند است بمناسبت سال نو میلادی

بشرح ذیل اهدا فرمایند.

۱- حسب الامر مطاع مبارک اعلیحضرت همایون شاهنشاه آریامهر

و علیاحضرت شهبانوی ایران پنج کیلو به حضرت رئیس جمهوری امریکا و بانو فورد.

۲- حسب الامر مطاع مبارک اعلیحضرت همایون شاهنشاه آریامهر و علیاحضرت شهبانوی

ایران پنج کیلو به حضرت ریچارد نیکسون و بانو.

۳- حسب الامر مطاع مبارک اعلیحضرت همایون شاهنشاه آریامهر و علیاحضرت شهبانوی

ایران چهار کیلو به بانو جانسون.

۴- دو کیلو از طرف اینجانب به جناب معاون رئیس جمهوری امریکا و بانو راکفلر.

قسمت سیاسی
قسمت اداری
قسمت کنسولی
قسمت فرهنگی و دانشجوئی
قسمت مالی
قسمت مطبوعاتی
وابستگی نیروهای مسلح

34.1

Telegram [Decrypted]
Received from: Ministry of Court

Emblem
Imperial Iranian Embassy
Washington

Number 3316
Date Received: 23/9/35

His Excellency Mr. Ardeshir Zahedi Honorable Ambassador of His Imperial Majesty the King of Kings Light of the Aryans

On the occasion of the Christian New Year the quantity of 20 kilos of Caviar was shipped by airplane to the Imperial Embassy, which we request to be gifted according to the following list:

1. In obedience to the auspicious order of His Imperial Majesty the King of Kings Light of the Aryans

and Her Majesty the Queen of Iran, 5 kilos to His Excellency President and Mrs. Ford.

2. In obedience to the auspicious order of His Imperial Majesty the King of Kings Light of the Aryans

and Her Majesty the Queen of Iran, 5 kilos to His Excellency and Mrs. Richard Nixon.

3. In obedience to the auspicious order of His Imperial Majesty the King of Kings Light of the Aryans

and Her Majesty the Queen of Iran, 4 kilos to Mrs. Johnson.

4. 2 kilos on my behalf to His Excellency Vice President of America and Mrs. Rockefeller.

Ghoosh Beigi and Jaleh and Elspeth

....

Received and orders executed

Caviars received inform Ministry of court, Mrs. Yazdanpanah - Signature

December 20, 1976

Political Section	☐
Administrative Section	☑
Cultural and Student Section	☐
Financial Section	☐
Press Section	☐
Armed Forces Attachés	☐

تلگرام [کشف]

شماره:

تاریخ دریافت:

سفارت شاهنشاهی ایران

واشنگتن ۲

رسیده از:

۵- دو گلدان از طرف اینجانب بجناب وزیر امور خارجه امریکا و بانو کیسینجر.

۶- دو گلدان از طرف اینجانب بجناب آقای اسپیرو آگنیو و بانو.

وصول را لطفاً باین وزارت اعلام فرمائید. [illegible]

۲۵۳۲/۶/۲۴ ۲۵۴

وزیر دربار شاهنشاهی

اسدالله علم

☐ قسمت سیاسی
☐ قسمت اداری
☐ قسمت کنسولی
☐ قسمت فرهنگی و دانشجوئی
☐ قسمت مالی
☐ قسمت مطبوعاتی
☐ وابستگی نیروهای مسلح

34.2

Telegram [Decrypted]
Received from: Ministry of Court

Emblem
Imperial Iranian Embassy
Washington

Number 3316
Dare Received: 23/9/35

2

5. 2 kilos on my behalf to His Excellency the Secretary State of America and Mrs. Kissinger.

6. 2 kilos on my behalf to His Excellency and Mrs. Spiro Agnew

Please inform this Ministry of its receipt stop

23/9/2535 253

Minister of Imperial Court
Assadollah Alam

Political Section ☐
Administrative Section ☐
Cultural and Student Section ☐
Financial Section ☐
Press Section ☐
Armed Forces Attachés ☐

JIM WRIGHT
12TH DISTRICT, TEXAS

Congress of the United States
House of Representatives
Washington, D.C. 20515

January 11, 1977

از شرف عرض پیشگاه مبارک شاهنشاه آریامهر گذشت
تاریخ

Hon. Ardeshir Zahedi
Anbassador of Iran
Imperial Embassy of Iran
Washington, D. C.

Dear Mr. Ambassador:

Thanks, very much indeed, for your great thoughtfulness in expressing your congratulations over my election as Majority Leader.

It isn't going to be an easy job. I didn't think it would be. But, then, I guess there isn't any sense of accomplishment in doing easy jobs.

So it makes me all the more appreciative that you would take time to extend your good wishes. I value your friendship and will be needing all your best wishes and your prayers.

Every good personal regard as always.

Sincerely,

Jim Wright

Jim Wright

Document 35
11 January 1977

Ardeshir Zahedi was always described not just as a gracious host and a generous friend but as someone who was attentive to every occasion in the lives of his friends, colleagues, and acquaintances, from birthdays and elections to anniversaries and moments of grief. On each occasion, he would find the requisite gesture of affinity or amity. This letter is one of hundreds of such examples available in the archive.

Document 36
1977

As the archive shows, Ardeshir Zahedi had a large coterie of friends, not only in the political and diplomatic elite but also among Western artists and writers, from Kirk Douglas (b.1916, actor) to Art Buchwald (1925–2007, columnist for the *Washington Post*). Ironically, in *Answer to History*, his last book written after the 1979 revolution, the shah, offering an analysis of where he might have gone wrong and why he lost the throne, suggests that Ardeshir Zahedi had in fact claimed to have many friends in Washington, and one of the shah's main mistakes, in his own reckoning, was not removing Zahedi from his post.

KIRK DOUGLAS

December 21, 1977

Ardeshir —

Dear ~~Ardeshir~~,

We miss you. You are so thoughtful to send us the delicious caviar and the wonderful book by Omar Khayam.

We hope all is going well with you for the holiday season and the New Year. Let's make a resolution to see each other more often in 1978. We would like that very much.

Again thanks and much affection, from both of us —

Kirk

The Honorable Ardeshir Zahedi
Ambassador to Iran
Imperial Embassy of Iran
3005 Massachusetts Ave. NW
Washington, D.C. 20008

4327 HAWTHORNE STREET
WASHINGTON, D. C. 20016

از شرف عرض پیشگاه مبارک شاهنشاه آریامهر گذشت
تاریخ بهمن ماه ۲۵۳۵ تهران

Dear Ardeshir,

Ann and I have just finished the caviar. We locked all the doors and pulled the cuttains across the windows. Ann made baked potatoes. Then we put butter on them--then we put the caviar on top--scoops and scoops of it. We cackled and chuckled as we ate the golden eggs of Iran. Outside the wind was blowing--our friends were freezing--people's cars wouldn't start up--old ladies were breaking their hips on the ice. But when you're eating caviar you forget about other people and think of yourself.

After I licked the bottom of the can and Ann licked the top, I lit up one of Cuban cigars from Davidov. The aroma permeats the room. We have now opened the book on Persia and going over it page by page.

Ardeshir we are very happy contented souls. Why can't everybody find happiness like this? If all the world could eat caviar and smoke Davidov cigars and look at pictures of Persia there would be no wars. There would nothing but love.

We are proof of it. I am

Your Obedient Servant

Art

Art Buchwald

January 22,1977

36.2

Document 37
26 January 1977

From the early 1970s, a loud chorus of critics, from Amnesty International to the Confederation of Iranian Students, began to criticize the shah's human rights record. The Iranian embassy was, as is evident from these notes, deeply involved in efforts to counter these allegations. Of particular importance were the articles and the testimony of Reza Baraheni (b. 1935), a prolific writer and dissident artist. It is important to note that the highly exaggerated and often repeated claim that Iran had more than 100,000 political prisoners was first made by Reza Baraheni in congressional hearings. Amnesty International, according to scholars, quoted the Baraheni testimony, and the Amnesty reports were subsequently cited in the echo chamber of the opposition. The actual number of political prisoners at the time was, according to many reports by visiting Western jurists and Amnesty officials, closer to 3,500.

MARSHALL, LEON, WEILL & MAHONY
1825 K STREET, N.W.
WASHINGTON, D.C. 20006

SYLVAN M. MARSHALL
EDWARD J. LEON
HAROLD WEILL
FRANK H. CONNELLY
HAROLD OBSTLER
ROBERT S. FRIEDMAN
BERNARD KAHN
JEROME LIPPER
MARVIN N. ROSEN*

(202) 223-9600
CABLE ADDRESS: "SYLVAN"
TELEX: 223380

NEW YORK OFFICE
LEON, WEILL & MAHONY
261 MADISON AVENUE
NEW YORK, N.Y. 10016
(212) 687-5707
CABLE ADDRESS
"WEILLEON" NEW YORK

LLOYD GEORGE SOLL
FRANCIS A. MAHONY
COUNSEL

*ADMITTED IN N.Y. ONLY

January 26, 1977

His Excellency
Ardeshir Zahedi
Ambassador of Iran
3005 Massachusetts Ave., N.W.
Washington, D.C. 20008

Dear Ardeshir:

You have asked for my legal opinion with respect to your options concerning certain public utterances by a Mr. Reza Barahani. I have examined the file provided to me by Dr. Tavallali and Counselor Moshavegh-Zade.

In my professional opinion, no direct action should be taken with respect to Mr. Barahani's appearance on the Barbara Walters show, because that occurred too long ago. Likewise, I do not counsel any activity with respect to his articles in "Penthouse" Magazine or the "New York Review of Books".

I believe that the attached letter should be sent to Mr. David Suskind, on whose program Mr. Barahani made a recent appearance. This letter may result in an invitation for your appearance on the same program; and if the conditions are acceptable, you may want to accept.

Having examined the text of Mr. Barahani's testimony before the Subcommittee on International Organizations of the House of Representatives Committee on International Affairs, I believe that there is no appropriate way that a direct response can be made. However, you may want to consider the possibility of inviting the Chairman of the Subcommittee, Honorable Donald Fraser, to visit Iran, perhaps with a balanced group of Members and staff. If an invitation is to be made, it could properly state that Iran does not tolerate any outside interference in its internal affairs, but that since the Subcommittee has received adverse reports, it is your belief that the best way for the Subcommittee to observe the truth is by a visit. In considering whether such an invitation should be extended, it should

37.1

be clearly understood that while you could insist that only Members and staff could comprise the group, and no outsiders, there would be no way that you could limit the places which they could visit in Iran, or the contacts which they might want to make there. In my opinion, the group should travel at the cost of the Congress, and no lavish entertainments should be offered; it should be a business trip.

Another step which could be taken, either as an alternative or in tandem, would be to invite a television personality of impeccable credentials and a reputation for objectivity (such as Walter Cronkhite or Barbara Walters) to visit Iran for the purpose of observing the matter of human rights, such visit to be culminated with an interview with Their Imperial Majesties. Again, in considering such an invitation, it should be clearly understood that it would be counterproductive to limit the places to be visited and the contacts to be made; you could not anticipate beneficial results from such a visit and interview if the personality was taken on a "guided" tour. Also, it should be understood that there could be no pre-conditions for the interview with Their Imperial Majesties, no pre-submission of the questions, and no limitation on the questions themselves. Again, the cost of the visit should not be borne by Iran.

I am at your disposal if you wish to discuss this matter with me in person.

Sincerely,

Sylvan

Sylvan M. Marshall

SMM/mo

Attachment

January 26, 1977

Mr. David Suskind
c/o Talent Associates
747 Third Avenue
New York City, New York 10017

Dear Mr. Suskind:

I write concerning that portion of your program of January 16, 1977, in which you show-cased Mr. Reza Barahani.

This is written in my capacity as Ambassador of Iran, but also as an Iranian citizen who loves and respects his country, his people and his sovereign.

And I write to you because I believe that you are an objective journalist, and that you have been misled. With respect to the telecast cited above, I wish to make some factual statements, and ask some questions; I shall then leave it to you to determine what course to follow, to set the record straight with your many viewers.

In Iran, all citizens are Iranians, and all receive equal treatment, regardless of their origins. It is contrary to our law for any person to preach separatism. Your interviewee has publicl admitted that he wrote and published an article in Iran, advocating separatism, thus commiting an illegal act. Rather than an indictment of our legal system, which pre-dates yours, it is a tribute to our justice that this man was detained for a little more than three months and then released. The fact that our legal system differs from yours does not render either one better or worse than the other.

I categorically deny that Mr. Barahani was tortured during his detention. I ask whether he exhibited to you any scars, which would have resulted ineradicably from the acts which he now describes? I ask you to remember that he said that his "hair was plucked out" of his face by "surgery scissors"; then I ask, if that was true, how could he now have the beard which you have seen?

Some time after his release, he was given an exit visa, and freely permitted to leave Iran. How does that square with your description of him as an "exile"? On your program, he insinuated that his departure from Iran was facilitated by undescribed activities by American writers. I state that his exit visa was given without the slightest pressure from anyone; and I ask you to check with those whom he mentioned, to inquire whether any action on their part was requested or needed.

Please examine the transcript of the telecast, to ascertain whether he provided you with the slightest proof of his "torture", or of his allegation that Iranian agents are harrassing him in the United States? If the Iranian police were as omnipresent and all-powerful as he contends, and if they had indeed taken the ridiculous decision to execute him, would they have any difficulty in locating this man, who appears on pre-announced television programs and who holds public meetings to slander the very Government which paid for his education and employed him? On your program, he claimed that in order to avoid harm to himself, he had to hide, by going from one corner of New York City to another; yet in the very same breath, he said that as soon as he received the alleged news that he was to be killed, he "held a press conference"! Is this credible to any logical person?

Above, I said that his education was paid for by Iran; I wish to amplify that. Because of his Azerbaijani origins, (Azerbaijanis speak a Turkish dialect), he was sustained by the Iranian Government when he attended a university in Turkey, for graduate studies. Upon his return to Iran, he was given a teaching post at the University of Teheran. Does that sound like discrimination against an ethnic minority?

All Iranians are poets, to some extent: but what evidentiary support did he give you for the assertion that he is Iran's "leading poet"? Did he show you any of his poems published by a responsible publisher? Did he produce any favorable reviews of his poetry, by serious critics? Or did you simply accept him on faith?

He asserted that he was confined "in the darkest, small hole" he had ever seen. Yet he tells you of his observations in all parts of the prison, and tells you of carrying others from place to place, at least inferring that he had the run of the place. Are these statements not self-contradictory?

Can a man who is blindfolded, and in the custody of four men in a car, reliably say that the car was being driven to the south of the city?

Did Mr. Barahani give you any evidence that he is working as a teacher or a writer, or even that he is respectably employed? Or can we more appropriately suspect that he is being sustained by elements which seek to drive a wedge between your country and mine? We firmly believe that the alliance which exists between our two countries is beneficial to both; we are fully aware, as is your Government, that there are forces which seek to destroy that relationship, for selfish purposes. Those forces are always prepared to exploit disgruntled people, using them to further dissidence. In other public forums, Mr. Barahani has given the real reason for his disappointment; he considered himself a contender for the position of head of his department at Teheran University, but was passed over in favor of a more experienced teacher-administrator. That obviously embittered him.

In public testimony, he has admitted that when his family visited him during his detention, he told them that he had not been tortured; he then tried to explain that away. He would have you believe that he was in virtual isolation; but the records show that he had frequent family visits, and that they brought him books for study and for writing. He asserted to you that reprisals are being taken against members of his family in Iran; but the fact is that his brother, Professor Ali Naqi Barahani, is a respected educator at the University of Teheran at this very moment, and has been for many years.

So that you may be aware of the views of your own Government concerning Iran's observance of the human rights of its citizens, I take the liberty of forwarding to you herewith the testimony of Honorable Alfred L. Atherton, Jr., Assistant Secretary of State for Near Eastern and South Asian Affairs, before the Subcommittee on International Organizations of the House of Representatives Committee on International Relations, September 8, 1976. You may be assured that although our history and laws differ from yours, our concern for the human condition of our people is no less than yours.

The length of this letter is dictated by my acute concern for the damage which can be inflicted upon the ties between our nations, when irresponsible, self-contradictory, exaggerated and untrue statements are broadcast, and in an effort to stimulate your sense of fairness.

I shall look forward to hearing from you in the near future.

Sincerely,

Ardeshir Zahedi
Ambassador

از عرض پیشگاه مبارک شاهنشاه آریامهر گذشت
تاریخ ۱۶ بهمن ۲۵۳۵

30 Rockefeller Plaza
New York, N.Y. 10020

Room 5600

CIrcle 7-3700

January 18, 1977

*

Dear Ardeshir,

I am writing this letter on behalf of Fritz Stern, Seth Low Professor of European History at Columbia University. Professor Stern, who has just published a major work on Bismark entitled Gold and Iron, is a leading historian in this country and is also well known in Western Europe. He has recently been decorated by the Federal Republic of Germany. He has been a friend and colleague of Henry Kissinger and Zbigniew Brzezinski for the last twenty years -- and both men support his present project.

With the help of the Ford Foundation and the personal support of McGeorge Bundy, Professor Stern is currently preparing a book on contemporary Europe, its politics at home and abroad, and its role in the world. In that connection he is interviewing leading statesmen, businessmen and scholars in different parts of the world. He has already talked with President Scheel and last April was invited by the German Government to speak at a memorial for the former Lord Mayor of Berlin - Ernst Reuter - with Chancellor Schmidt as the other speaker.

Professor Stern is planning to visit Teheran from March 2 to March 8. I know it would be of great value to him if he could speak to you before he leaves. He would also be deeply grateful for a chance to be received by His Majesty the Shah, if you felt that were feasible. He feels that such an interview would be of special importance to his work.

I should add that Professor Stern expects to leave the United States on January 22 and, if it were feasible for you, would change his other plans to come to Washington to talk to you on either the 20th or the 21st, though he assumes you will undoubtedly be thoroughly tied up on the 20th. He apologizes for this short notice, but will telephone your office on the afternoon of January 19 to see what might be possible.

I shall much appreciate anything you can do for him as he is truly an exceptional person.

With best wishes,

David

David Rockefeller

H.E. Ardeshir Zahedi
Embassy of Iran
3005 Massachusetts Avenue, N.W.
Washington, D.C. 20008

37.8

Document 38
27 January 1977

Both the shah and Ardeshir Zahedi kept close ties with Richard Nixon (1913–94), even after Watergate ended his presidency in 1972. This friendship extended to some of the Nixon's closest aids, assistants, and even relatives. Here, Rose Mary Woods (1917–2005), Nixon's long-serving private assistant, famous for her defiant refusal to testify against Nixon regarding the famous missing parts of the Watergate tapes, is a recipient of a kind letter from Zahedi.

از شرفعرض پیشگاه مبارک شاهنشاه آریامهر گذشت
تاریخ بهمن ماه ۲۵۳۵ تهران

January 27, 1977

Dear Mr. Ambassador:

I was delighted when I received your handsome Holiday Greetings Card. But, there are no words to really tell you just how much it meant to have you also remember me with the beautiful Honey Jar - complete with my initials and its own darling little Bee. Thank you so very much.

Believe me, I am most grateful for your friendship and all of us really appreciate the great friendship you have maintained with President Nixon. I am sure - as I think you are - that he will go down in history as one of our greatest Presidents. I just hope that he and his family will live to see the turning so that history will be written correctly and not by a biased media.

With deep gratitude and best wishes for good health, happiness and success in 1977,

Sincerely,

Rose Mary

Rose Mary Woods

His Excellency Ardeshir Zahedi
Ambassador Extraordinary and Plenipotentiary
Iranian Embassy
Washington, D. C.

BARRY GOLDWATER
ARIZONA

United States Senate
WASHINGTON, D.C. 20510

March 16, 1977

The Honorable Ardeshir Zahedi
Ambassador Extraordinary and
Plenipotentiary
Imperial Embassy of Iran
3005 Massachusetts Avenue
Washington, D. C. 20008

Dear Ardeshir:

May this one American add the thanks that rests in the hearts of all of us for what you did to help end that ridiculous and dangerous situation in Washington this past week. I hate to say this, but I think you believe it as I do, that terrorism is now a way of life and we are going to see more of it, not just confined to groups identified with those who perpetrated this recent one, but it's going to spread and, frankly, I don't have any answers.

We will all have to think about it and we'll have to pray to our Gods that stupidity will end and reason will enter. Otherwise what a few people want for themselves and feel they can gain by terrorism may begin a breakdown of the world's structure. In spite of all that, thank you from the bottom of my heart.

With warm wishes,

Barry

Barry Goldwater

Document 39
16 March 1977

Ardeshir Zahedi had developed close friendships with members of both political parties in the United States. One of his closest friends was Barry Goldwater (1909–98), a one-time presidential candidate and key member of Senate. The archives have many fascinating letters and memoranda of conversations detailing the close nature of this friendship and the kinds of discussion and consultations that went on between Zahedi and Goldwater.

Document 40
16 March 1977

Ardeshir Zahedi was, as is evident in the archives, in close contact with many American journalists and publishers, from the *Washington Post*'s Katharine Graham (1917–2001) to the Sulzberger family of the *New York Times*. These contacts included close ties to the Annenberg family of *Reader's Digest* fame. When the shah contemplated exile in the United States, the Annenbergs offered to make their palatial home available to him and his family. The shah was never issued the visa to settle in the United States—only one on humanitarian grounds, to seek medical help. His entry into the United States precipitated the hostage crisis.

MRS. ARTHUR HAYS SULZBERGER
1115 FIFTH AVENUE
NEW YORK, N. Y. 10028

March 16, 1977

My dear Mr. Ambassador:

I want to thank you once more for sending me a couple of years ago "Persia: Bridge of Turquoise." I am now re-reading it with real enthusiasm because I am planning to go to Iran at the end of April with my granddaughter Karen Sulzberger whom you know.

This will be the fulfillment of an old dream because I was raised on stories about Persia by a charming Irish governess who had been governess to the children of the French Ambassador to Persia at the beginning of the century. I know that, in spite of the great progress your country has made, I will find much of the past which always sounded so romantic to me as a child.

I hope that upon our return Karen and I will have the opportunity to tell you of our experiences.

Very sincerely,

H.E. the Ambassador of Iran,
the Hon. Ardeshir Zahedi
Embassy of Iran
Washington, D. C.

m

از شرف عرض پیشگاه مبارک شاهنشاه آریامهر گذشت
تاریخ ۱۱/۱۱/۳۶ تهران

THE WASHINGTON POST COMPANY

1150 Fifteenth Street, N. W., Washington, D. C. 20071

KATHARINE GRAHAM
Chairman of the Board

January 12, 1978

Dear Ardeshir:

Thank you for your letter about Dr. Sa'edi which I took the privilege of forwarding to Winthrop Knowlton and to my friend, Bob Bernstein, of Random House.

They were pleased to hear the news. You were good to give the matter prompt attention on your return from Tehran and in the face of the visit here today of Her Imperial Majesty.

I am most grateful for the intervention of His Imperial Majesty as, I know, are the distinguished American book publishers who signed the letter.

Sincerely,

Kay

His Excellency
Ardeshir Zahedi
The Ambassador of Iran
3003 Massachusetts Avenue, N.W.
Washington, DC 20008

Document 41
18 March 1977

In 1977, Ardeshir Zahedi played a key role in ending a potentially disastrous hostage crisis in Washington, DC. In the Hanafi Siege of 1977, a group of Sunni radicals took over three buildings and took 149 hostages. For his role in ending the crisis, he received many notes of gratitude, this one from John Silber (1926–2012), the storied president of Boston University.

BOSTON UNIVERSITY

147 BAY STATE ROAD BOSTON 02215

Office of the President

March 18, 1977

His Excellency, Ardeshir Zahedi
Ambassador of Iran
3005 Massachusetts Avenue, N.W.
Washington, D.C. 20008

Dear Mr. Ambassador:

On behalf of Boston University, I want to express our profound admiration of and deep gratitude for your courageous and skillful intervention in last week's events in Washington. I think it is very likely that two of Boston University's students are now alive because of the effectiveness of your intervention.

You and your colleagues have magnificently embodied the calling of the diplomat. A great many families around the world will remain forever in your debt.

Sincerely yours,

John R. Silber

JRS:nnt

Document 42
7 November 1977

Hubert Humphrey (1911-78), a famously liberal senator and a presidential candidate in 1968, was appreciative to find Ardeshir Zahedi's gifts of books and Persian caviar from the Caspian Sea. After the revolution, the Iranian regime's designated new head of mission accused Zahedi of making illegal gifts to American officials. After a lengthy FBI inquiry, which included subpoenas for every florist in the greater Washington, DC, area, it was determined that no illegal gifts were ever made to American officials.

HUBERT H. HUMPHREY
MINNESOTA

United States Senate
WASHINGTON, D.C. 20510

November 7, 1977

His Excellency
Ambassador Ardeshir Zahedi
Ambassador of Iran
Office of the Embassy
3005 Massachusetts Avenue
Washington, D. C. 20008

Dear Ardeshir:

You are a most thoughtful and generous man. First of all, we received your beautiful plant with the Birds of Paradise and other flowers on our return to Washington, and here the other day, came a generous package to satisfy the appetite and lift the spirits. I am most grateful.

I know of no one in this city who is more thoughtful of his friends than you.

Please convey to His Royal Highness my sincere friendship and good wishes.

Sincerely,

Hubert H.

Hubert H. Humphrey

Document 43
5 January 1978

Ardeshir Zahedi succeeded in developing close relations not just with several US presidents but also invariably with First Ladies, which began while they were in office and continued after they had left the White House—or even after they had lost their husbands. His ties with Jackie Kennedy (1929–94), Pat Nixon (1912–93), Lady Bird Johnson (1912–2007), and Nancy Reagan (1921–2016) were particularly interesting and enduring.

از شرفعرض پیشگاه مبارک شاهنشاه آریامهر گذشت
تاریخ [illegible]

Stonewall, Texas

January 5, 1978

Dear Ardeshir,

How thoughtful and generous you are! I could not be more appreciative or flattered by your beautiful gift. The elegant demitasse cup and silver saucer all but took my breath away as I eagerly pulled their wrappings away. I will treasure them and your kindness, as I do the many other times I have had cause to be grateful to you.

I know, too, it was through your efforts that my favorite caviar found its way here in time for festive Christmas celebrating. I thank you with all my heart and I hope that you will see that the enclosed letter reaches His Imperial Majesty in Iran.

With my deepfelt gratitude, once again, and my warmest hopes that all the days of this New Year are filled with peace and happiness,

Lady Bird

43.1

MRS. RONALD REAGAN (NANCY) IS THANKING YOU VERY MUCH FOR THE BEAUTIFUL SILVER PLACE CARDS, AND EXPRESSES HER'S AND HER HUSBAND'S CONERN ABOUT THE RECENT EVENTS IN IRAN. THEY BOTH WISH YOU WELL AND A HAPPY AND PEACEFUL NEW YEAR.

Dear Ardeshir,

Thank you so much for the beautiful silver place card holders - they're just lovely and I'll put them to good use!

We've thought of you so often in the last weeks, and our friends we met on our visit to Iran. My heart breaks to think of what is happening now.

I pray that everything will somehow work out all right.

Ronnie joins me in this as you know - also in thanks and in wishing you a happy, peaceful New Year.

Fondly,

Nancy

Mrs. Ronald Reagan
d.

Dear Ardeshir—

Thank you so much for the beautiful silver place card holders—they're just lovely and I'll put them to good use!

We've thought of you so often in the last weeks—and our friends we met on our visit to Iran—My heart breaks to think of what is happening now. I pray that everything will somehow work out all right—Ronnie joins me in this as you know—also in thanks—and in wishing you a happy, peaceful new year—

Fondly—Nancy

Mrs. Ronald Wilson Reagan

MORGAN GUARANTY TRUST COMPANY
OF NEW YORK
PO BOX 161
33 LOMBARD STREET, LONDON EC3P 3BH
TELEPHONE: 01-283 8888

London

ازشرفعرض پیشگاه مبارک شاهنشاه آریامهر گذشت
تاریخ ۱/۱۲/۳۶ تهران

THE RT. HON. LORD SHAWCROSS, G.B.E., Q.C.
Adviser on International Operations

30th January 1978

HE Mr Ardeshir Zahedi
The Imperial Iranian Embassy
Washington DC
USA

My dear Ardeshir:

I have just been reading a rather sensational "thriller" called "The Crash of '79". It is based upon an assumed economic and political collapse of the Western World brought on by the Shah launching a nuclear war on Saudi Arabia.

There are a great many personal references to His Majesty, his family and Ministers which are of a highly defamatory kind and I imagine that if a claim were made in the Courts here or in the U S where the book was first published, very heavy damages might be awarded. I assume, however, that His Majesty would not wish to be involved in litigation abroad. But I thought I would draw your attention to this very wicked attack in case you have not already seen it. The London publishers are Secker & Warburg.

I hope all goes well with you. We had a small party at Friston last week with several old friends of yours - eg. Nicky and Rupert and Diane Bridge - to enjoy some caviar I had been sent from Iran and we drank a health to you and the good times now over !

I hope to be coming to Washington in April and to see you there,

Yours ever

Hartley

Incorporated with limited liability in the State of New York, U.S.A.

Document 44
30 January 1978

Among Ardeshir Zahedi's closest friends was Lord Shawcross, the British prosecutor at the Nuremberg Tribunal (1902–2003). Other members of this influential British family were also close to Zahedi. The relationship was of consequence not only during Zahedi's ambassadorial appointments and his tenure as foreign minister, but after the revolution as well.

Document 45

On the eve of the revolution in 1979, Iran had a major earthquake. Many of Zahedi's friends offered notes of condolences, occasional gifts. Here is a letter from Douglas Fairbanks Jr.

From: Douglas Fairbanks, Jr.

575 PARK AVENUE
NEW YORK, N.Y. 10021

(212) 838-4900
CABLES: DOUGFAIR NEW YORK

از شرف عرض پیشگاه مبارك شاهنشاه آریامهر گذشت
تاریخ ۱۵/۸/۲۵۳۷ تهران

September 25, 1978

Personal

Dear Ambassador,

We have been so terribly upset and distressed by the awful convulsion of nature in Iran; that, and the amount of suffering which the earthquake has brought, that we want to send this small, inadequate token of our thoughts of the people, the country, and our charming host, who made our visit last year so memorable. I would like to make a check many times more than this is, but I've already gone way beyond my yearly budget for various charities and causes in which I am involved. Therefore, I hope it will, however small, prove acceptable.

Mary Lee joins me in warmest and best wishes and the hope that we will see you sometime in the near future.

Respectfully and sincerely
Doug Fairbanks

45.1

TELEGRAM

Mr. Douglas Fairbanks
The Vicarage
448 North Lake Way
Palm Beach, Florida 33480

January 11, 1979

My dear friend,

The contents of your very thoughtful letter of recent date were relayed to me in Tehran. It was very good indeed to hear from you and I just wanted to take this opportunity to convey my warmest thanks for your generous expression of friendship and support.

Your concern for His Majesty and for a peaceful resolution to the present difficulties is deeply appreciated.

With my warmest personal good wishes to you and Mary Lee for a bright and prosperous New Year.

As ever,

Ardeshir Zahedi

Document 46
9 January 1979

On the eve of the 1979 Revolution in Iran, a number of prominent Americans wrote letters of concern to Ardeshir Zahedi and sometimes also to the shah in Iran. The Rockefeller family had a long and complicated relationship with both the shah and Zahedi. The Rockefeller family played an important role in the eventual decision to admit the shah to the United States, an act that gave rise to the hostage crisis. This letter indicates the evolving and storied nature of this relationship leading up to the fall of the shah.

30 Rockefeller Plaza
New York, N.Y. 10020

Room 5600 Circle 7-3700

January 9, 1979

Dear Ardeshir: *

What Their Imperial Majesties and you have been going through in these last days and weeks, the friends who love you can only imagine -- it has to be one of the most tragic situations conceivable. Our prayers are with you. We respect and admire more than we can say your loyalty and devotion to Their Imperial Majesties and to your country.

I sent a hand-written note to Their Imperial Majesties last week via a friend who was going to Tehran.

In the midst of all this travail Happy and I were overwhelmed to receive the beautiful silver napkin rings and place card holders which you so thoughtfully sent to us. And the book on Persian carpets is magnificent. We will always treasure them as mementos of a great man and a great nation in a period of unbelievably trial.

This letter brings our support and expressions of affection and hope that in this New Year there may be a break in the clouds.

Sincerely,

Nelson

Nelson A. Rockefeller

His Excellency
Ardeshir Zahedi
The Imperial Embassy of Iran
3005 Massachusetts Avenue
Washington, D.C. 20008

January 22, 1979

I have just had an opportunity to read your article about the student demonstrators which appeared in the January 10 issue of the Manchester Union Leader and once again, I write to thank you for your untiring determination to set the record straight.

Of course this was only one small example of the sympathy and understanding which are so very characteristic of all your dealings but I did want you to know how very much it was appreciated particularly at the present time. You and Nancy are two wonderful people and I consider myself fortunate indeed to be counted among your friends. I look forward to seeing you both again very soon.

With my fondest wishes.

The Honorable Ronald Reagan
1669 San Onofre Drive
Pacific Palisades, CA 90272

Document 47
22 January 1979

Nancy and Ronald Reagan were among Zahedi's closest friends. As this and other letters in the archive indicate, the friendship began long before Reagan's presidential run.

MRS. WILLIAM P. ROGERS THANKS YOU VERY MUCH FOR THE MAGNIFICENT CARPET WHICH THEY LOVE SO MUCH, AND THE BOOK ON PERSIAN CARPET.

THEY FIND THE NEWS ABOUT IRAN VERY DISTURBING, HOWEVER, THEY WATCH IT EVERY DAY, AND SAW YOU ON T.V. ... VERY SELFISHLY THEY WANT YOU BACK IN WASHINGTON, BUT REALIZE YOUR VALUABLE SERVICES BACK HOME.

THEY WERE DISTRESSED ABOUT THE RECENT HAPPENING IN LOS ANGELES TO PRINCESS SHAMS' RESIDENCE, AND EXPRESS THEIR DEEP CONCERN.

Document 48
January 1979

One of Zahedi's closest friends among the American political elite, as well as an occasional legal adviser to him and to the Iranian embassy, was William Rogers (1913–2001, who eventually served as Nixon's secretary of state (1969–73). Zahedi's relationship with Rogers, both personal and professional, continued even after the 1979 Revolution. The incident referred to here is the fact that the residence of the shah's older sister, Princess Sham, was attacked by the shah's opponents on 30 December 1978 in Los Angeles.

ABOUT THE EDITOR

Abbas Milani is the Hamid & Christina Moghadam Director of Iranian Studies and adjunct professor at the Center on Democracy, Development and Rule of Law at Stanford University. He is also one of the founding co-directors of the Iran Democracy Project and a research fellow at the Hoover Institution. Until 1986, he taught at Tehran University's Faculty of Law and Political Science, where he was also a member of the board of directors of the university's Center for International Relations. After moving to the United States, he was for fourteen years the chair of the political science department at the Notre Dame de Namur University. For eight years, he was a visiting research fellow in University of California, Berkeley's Middle East Center.

His latest book is a collection he co-edited with Larry Diamond, *Politics & Culture in Contemporary Iran: Challenging the Status Quo* (Lynne Rienner Publishers, 2015). His publications in English include *The Shah* (Palgrave, 2012); *The Myth of the Great Satan: A New Look at America's Relations with Iran* (Hoover Institution Press, 2010); *Eminent Persians: Men and Women Who Made Modern Iran, 1941–1979,* 2 vols. (Syracuse University Press, 2008); *Lost Wisdom: Rethinking Persian Modernity in Iran* (Mage, 2004); and *The Persian Sphinx: Amir Abbas Hoveyda and the Riddle of the Iranian Revolution* (Mage, 2000). Milani has also written and translated numerous books in Persian.

Milani's more than 200 articles and book reviews have been published in journals, magazines, and newspapers.

He has been a member of the American Association of Political Science, the American Academy of Political and Social Science, and the Association of Iranian Studies.

Milani received his BA in political science and economics from the University of California at Berkeley and his PhD in political science from the University of Hawaii.

ACKNOWLEDGMENTS

I am immensely grateful to His Excellency, Ardeshir Zahedi, for his generosity, trust, and patriotic interest in preserving this remarkable collection for posterity. I must also thank Princess Mahnaz Zahedi, who has been inspiring in her humility, humanity, and support.

Eric Wakin is not only a dear friend and colleague, but his knack for history, his grace and efficiency as a director of the Hoover Archives, and his stewardship of the process of transferring the collection and making it available to scholars has been indispensable to the success of our effort, and to the completion of this book.

In every step of this long process, I have enjoyed the relentlessly efficient help of Mr. Franco Errico and of Ms. Roma Parhad, the program coordinator and associate director of the Iranian Studies Program at Stanford. Without their patience, their attention to details, and their willingness to manage the complications of this project, the book would still be lingering in the labyrinth of creation and production.

A special note of gratitude to Mr. Arman Saify who deftly managed the difficult task of deciphering many different handwritings of all the Persian texts, and diligently turned them into English.

I am greatly indebted to the administrative and technical staff of the Hoover Institution Library & Archives whose work greatly aided my research into this remarkable archival resource and preparation of materials for this book. I especially wish to thank Heather Hughes, who admirably served as project archivist for the Ardeshir Zahedi Papers. Many archival staff members were involved in the logistical handling and digitization of photos and documents selected for inclusion in this book, or were consulted during the editorial and production process, among them: Jean McElwee Cannon, Paige Davenport, Sally DeBauche, Fiore Irving, Daniel Jarvis, Lisa Nguyen, Sarah Patton, David Sun, and Diana Sykes. Special thanks to Lisa Nguyen and Paige Davenport for a timely discovery of a photo from the collection for use on the book's cover.

Additional thanks goes to the staff of the Hoover Institution Press who managed the project through all the stages toward publication, from manuscript to printed book: Barbara Arellano, Marshall Blanchard, Scott Harrison, Jennifer Navarrette (cover designer), John O'Rourke, and Alison Petersen. Hoover Press enlisted the expertise of outside talent for copyediting (Elizabeth Berg) and the layout/composition of the text pages (Howie Severson).

My deepest gratitude to all involved.

—ABBAS MILANI,
the Hamid and Christina Moghadam Director of Iranian Studies at Stanford University, and research fellow at the Hoover Institution

ILLUSTRATION REFERENCES

FIGURES

All photographs are from the Ardashīr Zāhidī [Ardeshir Zahedi] Papers collection in the Hoover Institution Library & Archives. Page location for each figure within this book is shown below, along with additional archival identifying information for each photograph.

Figure 1, page 4, Box 189, 2009c59_0189_004_022

Figure 2, page 6, top, Box 321, 2009c59_0321_002_008

Figure 3, page 6, bottom, Box 321, 2009c59_0321_002_007

Figure 4, page 10, Box 321, 2009c59_0321_002_001

Figure 5, page 13 top, Box 189, 2009c59_0189_004_009

Figure 6, page 13 bottom, Box 189, 2009c59_0189_004_008

Figure 7, page 14 top, Box 189, 2009c59_0189_004_006

Figure 8, page 14 bottom, Box 192, 2009c59_0192_014_009

Figure 9, page 18, photo by Louis Fabian Bachrach Jr., 2009c59_0177_06_001

Figure 10, page 20, Box 321, 2009c59_0321_002_004

Figure 11, page 25 top, Box 189, 2009c59_0189_004_020

Figure 12, page 25 bottom, Box 189, 2009c59_0189_004_021

Figure 13, page 27 bottom, Box 192, 2009c59_0192_009b_001_01

Figure 14, page 28 top, Box 192, 2009c59_0192_014_004_01

Figure 15, page 28 bottom, Box 192, 2009c59_0192_014_011

Figure 16, page 29 top, Box 258, 2009c59_0258_015a_001_02

Figure 17, page 29 bottom, Box 258, 2009c59_0258_015a_001_01

Figure 18, page 31, Box 189, 2009c59_0189_004_001

Figure 19, page 32, Box 192, 2009c59_0192_011_002

SELECTED DOCUMENTS

All documents are from the Ardashīr Zāhidī [Ardeshir Zahedi] Papers collection in the Hoover Institution Library & Archives. Page locations for the documents reproduced within this book are shown below, along with additional archival identifying information for each document image.

Document 1: on pages 42–67
1922–1924
1.1–1.15 Sheikh Khazal of Kurzestan: Despot or King without a Crown.
2009c59_001_015_001_001 to _015

Document 2: on pages 68–69
23 November 1935
2.1 State permission for installation of concert radio receiver in the home of Brigadier General Zahedi.
2009c59_001_001_002_001

Document 3: on pages 70–73
23 August 1953
3.1 Confidential advice to Zahedi from "Hirad" in regard to Hossein Makki's note to the shah. 2009c59_002_023_001_001

3.2 Note from Hossein Makki to the shah of Iran regarding Mohammad Mossadegh. 2009c59_002_023_001_002

Document 4: on pages 74–77
9 September 1953
4.1–4.2 Letter from Hassan Taqizadeh to General Zahedi. 2009c59_002_023_001_003 to _004

Document 5: on pages 78–79
15 September 1953
5.1 Letter to General Zahedi from a professor at the university. 2009c59_002_023_001_005

Document 6: on pages 80–87
6 October 1953
6.1–6.5 Correspondence from Great Britain seeking to resume diplomatic relations with Iran following the over-throw of Mossadegh government. 2009c59_002_023_001_006 to _009

Document 7: on pages 88–89
16 January 1954
7.1 Report of Anoushiravan Sepahbodi to A. Zahedi. 2009c59_002_023_001_011

Document 8: on pages 90–91
17 February 1954
8.1 Letter of Nasser Ghashghaei to Ardeshir Zahedi. 2009c59_002_025_001_001

Document 9: on pages 92–93
13 December 1954
9.1 Memorandum from Prime Minister to Mr. Abtin in re orders of Dr. Mofakham. 2009c59_002_023_001_010

Document 10: on pages 94–97
3 December 1955
10.1–10.2 Letter of Ali Asghar Hekmat to Ardeshir Zahedi. 2009c59_002_034_001_001 to _002

Document 11: on pages 98–99
1953–1955
11.1 Detailed account of gifts. 2009c59_002_019_001_001

Document 12: on pages 100–115
1954–1955
12.1–12.8 Outline of General Zahedi's career prepared in anticipation of his personal memoirs. 2009c59_002_019_001_002 to _010

Document 13: on pages 116–137
1953–1955
13.1–13.11 More of the outline General Zahedi prepared in anticipation of his personal memoirs. 2009c59_002_031_001_002 to _012

Document 14: on pages 138–139
1 April 1956
14.1 Letter to Ardeshir Zahedi from a cleric who had worked to overthrow Mossadegh. 2009c59_003_002_003_001

Document 15: on pages 140–141
19 August 1955
15.1 Letter from Shaban Jafari to Ardeshir Zahedi. 2009c59_003_003_001_001

Document 16: on page 142–143
12 October 1955
16.1 Letter from Hassan Ma'assar. 2009c59_003_002_001_001

Document 17: on pages 144–147
Around 1957–1958
17.1–17.2 Letter from Princess Ashraf to Ardeshir Zahedi. 2009c59_003_004_001_001 to _002

Document 18: on pages 148–151
17 February 1959
18.1–18.2 Ali Asghar Hekmat to General Zahedi. 2009c59_003_023_001_001 to _002

Document 19: on pages 152–153
13 June 1959
19.1 Letter of General Teymour Bakhtiar to General Zahedi. 2009c59_003_007_001_001

Document 20: on pages 154–157
30 January 1967
20.1–20.2 Letter from Ardeshir Zahedi as foreign minister to the shah reporting on foreign policy.
2009c59_007_002_003_015 to _016

Document 21: on pages 158–165
3 February 1967
21.1–21.4 Correspondence between Ardeshir Zahedi and the shah.
2009c59_007_002_003_010 to _013

Document 22: on pages 166–167
Approximately March 1967
22.1 Letter of Ardeshir Zahedi to shah of matters revolving around influence of Kermit Roosevelt.
2009c59_007_002_003_014

Document 23: on pages 168–179
11 June 1967
23.1–23.6 Digest of the shah's meeting with the Soviet ambassador regarding Soviet breech of bilateral agreement to use of Iranian air space.
2009c59_009_002_001_001 to _006

Document 24: on pages 180–191
Around 1967
24.1–24.6 Correspondence between Ardeshir Zahedi as foreign minister and Armin Meyer, US ambassador to Iran.
2009c59_007_002_003_001 to _006

Document 25: on pages 192–219
13 November 1968
25.1–25.14 Minutes of a meeting between the shah of Iran and the Saudi monarch, King Faisal.
2009c59_012_020_001_001 to _015

Document 26: on pages 220–227
25 January 1969
26.1–26.4 Zahedi reporting in minute detail his conversations with the Soviet ambassador. 2009c59_008_006_001_001 to _003

Document 27: on pages 228–237
10 February 1969
27.1–27.5 Letter from Ardeshir Zahedi, then foreign minister, to the shah of Iran.
2009c59_008_009_001_001 to _005

Document 28: on pages 238–239
28 July 1969
28.1 Letter in English from King Hussein of Jordan to Mohammad Reza Pahlavi, shah of Iran. 2009c59_011_003_001_001

Document 29: on pages 240–249
10 February 1970
29.1–29.5 Ardeshir Zahedi report to the shah of Iran.
2009c59_008_008_001_001 to _005

Document 30: on pages 250–265
2 March 1970
30.1–30.8 Ardeshir Zahedi report to the shah of Iran.
2009c59_008_001_001_001 to _008

Document 31: on pages 266–269
19 February 1974
31.1–31.2 Telegram to US Ambassador in Tehran requesting prevention of broadcasting 60 Minutes interview.
2009c59_041_007_001_002 to _003

Document 32: on pages 270–271
9 July 1974
32.1 Letter to Ardeshir Zahedi from US Senator Edward Wm. Brooke.
2009c59_019_002_001_001

Document 33: on pages 272–275
6 May 1976
33.1–33.2 Letters of Assadollah Alam (former prime minister of Iran) to the shah. 2009c59_041_007_002_001 and 2009c59_041_001_001_001

Document 34: on pages 276–279
20 December 1976
34.1–34.2 Documentation of gifts of caviar. 2009c59_041_008_001_001 to _008

Document 35: on pages 280–281
11 January 1977
35.1 Letter of thanks from US Representative James Wright to Ardeshir Zahedi. 2009c59_022_002_001_001

Document 36: on pages 282–283
22 January 1977
36.1 Letter of thanks from Kirk Douglas.
2009c59_0109_019_001

36.2 Letter of thanks from *Washington Post* columnist Art Buchwald. 2009c59_022_004_003_001

Document 37: on pages 284–291
26 January 1977
37.1–37.2 Letter to Ardeshir Zahedi, ambassador of Iran to US, from Sylvan M. Marshall, giving a legal opinion. 2009c59_022_004_001_002 to _003

37.3–37.7 Letter from Ardeshir Zahedi to David Susskind, US television producer, objecting to allegations made by Reza Baraheni. 2009c59_022_004_001_004 to _008

37.8 Letter to Ardeshir Zahedi from David Rockefeller. 2009c59_022_004_002_001

Document 38: on page 292
27 January 1977
38.1 Letter to Ardeshir Zahedi from Rose Mary Woods, secretary to President Richard Nixon. 2009c59_022_005_001_001

Document 39: on page 293
16 March 1977
39.1 Letter to Ardeshir Zahedi from US Senator Barry Goldwater. 2009c59_022_008_001_001

Document 40: on pages 294–295
16 March 1977
40.1 Letter to Ardeshir Zahedi from Mrs. Arthur Hays Sulzberger. 2009c59_022_008_002_001

40.2 Letter to Ardeshir Zahedi from Katharine Graham of the *Washington Post*. 2009c59_024_002_003_001

Document 41: on page 296
18 March 1977
41.1 Letter of gratitude to Ardeshir Zahedi from John R. Silber, president of Boston University. 2009c59_022_008_003_001

Document 42: on page 297
7 November 1977
42.1 Letter of gratitude to Ardeshir Zahedi from US Senator Hubert Humphrey. 2009c59_023_007_001_001

Document 43: on pages 298–300
5 January 1978
43.1 Letter of gratitude to Ardeshir Zahedi from Claudia A. "Lady Bird" Johnson. 2009c59_024_002_001_001

43.2 Telegram to Ardeshir Zahedi from Mrs. Ronald Reagan (Nancy). 2009c59_124_001_002_003

43.3 Letter to Ardeshir Zahedi from Mrs. Ronald Reagan. 2009c59_124_001_002_005

43.4 Handwritten note of thanks to Ardeshir Zahedi from Mrs. Ronald Wilson Reagan. 2009c59_124_001_002_006 to _007

Document 44: on page 301
30 January 1978
44.1 Letter to Ardeshir Zahidi from Lord Hartley William Shawcross. 2009c59_024_003_003_001

Document 45: on pages 302–303
25 September 1978
45.1 Letter to Ardeshir Zahedi from Douglas Fairbanks in regard to Tabas earthquake. 2009c59_025_002_001_001

45.2 Response to Douglas Fairbanks. 2009c59_123_007_001_001

Document 46: on page 304
9 January 1979
46.1 Letter of concern from Nelson A. Rockefeller. 2009c59_124_001_003_003

Document 47: on page 305
22 January 1979
47.1 Letter from Ronald Reagan to Ardeshir Zahedi. 2009c59_124_001_001_001

Document 48: on page 306
January 1979
48.1 Telegram from William Rogers. 2009c59_124_001_004_001